NEW TEEN TITANS

ARCHIVES ▾ VOLUME 2

ARCHIVE ▾ EDITIONS

DC COMICS

DAN DIDIO
VP-EDITORIAL

DALE CRAIN
SENIOR EDITOR-
COLLECTED EDITIONS

ANTON KAWASAKI
ASSOCIATE EDITOR-
COLLECTED EDITIONS

ROBBIN BROSTERMAN
SENIOR ART DIRECTOR

PAUL LEVITZ
PRESIDENT & PUBLISHER

GEORG BREWER
VP-DESIGN & RETAIL PRODUCT
DEVELOPMENT

RICHARD BRUNING
SENIOR VP-CREATIVE DIRECTOR

PATRICK CALDON
SENIOR VP-FINANCE &
OPERATIONS

CHRIS CARAMALIS
VP-FINANCE

TERRI CUNNINGHAM
VP-MANAGING EDITOR

ALISON GILL
VP-MANUFACTURING

LILLIAN LASERSON
SENIOR VP & GENERAL COUNSEL

JIM LEE
EDITORIAL DIRECTOR-
WILDSTORM

DAVID MCKILLIPS
VP-ADVERTISING &
CUSTOM PUBLISHING

JOHN NEE
VP-BUSINESS
DEVELOPMENT

GREGORY NOVECK
SENIOR VP-CREATIVE AFFAIRS

CHERYL RUBIN
VP-BRAND MANAGEMENT

BOB WAYNE
VP-SALES & MARKETING

THE NEW TEEN TITANS ARCHIVES
VOLUME 2

ISBN 1-56389-951-5

DC COMICS
1700 BROADWAY
NEW YORK, NY 10019

A WARNER BROS. ENTERTAINMENT COMPANY.

PRINTED IN HONG KONG.
FIRST PRINTING.

THE DC ARCHIVE EDITIONS

COVER PENCILS BY GEORGE PÉREZ
AND COVER INKS BY BOB WIACEK.

COVER COLOR BY JAMISON.

SERIES DESIGN BY ALEX JAY/STUDIO J.

PUBLICATION DESIGN BY PETER HAMBOUSSI.

COLOR RECONSTRUCTION BY JAMISON.

TABLE OF CONTENTS

TABLE OF CONTENTS

FOREWORD

ooks change as they grow. Or
at least they should. As time
goes on, the writer and artist
begin to feel more confident with
what they're doing. If they're lucky,
they know they've got something
that works so they don't mind taking
chances. Most important, they know
they've laid the proper groundwork
so if one experiment fails, it won't
spell instant disaster for the book.

That's TITANS #9-16 in a nutshell.

Back in 1981, sales of THE NEW
TEEN TITANS started high, dropped
with issues #2 and 3, then began to
zoom higher and higher starting with
issue #6. The readers were with us.
They saw something special,
something different was happening.
And, most important, the Titans
were attracting readers who hadn't
bought a DC comic in years. We
could have been content just writing
and drawing the same stories month
in and month out, but we weren't.
The ever-amazing George Pérez and
I both would get bored pretty quickly,
and, trust me, the readers, sensing
that, would not be far behind.

We knew this was the time for us
to push the envelope. TITANS would
hit its stride in what will be our third
Archive volume, but all the
groundwork was laid in issues #1-8
and confidently pushed along in
issues #9-16, the stories that are represented here.

George and I knew we had good
characters in Robin, Wonder Girl,
Changeling, Starfire, Cyborg and
Raven. We had spent a lot of pre-
publishing time creating and
developing them. And, as ex-Marvel
guys (Marv: *Spider-Man*, *Tomb of
Dracula*, among others; George:
Avengers and a zillion special
projects) who loved DC Comics and
its great history, we knew we could
take the best of Marvel (action and
soap opera) and blend it with the
best of DC (plot and story) and do
the kind of book we felt neither
company was then producing.

George and I were, and remain,
good friends. I think that was evident
in the early stories and that kept us
together as we struggled to expand
upon the consistency we had

developed. We would often start or finish each other's ideas, and all of it was without ego or the need to be number one. Our single goal was to make the book the star. Considering the number of Titans revivals that have since been attempted, I think we did exactly that.

The readers sensed our love for the stories and characters and the Titans quickly became DC's best-selling comic. Although what I'm about to bring up is business and not creative, I think it is still very important. DC introduced the idea of creator royalties at about the time of TITANS #11. Up until then we, and all other writers and artists in the business, did what we did for a standard page rate and nothing more. It was the same rate we'd get if our book sold or didn't sell. Well, THE NEW TEEN TITANS sold and we got royalties. Big royalties. Sometimes, other writers at the time would complain that we were getting royalties because we were put on a good-selling title and that they weren't getting extra money because they had been shoved off onto something that nobody cared about. When this happened, and it did more often than I'd now care to say, I always reminded them that at least two previous versions of the Titans had failed, and that because of those failures, as much as DC loved what we said we intended to do with the book, this new version of The Teen Titans was not expected to survive beyond six issues. Besides which, I said that George and I

created the Titans only expecting our page rates. Period. What we did we did for love. That we benefited from our work later was gravy.

Which brings us back to the reason we're all here. TITANS #9-16.

After a major cosmic storyline and a one-issue, all-character, no-action story, we decided to take on a standard DC villain and see what we could do with it. Because I was a huge Green Lantern fan I wanted to use The Puppet Master from GREEN LANTERN #1. Our story is nothing special, but the issue exists to introduce a number of strong character arcs that would take years to culminate. In issue #9 we set up Questor, Gar Logan's foil at home, even as we poured the cement for the upcoming Deathstroke/Changeling relationship. We also meet Sarah Simms and her school kids — introduced briefly in issue #8 — and spend time with Terry Long, Wonder Girl's future husband. At the time, some fans didn't like that Donna A) wasn't dating Dick Grayson, and B) was involved with a much older man. Speaking for myself, I thought Donna needed someone who was more mature. A less confident guy would never be able to survive in a relationship with the equally strong-willed and strong-armed Donna Troy.

Issue #10 brings back Deathstroke the Terminator, easily my favorite Titans bad guy, because deep down he wasn't all that bad. Well, he was for awhile, but he got better. Deathstroke had more shades of gray than any other villain I had ever previously created, so it's not all that surprising that this issue — which really sets up the Terminator/Changeling feud — is resolved four years later in one of my very favorite stories entitled, appropriately enough, "Shades of Gray."

What can I say about issues #11 and 12 after "I don't care if 'Clash of the Titans' is the most overused comic book title ever" (heck, I even used it on an old *Fantastic Four* script)? It was the *only* title I could have used.

I was and am a huge mythology buff. I've got too many books on mythology and not just of the Greek and Roman persuasion. Besides, how could I not have our teenaged Titans face the immortal Titans of myth? In many ways I think this two-part story helped cement the Titans' popularity. This is the issue where action and character all came together without any of the seams showing. The story also showed the Amazons of Paradise Island used, perhaps for the first time in a very long time, as real warriors and not just mannequins wearing flimsy long white gowns.

The best part about this story was that it got George Pérez excited about the ancient Greek myths. I may have helped light the mythological candle under him, but where he took it when he started writing and drawing his incredible run on WONDER WOMAN was all his. At any rate, this story was huge,

with multiple sets of gods, great wars, good characterization and unbelievable art. I'm extremely proud of it.

Issue #13 begins the Titans' second year of publication and is blessed with one of the best George Pérez Titans covers ever. It's one of the few pieces of Titans art I always wished I owned (George kindly gave me the original art for the covers of the first and last Titans issues, which are framed together and hang proudly on my office wall next to the framed lithographed CRISIS ON INFINITE EARTHS poster sent to me by the unbelievable Alex Ross).

Modestly, I believe that in this three-part story we did for The Doom Patrol what we had previously done with the Titans: we took a group that wasn't fondly thought of up at the office and showed everyone how great the Patrol could be. I used to love the original D.P. stories Arnold Drake, Bob Haney and Bruno Premiani spun for us way back when. The readers obviously agreed. The mail reaction to this story convinced DC to revive the Doom Patrol a short time later.

Issue #15 brings back and at the same time introduces one of my favorite villain teams ever, The Brotherhood of Evil. Influenced by the Arnold Drake originals, George and I created some new Brotherhood members that I think are every bit as good and goofy as the originals. I really like Plasmus, Houngan, Warp and Phobia.

After so many multiple-part stories, with issue #16 I wanted to go back to several done-in-one issues. In fact, in that issue's letter column I wrote, "We've already begun plans to 'scale down' the Titans a bit by pushing back the trip to Koriand'r's world until we've done some one-part, straighter stories." I felt then and now that sometimes comic-book stories, in an effort to always raise the stakes, keep getting larger and larger until there is nothing left for the readers to identify with. If all the people a super-hero meets have super powers of their own, it takes away the fragile layer of reality that we depend on. That's why characters like Sarah Simms, Terry Long and others exist: to ground the heroes in some manner of reality and to make the readers believe this could be happening right now around the corner, if only you can get there in time.

Long-running series need to be like roller coasters, with stories that move along faster than a speeding bullet followed by others that slow you down and remind you what you like about the characters even as you are being set up for the next major thrill. If you are constantly being shouted at you will eventually be numbed to everything. You gain perspective and have time for reflection only when there's some quiet.

Like issue #8's "Day in the Life" story, this issue is pretty much all-character, all the time. We send Raven off to college, which she goes to, drops out from, then returns to several times during my 16-year run on the book. It also introduces Franklin Crandall, a man who, well, not to ruin it for anyone who hasn't read the story before, but Starfire falls deeply and wildly in love with him. Koriand'r's people have always been shown to be highly emotional, for good and bad. This story targets Kory's personality and I think it does it well. As far as I know, this issue has never been a big fan favorite, but it's always been one of mine.

That's it for the second Titans Archive. I think George and I spent our second year solidifying our characters and our approach. Some of the stories are huge: Titans of Myth/Doom Patrol, while others are smaller, character-driven tales. One year into the run, George and I are beginning to show confidence in what we were doing and the willingness to keep changing what we thought super-heroes stories had to be like.

I hope you enjoy these stories as much as we did.

— Marv Wolfman

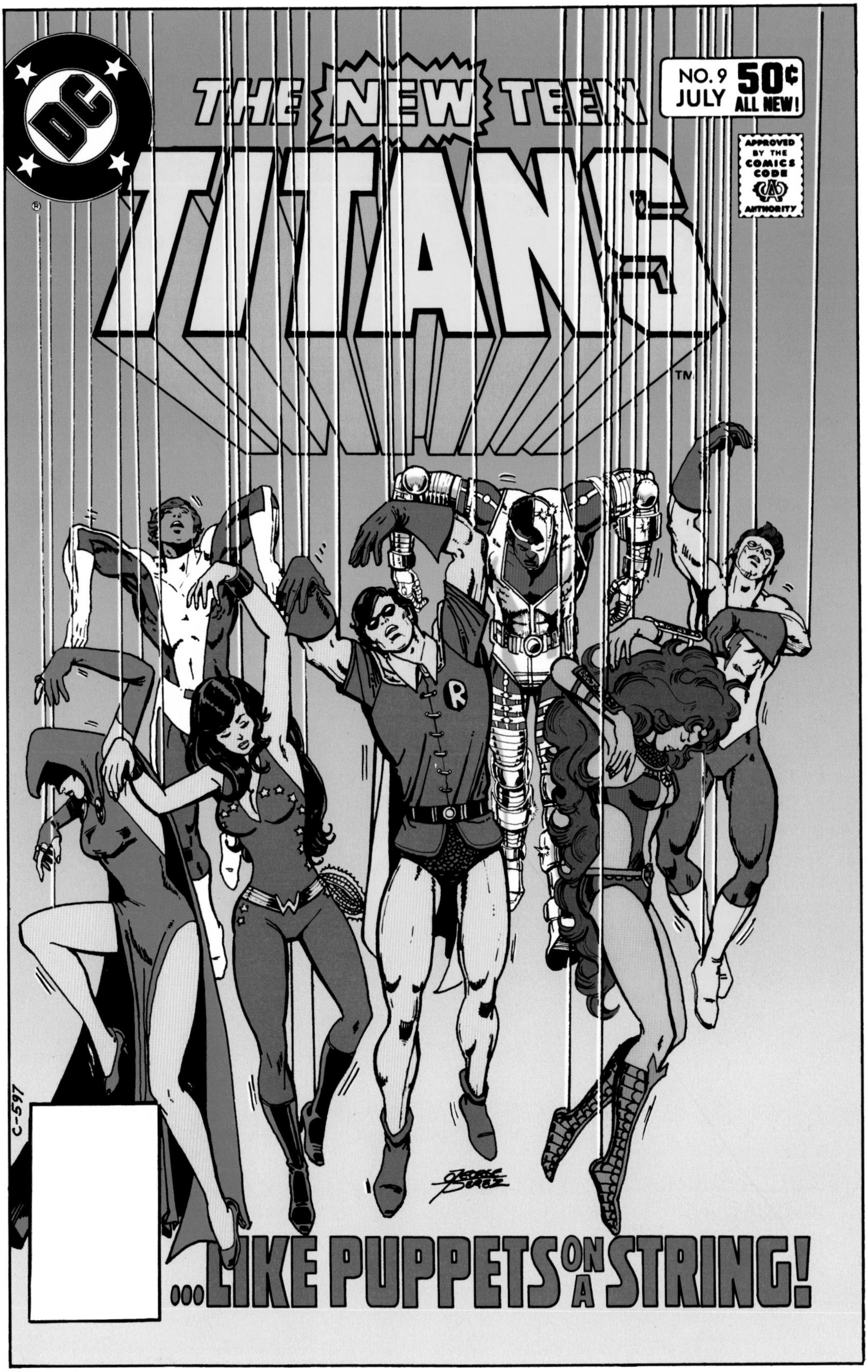
THE NEW TEEN
TITANS
NO. 9
JULY
50¢
ALL NEW!
APPROVED BY THE COMICS CODE AUTHORITY
C-597
...LIKE PUPPETS ON A STRING!

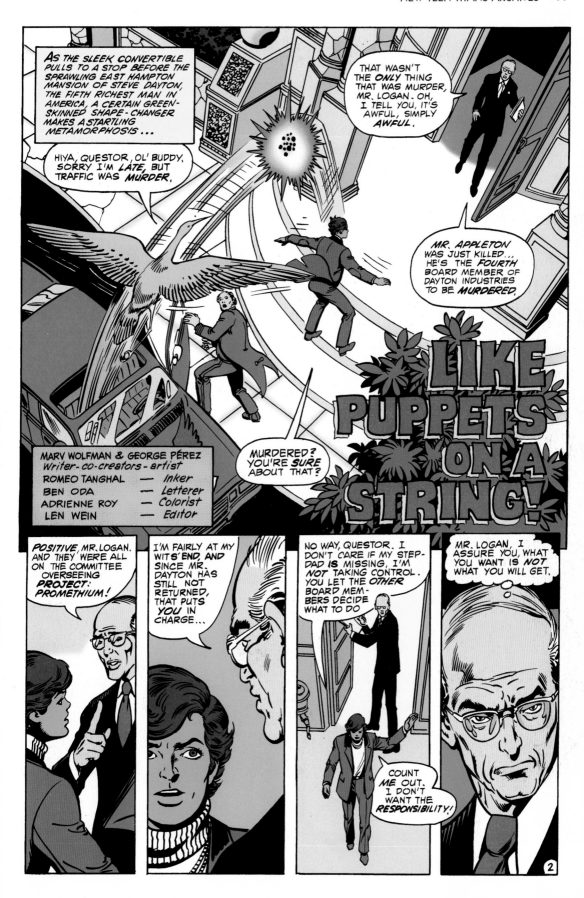

NUTS! EVERY TIME SOMETHING *GOOD* HAPPENS TO ME, SOMETHING'S GOTTA COME ALONG AND SCREW UP THE WORKS.

ALL I WANNA DO IS BE WITH THE OTHER *TITANS*, SO NATURALLY I GOTTA TAKE CHARGE OF DAYTON INDUSTRIES--

--WHICH IS MY *SECOND* MOST FAVORITE THING TO *DO* IN THE WORLD -- RIGHT AFTER *GARGLING RAZOR BLADES!*

IT'S ALL *YOUR* FAULT, POPS. YOU HADDA GO RUN OFF *LOOKIN'* FOR THE CREEPS THAT KILLED MY *STEP-MOM*--AND THE *REST* OF THE *DOOM PATROL*...

...INSTEAD OF STAYIN' HERE WHERE *I* NEED YOU.

MAN, I GO LOOKIN' FOR A NEW *FATHER*, AND WHAT DO I GET? *STEVE DAYTON,* ERRANT KNIGHT, WHO--

KLIK

UH-OH. SUDDENLY MY CHEST HAIRS ARE BRISTLING! WHY DO I HAVE THE SINKIN' FEELING SOMETHING *AWFUL'S* GONNA--

OH, CRIPES!

SUDDENLY, A FLASH OF LIGHT, AN EERIE ALTERING OF SHAPES, AND...

FIGGERS! EVEN IN MY OWN *ROOM*, I'M A TARGET FOR *MURDER!*

SHOOOM!

AND RODNEY DANGERFIELD SAYS *HE'S* THE ONE WHO GETS NO RESPECT! SHEESH!

SKUNGH!

ONLY THIS ISN'T *FUNNY!* SOMEONE'S USING ME AS A LIVING *SKEET TARGET* -- AND THAT'S NOT EXACTLY *HIGH* ON MY LIST OF *LIKES!*

OKAY, SOMEONE WANTS TO KNOW ME AS *GAR LOGAN, DECEASED.* BUT WHO? *WHY?*

3

AND, SHORTLY, IN DAYTON INDUSTRIES' LONG ISLAND LABORATORY...

...*ROBIN*, THE TEEN WONDER, HE'S CALLED. FRANKLY, THE ONLY *WONDER* ABOUT HIM IS HOW HE KEEPS HIS *LEGS* WARM IN THE WINTER.

ROBIN? YOU ARE THE BATMAN'S *PARTNER*, AREN'T YOU? WELL, FRANKLY, I HAVE MY *DOUBTS*, BUT AS LONG AS YOU ARE *HERE*...

PLEASE REMEMBER WHAT YOU WILL *SEE* HERE IS VERY *TOP SECRET*. ONLY A VERY FEW EVEN *KNOW* OF THE EXISTENCE OF *PROJECT: PROMETHIUM*.

PROMETHIUM? NAMED AFTER THE *ELEMENT?*

OH, NO... AFTER *PROMETHEUS*...

...THE MYTHOLOGICAL TITAN WHO GAVE *FIRE* TO MANKIND AND WAS PUNISHED BY THE GODS. HE WAS CHAINED TO A MOUNTAIN WHERE AN *EAGLE* WOULD EAT HIS *LIVER*.

EACH NIGHT THE LIVER WOULD *GROW BACK*, EACH DAY IT WOULD BE *EATEN* AGAIN.

EXACTLY, *EXACTLY!* THIS REGENERATING *LIVER*... REGENERATING *MATERIAL* IS WHAT WE TOOK OUR *NAME* FROM.

YOU SEE, *DAYTON INDUSTRIES* HAS PERFECTED A REGENERATING ...*SELF-GENERATING ENERGY SOURCE*.

BUT MONEY ISN'T *ALL*. IMAGINE USING PROMETHIUM *MEDICALLY*, TO REGENERATE *BODY PARTS!* I DARE SAY IN TIME IT COULD BE *POSSIBLE!*

WHAT WAS *DAMNATION* FOR PROMETHEUS WOULD BE A *GODSEND* FOR US.

AND THERE'S *MORE*, PROMETHIUM-COATED METAL ...CREATING A VIRTUALLY *INDESTRUCTIBLE* CAR TO ELIMINATE ACCIDENTS.

PERHAPS NOW YOU CAN SEE MY *PROBLEM*, EH? THERE ARE POTENTIAL *BILLIONS* TO BE MADE WITH PROJECT: PROMETHIUM.

MATTER REGENERATION-- IF HARNESSED *PROPERLY*, WOULD BE A *BOON*. IF USED IMPROPERLY, IT COULD BE A TERRIBLE *EVIL*.

WHY, A *NUCLEAR DEVICE* MADE WITH PROMETHIUM -- ITS ENERGY CONSTANTLY REGENERATING, CONSTANTLY SPREADING OUTWARD...

...COULD TEAR APART OUR PLANET, OR EVEN THE *UNIVERSE* ITSELF, I DARE THINK.

AND THAT IS WHY THE AWFUL *DEATHS* OF FOUR OF OUR COMMITTEE MEMBERS *BOTHERS* ME SO.

5

YOU SUSPECT THAT SOMEONE INTENDS TO *STEAL* THIS PROMETHIUM?

OH, YES, INDEED. I EVEN KNOW *WHO* THAT PERSON MIGHT *BE*.

ALVIN, PLEASE PUNCH IN THE *PROMETHIUM COUNCIL.*

AH, HERE WE ARE. THAT TOP GENTLEMAN IS *JEREMY THORNTON.* HE WAS SLAIN LAST NIGHT, DISCOVERED BY HIS GRANDSON THIS MORNING. SO *TRAGIC.*

HAROLD APPLETON WAS KILLED THIS MORNING. HE WAS A FINE, FINE MAN. AND BEFORE THEM, *ARTHUR KORDA* AND *SOREN WINSLOW* WERE SLAIN.

YOU SAID YOU SUSPECTED WHO THE *KILLER* MIGHT BE?

AH YES, MR. *JORDAN WEIR.* HE WAS A *SCIENTIST* ON THE PROMETHIUM TEAM, AND A MAN WITH A *PRISON RECORD,* I FEAR.

WEIR... THE NAME SEEMS FAMILIAR.

IT MIGHT BE TO ONE IN *YOUR*--UHH--PROFESSION. WHEN HE WAS A CRIMINAL, HE TENDED TO CALL HIMSELF THE *PUPPET MASTER,* THEN THE *PUPPETEER!*

THAT'S RIGHT. I REMEMBER *GREEN LANTERN* TELLING ME ABOUT HIM.* BUT HE SUPPOSEDLY GAVE UP HIS CRIMINAL CAREER YEARS AGO.

*GL FOUGHT THE PUPPETEER WAY BACK IN GL #1! --LEN.

MR. DAYTON HAS A RATHER--UHH--*LIBERAL POLICY* REGARDING HIRING *EX-CONVICTS.* AND MR. WEIR'S *BRILLIANCE*...WELL, THAT MUCH IS *UNQUESTIONABLE.*

WELL, *SOMEONE* SHOULD HAVE QUESTIONED HIM AND I GUESS *THAT* NOW FALLS TO ME.

HOLD ON, LEGS. YOU'RE NOT GOIN' ANYWHERE WITHOUT *ME.* I GOTTA GET *OUTTA* THIS PLACE BEFORE I GO *BONKERS!*

OH, I DO HOPE I HAVEN'T MADE A *MISTAKE* IN THIS, SUPER-HEROES? HMPPH!

WHAT IS THIS WORLD *COMING* TO?

ROBIN GLIDES THROUGH NEW YORK'S EAST EIGHTIES ON A NYLON-THIN STRAND OF IMPOSSIBLY STRONG CORD, HIS ACTIVE MIND SORTING THROUGH A THOUSAND BITS OF STORED-AWAY INFORMATION...

THIS IS WEIR'S LAST KNOWN *ADDRESS*. WE MIGHT STILL *FIND* HIM HERE.

SURE! IF THAT GUY'S *MURDERIN'* THE FOLKS AT *D.I.*, WE'D PROP-ABLY STAND A BETTER CHANCE OF FINDING *VALERIE BERTINELLI* THAN HIM.

C'MON, KILLERS DON'T HANG AROUND *WAITING* TO BE *CAUGHT*.

HE *MIGHT*, IF HE THINKS HE'S *SMARTER* THAN THE POLICE BESIDES, ONE THING BATMAN *TAUGHT* ME WAS NEVER OVERLOOK THE *OBVIOUS*.

WINDOW'S *OPEN?* ROBBIE, THIS COULD BE A *TRAP*.

I DUNNO, BUT SOMETHING JUST DOESN'T FEEL *KOSHER*.

GAR, TURN *SLOWLY*...WE'RE NOT *ALONE*.

REALLY? WHO'S *WITH* US? THE *KUKLAPOLITAN PLAYERS?*

NO! THE-MAN-WHO-IS-GOING-TO-*KILL*-YOU!

YOU DUCK, PAL. *ME*, I'M GOIN' AFTER *JERKO!*

GAR-- *DUCK!*

NO!

C'MON, THE ONLY WAY TO *STOP* THIS CREEP IS TO STOP 'IM *COLD!*

BLEECH! WHAT'S THIS NERD *MADE* OUT OF ANYWAY?

PTUI

DIDN'T YOU HEAR THE *MECHANICAL TONE* TO HIS VOICE?

HE'S NOT *REAL!* AND *THAT* MEANS--

--WE'D BETTER GET THE BLAZES *OUTTA* HERE --AND *FAST!*

⑦

TOGETHER, THE TWO TITANS LUNGE FOR THE OPEN WINDOW...

WHY ARE WE TURNIN' TAIL? WE COULD'A STOPPED THAT SHMOE!

IS THIS AN ACT OR ARE YOU REALLY THIS THICK?

WE'RE DEALING WITH THE PUPPETEER...AND THAT PUPPET BACK THERE HAD TO BE A--

BLAMMO

DO I HAVE TO CONTINUE?

NOPE! I GET THE PICTURE....IN TECHNICOLOR, TOO.

HOLLLEEE! WHAT TH--?

MASTER! THEY ELUDED US... A SECOND TIME.

SHALL WE UNLEASH THE ASSAULT TEAM?

NOT YET, LITTLE ONE. BESIDES, IT MIGHT ALREADY BE TOO LATE FOR THAT.

IT APPEARS LOGAN HAS ALREADY INVOLVED THE TITANS.

AS THE H.I.V.E. WARNED YOU HE WOULD, PUPPETEER.

YOU FAILED TO GET US THE PROMETHIUM FORMULA...

FAILED? THIS IS ONLY A SETBACK, AND NOT EVEN A MAJOR ONE.

YOU WERE WARNED THAT IF LOGAN LIVED, THE TITANS WOULD INTERFERE WITH OUR PLANS.

WE TRIED TO DESTROY THAT GROUP EARLIER, KNOWING THAT PROJECT: PROMETHIUM WAS SOON TO BE COMPLETED. OUR AGENT, THE TERMINATOR, FAILED.*

HE FAILED. I WON'T.

* CHRONICLED IN TITANS #2:--LEN AGAIN!

8

BESIDES, THE SET-UP IN MY *HOME* WAS MERELY A TEST OF SKILLS THAT I *EXPECTED* THE TITANS TO EVADE. I SIMPLY WISHED TO OBSERVE THEM IN ACTION.

YOU SEE, I HAVE ALREADY *PERFECTED* A CERTAIN DEVICE WHICH WILL RENDER THEM ALL BUT *INOPERATIVE.*

I GUARANTEE THAT, BY TONIGHT, THE TITANS WILL BE *DEAD*--

--AND THEIR *ASSASSINS* WILL BE THE TITANS *THEMSELVES!*

HAW! HAW! HAW!

ACROSS TOWN, IN THE WEST SEVENTIES...

...ALL RIGHT, KIDS, LET'S PUT EVERY-THING *AWAY.*

CLASS IS *OVER.*

SOMETHING *WRONG,* RONALD?

AW, NO, MISS SIMMS, JUST, DO WE GOTTA GO *HOME?* I *LIKE* IT HERE WITH MR. STONE AN' THAT OTHER LADY AN' YOU.

C'MON, YOU WANNA *FREEZE* YER *BUTT* OFF? BUTTON UP OR YOU'RE AN *INSTANT POPSICLE.*

YOU STILL HAVEN'T EXPLAINED WHY YOU *ASKED* ME HERE, *VICTOR.*

HAVEN'T *GUESSED* YET, WITCH-LADY?

MISS RAVEN... MR. STONE, WELL, HE SAID YOU C'N MAKE PEOPLE FEEL *BETTER* JUST BY *TOUCHIN'* 'EM.

WELL, I DON'T HAVE A *HAND* AN' MY MOM AN' DAD, WELL, THEY DON'T HAVE THE *MONEY* FOR A NEW ONE.

NEW HAND? OH, A *MECHANICAL* ONE...?

OH, DEAR ONE, IF ONLY MY POWERS COULD *HELP* YOU... BUT THAT IS SO FAR *BEYOND* WHAT I CAN DO.

BUT, YOU'RE A *SUPER-HERO* AN' SUPER-HEROES CAN DO *ANYTHING.*

I WISH WE *COULD.* I WISH THERE WERE A WAY OF *STOPPING* ALL THE *HURTS* PEOPLE SUFFER, BUT WE *CAN'T.*

9

ALL THEY CAN DO IS THEIR *BEST* AND THAT'S ALL *ANY* OF US CAN DO, SUPER-HERO OR *ORDINARY* PERSON.

DO YOUR BEST WITH WHAT YOU'VE *GOT* AND EVERYTHING ELSE WILL *TAKE CARE* OF ITSELF.

SARAH'S TEACHIN' 'EM THAT MEBBE THEY DON'T *NEED* TWO HANDS OR TWO LEGS TO BE *NORMAL*.

AND SHE'S DOIN' A BLASTED GOOD *JOB* OF IT, TOO.

WE *TRY*, THOUGH IT'S NOT *EASY* ANYMORE. THERE'S ONLY SO MUCH MONEY AND IT DOESN'T GO *FAR*. BUT I *LOVE* THESE KIDS AND I'VE GOT TO AT LEAST *TRY*.

AND SINCE *VIC'S* BEEN HELPING OUT, MY WORK'S BEEN THAT MUCH *EASIER*.

THEY SEE HIS *MECHANICAL PARTS*, THEY KNOW HE'S A *SUPER-HERO*, AND THEY THINK, WELL, MAYBE THEIR ARTIFICIAL HAND OR LEG ISN'T THAT *BAD* AFTER ALL.

CAN IT, LADY, YER GONNA BLOW MY *IMAGE*. THE OTHER TITANS'LL NEVER LET ME *FERGET* THIS.

I DON'T KNOW, BUT IF THEY DON'T *LOVE* YOU LIKE I *DO*, IT'S *THEIR* PROBLEM.

SEE YOU *TOMORROW*?

SURE. IF I AIN'T OUT *SAVIN' THE EARTH* OR SOMETHIN'!

YOU BROUGHT ME HERE TO *HELP* THOSE CHILDREN? SURELY YOU MUST'VE *KNOWN* MY POWERS WERE *USELESS* HERE.

YEAH, I *KNEW* IT--BUT THEY KEPT *ASKIN'!* THEY THOUGHT BEIN' A SUPER-HERO MEANT YOU COULD DO *ANYTHIN'!* GUESS THEY KEPT HOPIN' FER A *MIRACLE*.

I BROUGHT YOU HERE TO SHOW 'EM THE ONLY *MIRACLE* THEY'RE GONNA FIND IS IN THEIR OWN *COURAGE*.

YOU ARE AN *ENIGMA*, VICTOR, YOU ARE A VERY COMPASSIONATE MAN. YOU ARE *WELL-EDUCATED*, YET YOU SHOW NEITHER SIDE TO YOUR *FRIENDS*.

YOUR *SPEECH*...

Y'MEAN SOMETHIN'S *WRONG* 'CAUSE I USE *SLANG*? LISSEN, WITCH-LADY, IT MAKES ME FEEL *COMFORTABLE*.

MEBBE I GOTTA *LOOK* LIKE A BLASTED ROBOT, BUT DO I GOTTA *TALK* LIKE ONE, TOO?

SHADOWS...

SHADOWS MOVE... SHIFT... SEEM ALMOST *ALIVE*...

10

YET, STILL YOU BUILD *WALLS* AROUND YOU...ALMOST *DENYING* YOUR HUMANITY.

KLIK KLIK KLIK KLIK

LISSEN, I CALLED YOU DOWN TA TALK TO THOSE *KIDS*, NOT TA PLAY *DR. BROTHERS* WITH MY *HEAD*, GOT THAT?

SO WHY DON'T YOU JUST KEEP YOUR-- *EH*?

HOLD ON, SOMETHING'S...

WHAT *IS* IT, VI--

--*VICTOR*?!?

"*PUPPET B-13*... ATTACH THE *NEURAL* CONNECTORS!"

CHRISTMAS! SOME KINDA *PUPPET*...MAKIN' LIKE THE *BOSTON STRANGLER!*

RAVEN, GET THIS THING *OFF'A*--

AAARGGHHH!

SPOOO OOMM!

"CONNECTION COMPLETE. CONTROLLING ALL NEURAL ACTIVITY. BRAIN CIRCUITRY UNDER EQUAL CONTROL. THE CYBORG IS MINE!"

VICTOR? CAN YOU HEAR--?

STRANGE...HE'S *FALLEN*, YET I CAN SENSE NO *PAIN*, NO *DAMAGE*. STILL, AN EXPLOSION OF THAT *INTENSITY*...

"RISE! RISE! AND DESTROY THE WOMAN!"

HELPLESS, MINDLESS, LIKE A PUPPET ON A STRING, CYBORG RISES TO HIS FEET...

FROM THE BALLS OF CYBORG'S FEET, STEEL GRAPPLERS EMERGE, ANCHORING HIM TO THE HARD GROUND...

MIGHTY STEEL-JACKETED MUSCLES TENSE. HYDRAULIC-POWERED FINGERS DIG DEEP INTO THE MOIST WOOD.

11

THERE IS A BONE-CRUNCHING YELP AS CYBORG HEAVES THE MIGHTY OAK WITH A POWER THAT FAIRLY BEGGARS DESCRIPTION...

SHOOOSSMM!

BUT, THE EMPATHIC WOMAN KNOWN AS RAVEN SIMPLY VANISHES IN A CLOUD OF MYSTIC EBON SMOKE...

THEN, JUST A MOMENT *LATER*...

HE MOVES STIFFLY, AS IF *CONTROLLED* ...YET THAT WOULD EXPLAIN WHY I CAN SENSE *NOTHING* IN HIS SOUL.

THE OTHER TITANS MUST BE *ALERTED*, FOR I SENSE A MOST DEADLY *DANGER* LURKING...

I CANNOT HOPE TO *TELEPORT* ACROSS THIS COUNTRY...CANNOT POSSIBLY SHIFT THROUGH THE *DIMENSIONS* TO SUCH A DEGREE...

MY *SOUL-SELF* IS NEEDED NOW.

AND, LIKE THE GREAT BLACK SHADOW IT IS, THE VERY *ESSENCE* OF RAVEN'S SOUL RISES FROM HER SEMI-CONSCIOUS FORM, ARCING ACROSS THE SKIES TOWARD A GOAL MORE THAN A THOUSAND MILES AWAY...

WITHIN MINUTES SHE TRAVERSES THE GREAT DISTANCE BETWEEN EAST COAST NEW YORK AND THE MIDWESTERN CITY OF BLUE VALLEY...

... WHERE SHE SEEKS THE FIRST MEMBER OF THE *NEW TEEN TITANS*...

12

THEN, HAVING FOUND WHAT SHE HAS COME FOR, HER ASTRAL IMAGE DESCENDS TOWARD THE GROUND...

OH, HEAVENS! RAVEN! SOMETHING MUST BE UP.

BUT IF SHE CALLS OUT TO ME, SHE'LL BLOW MY SECRET IDENTITY!

W-WALLY? WHAT IS THAT THING?

ONLY ONE CHANCE... GOT TO PLAY IT FOR ALL IT'S WORTH.

RUN, SUSIE-- I'M CALLING THE POLICE!

RAVEN DIDN'T FOLLOW... SHE MUST'VE UNDERSTOOD, THANK GOODNESS.

I JUST DON'T WANT THE PROBLEMS OF HAVING THE WORLD KNOW KID FLASH IS ALSO WALLY WEST.

HIS FINGER DARTS TO HIS SPECIAL RING, AND FROM WITHIN, A COMPRESSED COSTUME EXPANDS ON CONTACT WITH THE AIR...

THEN... RAVEN... ...WHAT IN BLAZES-- --IS GOING ON? WHY ARE YOU HERE?

THERE IS TROUBLE, WALLACE ...BEYOND ANY I HAVE EVER BE-FORE ENCOUNTERED.

I NEEDED THE TITANS, I NEEDED YOU.

I TOOK A LEAVE OF ABSENCE, YOU KNOW THAT!

BUT SOME-THING HAS TAKEN CONTROL OVER VICTOR. HE TRIED TO SLAY ME.

OOOOKAYYY! THAT CHANGES THINGS!

13

YOU SEARCH OUT VICTOR WHILE I FIND DONNA AND THE PRINCESS. WE'LL LOCATE THE OTHERS IF THEY'RE NEEDED.

BUT BE CAREFUL, WALLACE-- HE'S DANGEROUS!

SO I'M A SUPER-HERO AGAIN. MAYBE IT'S JUST AS WELL. I STILL HAVEN'T DECIDED WHAT I WANT... TO BE KID FLASH OR JUST PLAIN WALLY WEST.

THE PROBLEM IS, CAN I GO BACK TO BEING A REAL PERSON? HAVE I BEEN A SUPER-HERO TOO LONG?

GOD, IF ONLY I COULD SEE INTO THE FUTURE... KNOW WHAT I SHOULD DO...

IN A SMALL RENTED NEW YORK PHOTO STUDIO...

GOTTA *TELL* YOU, KORIAND'R, I STILL HAVEN'T GOTTEN OVER THE FACT THAT YOU'RE AN *ALIEN.*

I MEAN, YOU'RE NOT A LITTLE GREEN MAN WITH *TENTACLES* OR ANYTHING.

WHY, *THANK YOU,* TERRY LONG. NEITHER ARE *YOU.*

TOUCHÉ! GUESS I *DESERVED* THAT, HUH?

TERRY, DO YOU AND DONNA *TALK* ABOUT SUPER-HEROING? ABOUT *FIGHTING?*

NO WAY! DONNA KNOWS *SO MUCH,* SHE'S *SEEN* AND *DONE* SO MUCH -- WE TALK ABOUT *EVERYTHING.* WHY?

I WAS *WONDERING,* DO YOU *LIKE* DONNA?

LIKE? I LOVE HER! I WAS A LITTLE *TAKEN ABACK* WHEN SHE TOLD ME WHO SHE *WAS,* BUT...

YEAH. TERRY THOUGHT I WAS *OLDER...,* LIKE *HIM.* HE'S *ANCIENT,* YOU KNOW. AT LEAST *29!*

NOW, IF YOU'VE FINISHED *SNOOPING,* KORY, I'LL SHOW YOU YOUR CONTACT PRINTS...

BUT...

DONNA... KORIAND'R. THE TITANS ARE IN *TROUBLE...*

RAVEN--?

BLAST! A PERFECT EVENING *BLOWN!*

TERRY, YOU *WON'T MIND...?*

SURE, BUT ONLY BECAUSE YOU WON'T BE *NEAR.* LOOK, I'VE GOT *PAPERS* TO GRADE. JUST BE *CAREFUL,* OKAY?

YOU *TOO,* LOVE. I KNOW HOW THOSE *COLLEGE CO-EDS* GET WHEN YOU *FLUNK 'EM!*

A MOMENT PASSES, AND...

WELL, WHAT DO YOU *THINK,* KORY? ISN'T HE A *DREAM?*

HE SEEMS A *NICE* MAN. DO YOU *LOVE* HIM?

HE'S KIND AND UNDERSTANDING, AND, KORY... HE CAN REALLY MAKE ME *LAUGH.*

I CAN'T THINK OF *ANYONE* I'D RATHER SPEND THE REST OF MY *LIFE* WITH.

AND, WATCHING, TERRENCE LONG SMILES AS THE TWO SLIM FIGURES FADE INTO THE AFTERNOON MISTS...

14

MEANWHILE, BACK AT A CERTAIN PUPPETEER'S *LABORATORY...*

SIMPLY PERFECT. *ANOTHER* OF YOUR TITANS FRIENDS HAS SHOWN UP, LOOKING FOR THE *CYBORG,* I WOULD ASSUME.

WELL, HIS METAL-CLAD FRIEND SHOULD BE *RETURNING* IN A MOMENT...

...WITH THE *SPECIAL WEAPON* I GAVE HIM.

I *TOLD* YOU, PAL -- YOUR H.I.V.E. BUDDIES WOULDN'T BE *DISAPPOINTED.*

THE PUPPETEER KNOWS WHAT HE'S *DOING!*

AND...

HERE COMES *RAVEN...* READY TO *REMERGE* WITH HER REAL *BODY.*

EVERY TIME I *SEE* HER, ALL MY DOUBTS *RETURN.*

HE TURNS IN A... FLASH. BUT, IT IS ALREADY *TOO LATE.*

IN AN INSTANT, HIS BODY IS NUMB. HE TRIES TO VIBRATE AT SUPER-SPEED TO *ESCAPE* THE ELEC-TRICAL HELL THAT HOLDS HIM IN A PAINFUL GRIP, BUT HE FINDS HE CANNOT *MOVE.*

I STILL DON'T KNOW IF SHE *CARES...* OR IF IT'S ONLY *ME.* I JUST DON'T UNDERSTAND OUR *RELATIONSHIP...*

AND, WHAT'S *WORSE,* SHE WON'T GIVE ME A SINGLE *CLUE.*

AHHHH, I AM *WHOLE* AGAIN!

BUT WHAT HURTS HIM EVEN MORE IS THE FACE OF HIS *COWARDLY ATTACKER...*

STILL, THE SHOCK QUICKLY *VANISHES...*

I *LOOKED EVERYWHERE,* RAVEN, BUT VICTOR'S *NOT HERE.* ARE YOU SURE THIS IS THE *PLACE?*

AZAR PROTECT US! WALLACE-- *BEHIND YOU!*

...REPLACED A MOMENT LATER WITH THE BLANK STARE OF A MIND-CONTROLLED *KID FLASH.*

15

"ATTENTION: TWO TARGETS APPROACHING. GET READY!"

RAVEN, WHAT'S *GOING ON* HERE?

GET BACK, *BOTH* OF YOU, CYBORG AND KID FLASH ARE BEING *CONTROLLED* SOMEHOW.

"NOW! *FIRE!*"

WHOOMP!

IT IS *TRUE*, THEN... CYBORG IS NOW MY *ENEMY.*

EVEN IF SOMEONE IS *FORCING* HIM TO ATTACK ME, I CANNOT *ALLOW* THAT!

I MUST *FIGHT BACK*... WITH ALL MY *STAR-BORN POWER!*

BUT...

WHOOOMM!

I HAVE NO *CHOICE* NOW... I CANNOT ALLOW THEM TO *DEFEAT* ME.

SKREEE

THE ALIEN PRINCESS IS GRIM AS SHE FIRES STARBOLT AFTER DESTRUCTIVE STARBOLT. BUT THEN, UNEXPECTEDLY...

X'HAL'S *BLOOD!!* MY *THROAT--!*

DONNA--DRAGGING ME DOWN WITH HER *MAGIC LASSO--!*

CAN'T FIGHT WITH IT *BINDING* ME...

HER *PUNCH*... NEVER FELT SUCH *POWER* BEFORE! SHE'S IM-POSSIBLY *STRONG!*

AGGHH!

KROOM!

STILL, I MUST *RESIST!*..

16

BUT IT IS MUCH TOO LATE FOR RESISTANCE, FOR...

"WE HAVE THEM NOW. ONLY THE BLACK-CLOAKED ONE KNOWN AS RAVEN HAS RESISTED MY CONTROL!"

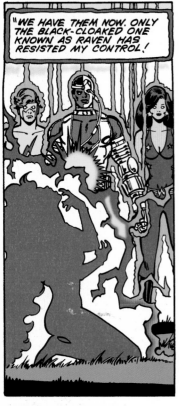

"SHE WILL FIND THE FINAL TWO TITANS... SHE WILL SEEK THEIR AID. BUT YOU, MY PUPPETS, YOU WILL FOLLOW HER..."

"YOU WILL FIND THOSE OTHER TITANS ...AND YOU WILL DESTROY THEM AND THEN DESTROY YOURSELVES AS WELL!"

AND THEY WATCH IN OBEDIENT SILENCE AS RAVEN DRAPES HER CAPE ABOUT HER SLENDER FORM AND VANISHES...

... TRAVELLING 'TWIXT DIMENSIONS AS EASILY AS YOU MIGHT CROSS 'TWEEN STREETS...

AND, OBSERVING ALL THAT HAS TRANSPIRED...

THEY WILL FOLLOW HER, MASTER?

INDEED THEY WILL, LITTLE FRIEND...THEY'LL FOLLOW HER STRAIGHT TO OUR LAST TWO TITANS...

...ROBIN AND GAR LOGAN, THE ONE WHO BEGAN THIS LITTLE BATTLE IN THE FIRST PLACE.

THEY WILL BE DOWNED AND THEN, BEFORE WE DESTROY THEM ALL, WE'LL USE THEIR POWER TO TAKE POSSESSION OF PROJECT: PROMETHIUM ITSELF.'

WE'VE WON, LITTLE ONE.' WE'VE WON!

MEANWHILE, IN THE MANHATTAN OFFICES OF DAYTON INDUSTRIES...

...WEIR KILLED YOUR FIRST TWO BOARD MEMBERS TO INTIMIDATE YOU... TO FORCE YOU INTO GIVING HIM THE SECRET OF PROMETHIUM...

INTIMIDATION? C'MON, YOUNGSTER, THAT SOUNDS FAR-FETCHED TO ME. YOU CAN'T INTIMIDATE AN ENTIRE CORPORATION.

YOU CAN IF YOU POSSESS HIS POWER.

NONSENSE, LAD, POPPYCOCK! I REMEMBER WEIR ... A SLIGHT MAN, HARDLY A THREAT.

NO, THOSE MURDERS WERE, WELL, SIMPLY COINCIDENCE, NOTHING TO CONCERN US.

17

BUT, AS ROBIN GRITS HIS TEETH, READY TO PROTEST...

CHANGE MY SOCKS! IT'S *RAVEN!*

GARFIELD! ROBIN! YOU MUST *COME* WITH ME *QUICKLY!*

THE *OTHERS* HAVE BEEN TAKEN OVER BY *FORCES UNKNOWN.*

TAKEN OVER? IT'S GOTTA BE *THE PUPPETEER...* THAT WAS HIS *M.O.** THE LAST TIME.

IF HE'S CONTROLLING THE TITANS, HE CAN MARCH RIGHT IN HERE AND *TAKE* THOSE PRECIOUS PLANS... UNLESS WE CAN DO SOMETHING *FAST!*

M.O. — METHOD OF OPERATIONS. — LEGAL LEN.

TOO LATE, ROBIN. EVEN BEFORE YOU CAN *BEGIN* TO FORMULATE A PLAN...

UH-OH--IT ALL JUST HIT THE *FAN,* ROBBIE, THAT'S ONE'A STARFIRE'S *STARBOLTS!*

SKREEEEEEEEEEEE EK!

SHE'S OBVIOUSLY BEING *CONTROLLED!* HER MOVEMENTS ARE TOO *STIFF* TO BE NATURAL.

CHANGELING, CIRCLE *AROUND* HER WHILE I HIT FROM THE *FRONT!*

NO USE, SHE ISN'T EVEN *SLOWING DOWN.*

HIS HAND FLASHES TOWARD HIS UTILITY BELT, EXTRACTING HIS BATA-RANG IN LESS THAN A SECOND, THEN...

RAVEN, CLEAR EVERYONE *OUTTA* HERE. THE OTHERS HAVE TO BE RIGHT *BEHIND* HER!

HURRY, ALL OF YOU, WHILE STARFIRE'S ATTENTION IS TURNED TOWARD *ROBIN.*

THERE MUST BE NO DELAY-- *RUN* FROM HERE NOW!

OH, LORD... MY *LEG.* SHE REALLY WRECKED MY *LEG.*

C'MON! HELP ME GET JIM *OUTTA* HERE!

18

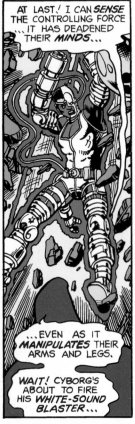

AT LAST! I CAN SENSE THE CONTROLLING FORCE ...IT HAS DEADENED THEIR MINDS...

...EVEN AS IT MANIPULATES THEIR ARMS AND LEGS.

WAIT! CYBORG'S ABOUT TO FIRE HIS WHITE-SOUND BLASTER...

CYBORG'S ATTACK COMES SWIFTLY, BUT THE MAID OF MYSTICISM VANISHES EVEN AS A MILLION DECIBELS OF WHITE SOUND BLASTS THE SPOT WHERE SHE HAD STOOD JUST INSTANTS BEFORE...

ONLY CHANCE IS TO GET CYBORG'S INNER CONTROLS ...CRIPPLE HIM...

BUT...

SO MUCH FOR THAT IDEA!

EVEN AS THE ACROBATIC ACE SOMERSAULTS TO SAFETY...

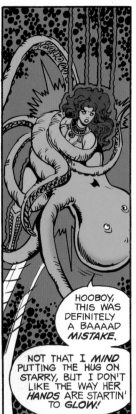

HOOBOY, THIS WAS DEFINITELY A BAAAAD MISTAKE.

NOT THAT I MIND PUTTING THE HUG ON STARRY, BUT I DON'T LIKE THE WAY HER HANDS ARE STARTIN' TO GLOW!

CHANGELING'S OCTOPODAL GRIP WEAKENS FOR A MOMENT AS HIS BODY TENSES, PREPARING ITSELF FOR MIND-NUMBING STARBOLT BLAST...

WHILE OUTSIDE, ANOTHER MINDLESS HUMAN MARIONETTE RACES UP THE SIDE OF DAYTON INDUSTRIES' CORPORATE HEADQUARTERS...

HE TRIES TO RESIST, BUT RESISTANCE IS USELESS. HE IS HELPLESS AGAINST THE PUPPETEER'S POWER.

AND SO, INSTEAD OF RESISTING, ALL HE DOES IS JOIN THE FIGHT...

JUST GREAT! NOW IT'S TWO AGAINST ONE!

NOW I'M REALLY GETTIN' TICKED OFF!

ONCE MORE THE CHANGELING'S FORM METAMORPHOSES AND...

IF I HURT WALLY, I'LL APOLOGIZE LATER, BUT RIGHT NOW I'M FIGHTING FOR MY SKIN!

AND THAT'S SOMETHING I'VE BECOME VERY ATTACHED TO THESE PAST YEARS!

MY CURRENT SKIN EXCEPTED, OF COURSE!

19

VIC STONE'S EYES *BULGE.* HE STAGGERS, SWAYS, THEN FINALLY COLLAPSES...

HE'LL *LIVE,* BUT HE'LL PROBABLY NEVER *FORGIVE* YOU.

I'LL WORRY ABOUT *THAT* WHEN WE'RE *SAFE.*

YOU KNOCKED HIM OUT.

C'MON, WE'RE NOT OUTTA THE COW CHIPS *YET*--

--WE STILL HAVE TO PUT DOWN *WONDER GIRL!*

LISTEN TO ME, WONDER GIRL. WE'RE YOUR *FRIENDS*...YOU DON'T WANT TO HURT *US!*

ROBIN IS DIVERTING HER ATTENTION... *CONFUSING* HER. HER AMAZON INNER STRENGTH IS *FIGHTING* THE PUPPETEER'S POWER, BUT IT ISN'T *ENOUGH!*

SHE NEEDS *ME!*

RAVEN'S SOUL-SELF DRAPES ITSELF ACROSS THE AMAZON'S SHOULDERS WITH AMAZING GRACE. IT *HANGS* THERE, HOLDING THE SUDDENLY PARALYZED FIGURE IN AN UNSHATTERABLE SPELL...

TO *EXPLAIN* WHAT HAPPENS NEXT IS *IMPOSSIBLE.* YET, AS THE ASTRAL IMAGE AT LAST *RISES*...

...IT LEAVES A VERY *DEFEATED* WONDER GIRL IN ITS WAKE...

WONDER GIRL, ARE YOU ALL RIGHT? PLEASE, *SPEAK*... CAN YOU *SPEAK*...?

OOOOH, WHAT *HAPPENED?* WHAT DID I *DO*...?

THE SAME THING *ALL* OF US DID, LADY, WE GOT *USED!*

BUT WE'RE *FREE* NOW, FREE TO *FIGHT BACK,* READY TO DESTROY OUR FOES!

DESTROY'S A LITTLE TOO *PERMANENT* FOR ME, STARFIRE, BUT I AGREE WITH THE *GENERAL IDEA.*

SO HOW DO WE FIND THE *PUPPETEER?* HE'S PROBABLY NOT LISTED IN THE YELLOW PAGES UNDER "BADDIES"!

YOU JUST FOLLOW *ME,* I'LL TAKE CARE OF THE *REST!*

21

AND, IN THE PUPPETEER'S PRIVATE *LABORATORY...*

THEY'RE *FREE,* MASTER.

I *KNOW!* I *KNOW!* BUT IT'S NOT THE *TITANS* I'M WORRIED ABOUT. IT'S THE *H.I.V.E.*

I *FAILED* THEM AND THEY DON'T *ACCEPT* FAILURE.*! BLAST!* I KNEW I SHOULD NEVER HAVE *JOINED* THEM...

LITTLE ONE, I SUGGEST WE *PREPARE* OURSELVES. I WOULD ASSUME THE *H.I.V.E.* WILL BE SENDING THEIR *ASSASSINS* AFTER US...

I WENT STRAIGHT FOR SO LONG. *DAMN!* BUT THEY APPEALED TO MY *EGO...* TO MY *GREED.*

CRASH!!

THEY'RE *HERE!* WELL, THEY'LL LEARN I'M NOT *HELPLESS.* NOT HERE IN MY *PLAYROOM!*

HELPLESS, *NO...* STUPID, DEFINITELY *YES.*

WHY DO WE *STAND* HERE? LET US *TAKE* HIM!

YOU *HEARD* THE LADY, WEIR. I SUGGEST YOU *GIVE UP* BEFORE WE LET HER *LOOSE* ON YOU.

THE TITANS?!? B-BUT *HOW?* YOU *COULDN'T* HAVE FOUND ME!

SURE WE COULD, POPS! BY FOLLOWING YOUR *ENERGY VIBRATION RESIDUE...* IT LED US STRAIGHT *HERE...*

HMMM. THIS COULD BE *FORTUITOUS,* YOU KNOW, MY *H.I.V.E.* FRIENDS MIGHT NOT YET BE *DISAPPOINTED.*

YOU SEE, THIS WORKSHOP IS *MINE!* MY *SOLDIERS* ARE HERE...

...AND THEY ARE MOST ANXIOUS TO *MEET* YOU!

22

THERE IS A MECHANICAL WHIRRING AS THE WALL BEHIND THE TITANS SLIDES *OPEN...*

GREAT HERA! I DON'T *BELIEVE* IT!

THOSE ARE *SOLDIERS?* BUT--?

SOLDIERS *READY!* DESTROY THEM *NOW!*

THEY'RE NOT WHAT THEY *SEEM* TO BE, STARFIRE. REMEMBER WHAT *GAR* TOLD US *ATTACKED* HIM. THEY'RE MORE *DANGEROUS* THAN THEY MIGHT SEEM!

DESPITE WHAT THEY MAY *LOOK* LIKE, THEY AREN'T *KIDS' TOYS* OR *PUPPETS!*

THEY'RE WEAPONS-- *WEAPONS DESIGNED TO KILL!*

FWIPP

THEY FIGHT NOW, *FREE OF ALL RESTRAINTS...*

SPOK

BLAM

STIPP

BAM

STARFIRE'S *STARBOLTS* LASH OUT WITH *UNMERCIFUL ABANDON.*

SKREEE

HER *LUSH LIPS* CURL UP IN *CRUEL SAVAGERY.*

THIS ALIEN PRINCESS COMES FROM A *WARRIOR RACE* AND THIS BATTLE IS SOMETHING SHE DEEPLY *RELISHES.*

THE OTHERS LASH OUT WITH *EQUAL FEROCITY.* THEY HAVE BRED THEM- SELVES TO HONOR ALL *LIFE,* BUT THESE *TOYS,* THESE MECHANICAL *PUPPETS,* ARE ONLY A *BLASPHEMY...*

SO THEY ATTACK WITH ALL THEIR *INCREDIBLE POWER...*

...BE IT *STRENGTH* OR *ENERGY...*

23

...OR EVEN A POWER THAT *DEFIES ANY PLAUSIBLE EXPLANATION...*

FOR SEVERAL INTERMINABLE MINUTES, THE BATTLE RAGES, THEN...

THERE AIN'T MANY *LEFT*, SHORT-PANTS! WE'RE *SMASHIN'* 'EM ALL!

DON'T CELE-BRATE *YET*, CYBORG -- WE'RE STILL VASTLY *OUTNUMBERED!*

ATTACKED BY *TOYS!* THIS IS *INSANE!*

I'LL PUT UP WITH IT *NO LONGER!*

HER COLD EYES BLAZING WITH BATTLE-LUST, STARFIRE LETS LOOSE A DEADLY, DESTRUCTIVE SWEEP OF UNBRIDLED STARPOWER.

IN A SEARING, AGONIZING MOMENT, ALL DEFIANCE IS SUDDENLY, INSTANTLY ENDED...

THAT IS THE WAY ONE *FIGHTS*, MY FRIENDS. YOU FIGHT TO *WIN*. ANYTHING LESS IS *SENSELESS!*

I DON'T *UNDERSTAND*. THE PUPPETEER SEEMED TO BE *AFTER* US, BUT I THOUGHT HE WANTED SOME *PLANS* OR SOMETHING.

SO HE'S A *GREEDY* LITTLE DEVIL... HE WANTED *BOTH!*

SPEAKING OF HIM, WHERE THE HECK HAS THE PUPPETEER *FLED?* HE'S *GONE!*

WHERE? TO FIND HIM NOW, YOU HAVE TO LOOK FAR ACROSS TOWN, WHERE...

WE LOST *AGAIN*, MASTER. HAVE YOU FORMED YOUR *CONTINGENCY PLAN?*

YEAH, *YEAH.* JUST GET ME OUT OF THIS *CITY...*

AS FAR AWAY FROM THE *H.I.V.E.* AS YOU CAN. THEN I CAN PUT THE FINAL TOUCHES ON MY *ULTIMATE PLAN.*

24

BELIEVE ME, LITTLE ONE, THEY HAVEN'T HEARD THE *LAST* OF *THE PUPPETEER!*

ATTENTION! TARGET IS *WITHIN RANGE.*

THEN WHAT ARE YOU *WAITING* FOR, NUMBER NINE? *SHOOT!*

AND REMEMBER, THE *H.I.V.E.* DOES NOT TOLERATE *FAILURE...* FROM *ANYONE!*

NEXT ISSUE: PROMETHIUM: UNBOUND!

SURELY YOUR VARIOUS *AGENCIES* HAVE THE INFORMATION YOU REQUIRE?

IF THEY *DID*, WINTERGREEN, I WOULDN'T BE *SITTING* HERE NOW.

YOU SEE, I'VE GOT THESE TWO *PROBLEMS*... THE FIRST IS THAT *CONTRACT* I TOOK OUT WITH THE *H.I.V.E.* -- I SWORE I'D *KILL* THE TITANS ...AND I CAN'T GET *OUTTA* THAT.

THE OTHER IS HOW TO HANDLE THIS *PROMETHIUM GAMBIT*... AND GET BACK AT THE *H.I.V.E.* AT THE SAME TIME...

STILL BURNIN' OVER THE WAY THEY *CONNED* ME INTO *WORKING* WITH THEM.*

YEAH, TWO *PROBLEMS*... AND I'VE GOT TO FIND TWO ANSWERS-- *QUICKLY!*

MR. WILSON, SIR?

*AS SHOWN IN *TITANS #2*.--LEN.

DR. BENSON HONEYWELL, MY LAB CHIEF! YOU GO OVER THOSE *PROMETHIUM PLANS* YET, HONEYWELL?

OH, YES SIR, ALONG WITH MY ASSISTANT, *BLEEKER*.

QUITE *FASCINATING*, THIS PROMETHIUM, SIR... THE IDEA OF A CONTINUALLY-REGENERATING *ENERGY SOURCE*...ITS POTENTIAL FOR DESTRUCTION... *INCREDIBLE*, SIR...

EXCEPT, SIR, THERE IS SOMETHING YOU SHOULD *KNOW*... IT MAY VERY WELL *ALTER* YOUR PLANS...

DON'T KEEP IT TO *YOURSELF*, HONEYWELL. WHAT *IS* IT?

AND ON THAT QUESTION, WE *PAUSE*...

...AND *RETURN* TO OUR STORY SEVERAL DAYS LATER, IN THE MID-PACIFIC, WHERE A NAVY TRANSPORT SUDDENLY FINDS ITSELF IN THE MIDDLE OF AN UNDECLARED *WAR*...

BLOOM!

BAMMO!

SPOOOOOMM!

THE ATTACKING JETS CAME FROM NOWHERE. NOT EVEN THE CARRIER'S RADAR SPOTTED THEM BEFORE THE FIRST SALVO DROPPED AND EXPLODED.

PANIC WAS INSTANTA-NEOUS AS THE CARRIER'S FLEET OF BATTLE-READY FLIERS LAY IN SUDDENLY RUINED, TWISTED TANGLES OF STEEL.

WITHIN TWO MINUTES, FIFTEEN CREW MEMBERS WERE SERIOUSLY INJURED. THREE WOULD LATER DIE OF COMPLICATIONS.

...BLAST IT, GENERAL, WE'RE BEING ATTACKED! I DON'T KNOW WHO'S ATTACKING... I DON'T EVEN CARE!

I NEED HELP HERE ... AND I NEED IT NOW!

BUT MORE THAN A THOUSAND MILES AWAY, AT BASE OPERATIONS...

WE'RE TALKING ABOUT CARRIER F-16?

THAT'S IT, WILKINS. WE'VE GOT TO FIND OUT IF THE RUSSIANS ARE BEHIND THIS, OR...

W-WE CAN'T, SIR...COMMU-NICATIONS...THEY JUST WENT DEAD, SIR.

AND, SIR... F-16... ISN'T THAT SHIP CARRYING...

...A THERMONUCLEAR WARHEAD?

WILKINS' SUPERIOR NODS GRIMLY AS HIS TREMBLING HAND REACHES FOR A BRIGHTLY-COLORED CRIMSON PHONE.

MEANWHILE, AS THE F-16 LIES LIMPLY IN THE VAST PACIFIC, UNDER THE CALM BLUE WATERS, SILENT AS A SCHOOL OF FISH, A SQUADRON OF TRAINED FROGMEN SWOOP TOWARD THE SMOLDERING HULK, ALL MINDS FOCUSED ON THE TASK AT HAND...

3

AND, BEFORE YOU BEGIN ASKING TOO MANY *QUESTIONS*, LET'S LOOK IN ON A VAST *ESTATE* IN LONG ISLAND'S FAMED *EAST HAMPTON*...

BUT, MR. LOGAN, WE NEED YOU IN THAT *BOARD MEETING*. WITH THE MAIN PLANS FOR PROJECT: PROMETHIUM *STOLEN*...

YEAH, YEAH, I KNOW... THEY COULD BE *DANGEROUS*. LOOK, WE'VE GOT *MICROFILM* COPIES...

THAT ISN'T THE *POINT*, SIR... MR. DAYTON PLACED YOU IN *CHARGE* OF HIS COMPANY ... YOU SHOULD--

QUESTOR, OLD *BUDDY*, I RESIGN, QUIT, BUG-OUT, LEAVEAY-VOUS, SHUFFLE OFF,... IN SHORT, *YOU* TAKE OVER.

I GOT *BETTER* THINGS TO DO WITH MY TIME... AND RUNNIN' A MULTI-ZILLION-DOLLAR CORPORATION COMES *SECOND* ON MY LIST... AFTER *EVERYTHING ELSE*.

YOU WANT A *KID* RUNNING THAT PLACE, CALL *RICHIE RICH*. JUST LEAVE *ME* ALONE.

SHEESH!

TAKE IT *EASY*, SALAD-HEAD... YOU'RE GONNA *BLOW A GASKET*...

KNOCK IT OFF, STONE. DON'T YOU HAVE ANY-THING *BETTER* TO DO THAN HANG AROUND *HERE*...?

NAH. I DIG PLAYIN' "*STAR ATTACK*" ON YER FIVE-FOOT T.O.

GO GET A TUNE-UP OR A *LUBE JOB* OR SOMETHING.

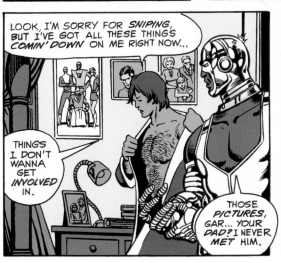

LOOK, I'M SORRY FOR *SNIPING*, BUT I'VE GOT ALL THESE THINGS *COMIN' DOWN* ON ME RIGHT NOW...

THINGS I DON'T WANNA GET *INVOLVED* IN.

THOSE *PICTURES*, GAR... YOUR *DAD*? I NEVER *MET* HIM.

THAT'S MY *STEP-DAD* ... HIM AND THE *DOOM PATROL*.

OH, YEAH... I KEEP FOR-GETTING YOU WERE A *BIG SHOT* WITH THEM A FEW YEARS BACK-- THE ONLY SUPER-HERO DRESSED IN *PAMPERS*, RIGHT?

NEVER WAS SURE HOW YOU GOT *INVOLVED* WITH 'EM, THOUGH.

4

HOW? COULDN'T HELP IT... Y'SEE, MY FOLKS WERE *BIOLOGISTS* WORKING IN AFRICA. WELL, I CAME DOWN WITH THIS CRAZY DISEASE CALLED *SAKUTIA*...

"TO SAVE ME, MY DAD USED SOME KIND'A GIZMO ON ME... ONLY IT TURNED ME INTO A *LIVING LAWN*... BUT GREEN WASN'T ALL IT MADE ME.

"ONLY I WAS ABOUT *TEN* AT THE TIME... AND TOO *DUMB* TO KNOW WHAT TO DO WHEN MY PARENTS WERE CAUGHT IN A STORM.

"WELL, A YEAR LATER, I WAS FOUND BY NILES CAULDER, THE *BIG ENCHILADA* OF THE *DOOM PATROL*..."

"NO, I FOUND I COULD ALSO CHANGE *SHAPES*... INTO *ANIMALS*. OTHER HEROES FLY, HAVE *SUPER-STRENGTH*. I BECOME A LIME-JELLO MONGOOSE! IT FIGGERS.

"BECAUSE OF ME... BECAUSE I COULDN'T HELP 'EM... THEY *DIED*...

FOR AWHILE I *HUNG AROUND* WITH THEM. BUT, WHEN ONE OF THEIR MEMBERS, RITA FARR -- *ELASTI-GIRL* -- GOT MARRIED TO *STEVE DAYTON*, THEY DECIDED THEY WANTED TO *ADOPT* ME.

SUDDENLY I HAD A WHOLE *NEW FAMILY*, GOTTA TELL YOU, IT WAS A *REAL GOOD FEELIN'*

"SHE THREATENED TO *OFF* THIS JOINT CALLED *CODSVILLE, MAINE*, POPULATION 14... IF THE PATROL DIDN'T SACRIFICE *THEMSELVES* INSTEAD.

"FOR *FOURTEEN* PEOPLE THEY DIDN'T EVEN KNOW... THE PATROL, AND MY *MOM* -- DIED... JUST LIKE THAT."

SO, NATCH, IT COULDN'T *LAST*. MADAME ROUGE, A *NASTY* IF YOU EVER SAW ONE, *CAPTURED* THE DOOM PATROL.

*FLASHBACKS COURTESY OF DOOM PATROL #'S 100 & 121.

5

MY STEP-DAD TOOK OFF, *SEARCHING* FOR ROUGE AND HER PARTNER.... AND IN THAT TIME WE LEARNED *CLIFF STEELE, ROBOTMAN,* DIDN'T DIE.

SPEAKING OF CLIFF... I GOT A *MESSAGE* IN TO HIM. HOLD ON, WILLYA, VIC?

A SPECIAL PHONE-CODE IS PUNCHED INTO A COMPUTER CONSOLE, AND THEN, SECONDS LATER...

HEY, GREENIE, WHAT'S *COOKIN'*?

NOT *MUCH,* CLIFF. ANY LUCK IN FINDING MY STEP-DAD?

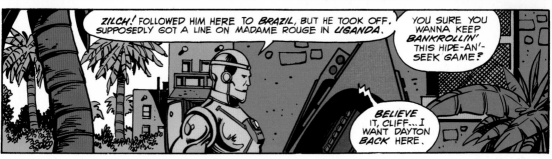

ZILCH! FOLLOWED HIM HERE TO *BRAZIL,* BUT HE TOOK OFF. SUPPOSEDLY GOT A LINE ON MADAME ROUGE IN *UGANDA.*

YOU SURE YOU WANNA KEEP *BANKROLLIN'* THIS HIDE-AN'-SEEK GAME?

BELIEVE IT, CLIFF... I WANT DAYTON *BACK* HERE.

OKAY, GREENS, IT'S YOUR *BUCKS.* BY THE WAY, TELL YOUR LAB GUY'S *THANKS.* IF I GOTTA BE *TRAPPED* IN A ROBOT BODY, I REALLY PREFER *THIS* ONE.

SIGNIN' OFF, AND TAKE CARE, SQUIRT.

ROBOTMAN? HE'S ALMOST LIKE *ME.* IS THAT WHY LOGAN...?

CLIFF'S SOME *GUY,* ISN'T HE, VIC?

Y'KNOW, FOR AWHILE I DIDN'T EVEN WANNA *SPEAK* TO HIM ...SEEIN' *HIM* REMINDED ME OF MY *STEP-MOM* AND ALL MY PROBLEMS...

AND WHEN THE *TITANS* WERE FORMED... WELL, SEEIN' *YOU* SORTA *REMINDED* ME OF CLIFF... I REALLY *HATED* YOU FOR AWHILE BACK THEN.

BUT THEN I GOT TO *KNOW* YOU... WE BECAME *FRIENDS,* AND BECAUSE OF YOU, VIC... I WAS ABLE TO CALL *CLIFF* AGAIN...

...ABLE TO *LOOSEN* UP AND OFFER HIM A *JOB...*

WITHOUT *KNOWIN'* IT, PAL ... YOU *HELPED* ME ...REALLY *HELPED* ME.

THANKS.

6

IN MANHATTAN, IN THE WEST EIGHTIES, MISS SARAH SIMMS SHOPS FOR HER SUPPER...

GAWD! 89 CENTS! IT WAS ONLY 75 CENTS LAST WEEK.

I SPEND SO MUCH *MONEY*, MY WALLET'S DYING OF *MALNUTRITION!*

MOM! HEY, IT'S MISS SIMMS, MY *TEACHER* AT THE SPECIAL SCHOOL!

HELLO, MISS SIMMS, I'M *MRS. GRAHAM*, JIMMY'S *MOTHER*. I HAVE TO SAY YOU'VE DONE *WONDERS* WITH JIMMY...

AFTER HIS *ACCIDENT* I DIDN'T THINK HE'D *EVER* GET USED TO HAVING A *PROSTHESIS* INSTEAD OF A *REAL* HAND, BUT YOU...

... YOU TURNED HIM *AROUND*... AND I *THANK* YOU... TRULY *THANK* YOU.

IT'S MY *PLEASURE*, MRS. GRAHAM ... *REALLY*.

WOW! I'M *BROKE*, BUT I'M *HAPPY*. IT'S WORTH *SO MUCH* TO SEE A KID LIKE THAT SO *HAPPY* AFTER WHAT HE'S GONE THROUGH.

GUESS I DON'T *MIND* NOT HAVING MONEY... BUT DO I REALLY HAVE TO BE *SO* BROKE ALL THE TIME?

OH, WELL ...

IT COULD BE *WORSE*, I GUESS... *MOST* OF THE GIRLS I GREW UP WITH AREN'T DOING *ANYTHING* THEY REALLY WANT TO DO... ANYTHING THEY *ENJOY.*

MY HOME MAY BE UNHEATED AND COLD, BUT I'VE GOT MORE THAN ENOUGH WARMTH *INSIDE*... WARMTH, HAPPINESS, AND *CONTENTMENT.*

LISTEN TO ME, I SOUND LIKE *MISS MARY SUNSHINE*. OH, WELL... MAYBE I *AM*... MAYBE I--

GOOD DAY, MISS SIMMS...

THEN, SUDDENLY, VICIOUSLY...

GOOD DAY, AND GOOD-BYE!

MMFMMF FFFM!

7

SOMEWHERE IN THE *MIDDLE EAST*. NIGHT: THE SLEEK PRIVATE JET LANDS AT THIS HIDDEN *AIRSTRIP* A HUNDRED MILES FROM THE NEAREST VILLAGE.

IT *REFUELS* WHILE WAITING FOR ITS *PASSENGERS* TO ARRIVE. SURROUNDING THE JET, ARMED GUARDS KEEP THEIR EYES PEELED FOR ANY UNWANTED *OBSERVERS.*

BELOW ARE TWO UNWANTEDS:

HARRY, IT MUST BE A *CONVENTION* DOWN THERE... EVERY BLAMED *TERRORIST* IN THE COUNTRY.

YOU THINK THEY'RE ARRANGING A *STRIKE?*

NAH, DON'T *THINK* SO ... IT LOOKS LIKE *BUSINESS* AND FROM THE FLIGHT PLAN WE SAW...

IT'S ABOUT TIME WE RADIOED *WASHINGTON*... I'VE GOT A BAD *PREMONITION.*

WHICH COMES *TRUE* JUST MOMENTS LATER, AS...

MMFMFF MMF

WASHINGTON'S *NOTIFIED,* HARRY... HARRY?

YOUR FRIEND IS *DEAD,* AMERICAN...

...AND YOU SHALL *JOIN* HIM-- *NOW!*

ARGGHHH!

LENINGRAD: BORIS BATTINOV, TERRORIST FOR THE *K.G.B.,* BOARDS A SMALL JET, HIS MISSION AND DESTINATION KNOWN ONLY TO A VERY FEW WITHIN THE *KREMLIN PRESIDIUM.*

KOREA: CHUNG LO OF KOREA'S CRIMINAL ORGANIZATION, *ZATZU,* CLUTCHES THE ATTACHE CASE FILLED WITH FIVE MILLION DOLLARS, SWISS, AS HE BOARDS HIS PRIVATE *JET.*

WHILE IN *LIBYA,* A CERTAIN FORMER HEAD OF STATE WITH DESIRES OF WORLD CONQUEST ALSO PREPARES TO FLY WESTWARD.

ALL THESE PEOPLE, AND MORE THAN ONE HUNDRED OTHERS *LIKE* THEM, ARE WINGING THEIR WAY SECRETLY TO *AMERICA.*

THEY ARE *NOT* COMING TO THROW A *PARTY.*

⑧

MEANWHILE, CUTTING A FLAMING SWATH ACROSS THE BLUE SKIES OF MANHATTAN COMES THE LITHE, GOLDEN FIGURE OF THE ALIEN PRINCESS KORIAND'R, ALSO KNOWN AS STARFIRE...

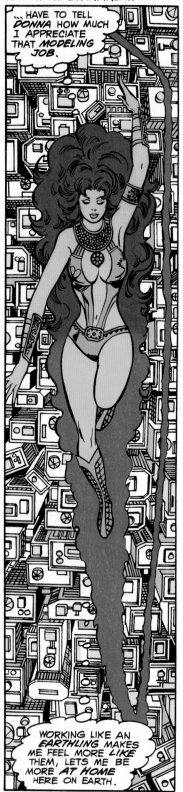

...HAVE TO TELL DONNA HOW MUCH I APPRECIATE THAT MODELING JOB.

WORKING LIKE AN EARTHLING MAKES ME FEEL MORE LIKE THEM, LETS ME BE MORE AT HOME HERE ON EARTH.

AND THIS IS MY HOME NOW, FOR I HAVE NO REAL REASON TO WANT TO RETURN TO TAMARAN... THOUGH I DO MISS MY PARENTS... MY BROTHER.

STRANGE, THINKING OF RYAND'R MAKES ME THINK OF MY SISTER.

I THOUGHT I'D LONG AGO BLOTTED HER FROM MY MEMORY.

THAT TRAITRESS... FOR WHAT SHE DID TO TAMARAN, WHAT SHE LATER DID TO ME...

...I SWEAR I'D SLAY HER IN A MOMENT IF I HAD THE CHANCE.

THERE SHE IS. BEAUTIFUL KID, TOO.

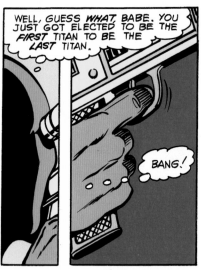

WELL, GUESS WHAT, BABE. YOU JUST GOT ELECTED TO BE THE FIRST TITAN TO BE THE LAST TITAN.

BANG!

HUNH?

PERFECT... DIRECT HIT! AND WHY NOT? WHEN I GOT MY BRAIN POWER INCREASED 90%...

...IT NOT ONLY MADE ME STRONGER AN' FASTER THAN ANYONE ELSE ON EARTH--

--BUT IT INCREASED ALL MY SENSES A THOUSANDFOLD!

SO NOW-- THE TERMINATOR NEVER MISSES!

9

SOMETHING *HIT* ME ...*ATTACKED* ME. THE *CITADEL?* HAVE THEY *FOUND* ME AGAIN?

I DON'T HAVE ANY OTHER *ENEMIES* HERE ON EARTH, OR--

KRAASH!

FRUIT STAND

YOU? YOU'RE THE ONE WHO CALLED HIMSELF *THE TERMINATOR!*

YOU *REMEMBER,* GOLDIE? I SHOULD BE *FLATTERED!*

ANYWAY, BABE, I'VE GOT A LITTLE *MESSAGE* FOR YOU AND YOUR BUDDIES, AND I FIGGERED *THIS* WAY WAS CHEAPER THAN A *PHONE CALL.*

TERMINATOR, YOU ARE *MAD!*

YOU *ATTACKED* ME AND THINK I'M GOING TO SIT HERE LISTENING TO SOME *MESSAGE?*

SKREEEEEK

WELL, THE OTHERS AREN'T HERE TO *STOP* ME, TERMINATOR... NO ONE ELSE IS HERE TO *PREVENT* ME FROM *FIGHTING BACK!*

ON TAMARAN WE TRY TO *AVOID* THE FINAL BATTLE, BUT, WHEN WE FIGHT-- *WE FIGHT TO THE FINISH!*

BABE, THAT'S JUST WHAT I HAD *IN* MIND!

THE TERMINATOR'S HAND SQUEEZES THE RIFLE'S TRIGGER...

AND...

A DOZEN PELLETS, PERHAPS *MORE.* I NEED TO SPREAD MY *STARBOLT BEAM WIDE* ...SETTING UP A *FLAK PATTERN* TO ACT LIKE A *SHIELD!*

SPAM! SBTT! BLAM! SPTAM! SPAM!

THERE! THOSE LEADEN MISSILES *DETONATE* LONG BEFORE THEY *REACH* ME.

⑩

HE IS *DANGEROUS* AND MUCH *FASTER* THAN I REMEMBERED. I MUSTN'T ALLOW HIM TIME TO *COUNTER* MY ATTACK.

STILL, HE *AVOIDS* MY STARBOLTS AS IF THEY WERE *STANDING STILL*. HIS REFLEXES ARE *ASTOUNDING!*

OR HAVE I *SLOWED DOWN* THESE PAST YEARS? I HAVE NOT GONE THROUGH THE *RITUALS* TAUGHT TO ME BY THE *OKAARAN WARLORDS* SINCE THE CITADEL FIRST TOOK ME AS THEIR *SLAVE!*

YOU'RE *GOOD*, GOLDIE. I'LL GIVE YOU *THAT* MUCH. GOOD, BUT NOT GOOD *ENOUGH!*

ACKKK!

SOK

HIS PUNCH *HURT*... MUCH MORE THAN IT *SHOULD* HAVE. I HAVE TO RESUME MY *TRAINING*... EVEN HERE ON *EARTH!*

TERMINATOR, YOU DO NOT *WIN* A BATTLE BY *TALKING* YOUR OPPONENT TO DEATH!

DON'T *INTEND* TO, DEAR. WHEN IT *COMES DOWN* TO IT, I'LL WIN BECAUSE I'M *BETTER*...

...FASTER, AND DAMN *SNEAKIER!*

I DON'T *PLAY FAIR*, BEAUTIFUL!

BUT I *DO* PLAY FOR *KEEPS!*

SKRAKK

11

HIS EXPLOSIVE DEVICE *MISSED* ME... AND NOW HE *RUNS*, THINKING HE'LL *ESCAPE!*

WHAT *ARROGANCE*... TO THINK I'D LET HIM ELUDE ME SO *EASILY* THAT--*EH?*

OH, MY GOD... *WATCH OUT!*

THAT *BUILDING!* OF COURSE... THE TERMINATOR WASN'T ATTEMPTING TO *DESTROY* ME WITH THAT BOMB--

--HE USED IT TO *DELAY* ME!

HE KNOWS I CAN'T CHASE *HIM* AND SAVE THOSE POOR *PEOPLE* AT THE SAME TIME.

HMMM, THEY'RE ALREADY *PANICKING*... LOSING *CONTROL* OVER THEIR ACTIONS.

AMAZING! YOU'D THINK THEY'D BE *TAUGHT* AS *CHILDREN* HOW TO HANDLE EMERGENCIES... BUT *NO*-- ALL THEY DO IS *REGRESS* INTO CHILDREN.

ALL OF YOU, PLEASE *LISTEN* TO ME... THERE IS NO REASON TO *RUN*... NO REASON TO *PANIC*. I CAN *HELP* YOU.

NO GOOD! THEY DON'T KNOW WHO I AM... AND MY STRANGE *APPEARANCE* ONLY SERVES TO FRIGHTEN THEM *MORE*.

THEREFORE I'VE GOT TO ACT MORE *QUICKLY* THAN I THOUGHT...

NEVER TRIED ANYTHING LIKE THIS *BEFORE*... BUT I HAVE TO *HARNESS* MY STARBOLT POWERS... PROJECT THEM IN AS *WIDE* A FIELD AS I CAN...

...AND REDUCE THIS STONE DEBRIS TO *ASH* BEFORE IT COMES HURTLING TO THE GROUND.

THE GREAT SHIMMERING RAY SPREADS WIDE... ⑬

AND... IT IS *OVER*, AND HE IS *GONE*, BUT--

--WHY DID HE *ATTACK* ME IN THE FIRST PLACE? AND WHY DIDN'T HE *KILL* ME WHEN HE HAD THE *CHANCE*?

AS THE ANSWER CAN-NOT BE DIS-COVERED WITH *STARFIRE*, LET'S MOVE ACROSS TOWN, WHERE...

WINTERGREEN, EVERYTHING PANNED OUT LIKE A *PROSPECTOR'S DREAM*, THE TRANSMITTER'S IN PLACE.

SIR... YOU HAVE A RATHER URGENT *MESSAGE*-- FROM *THE H.I.V.E.!*

AND... TERMINATOR, YOU STOLE PLANS TO WHICH WE HAD *PRIOR CLAIMS!* WE WISH THEM GIVEN TO US-- *IMMEDIATELY.*

YOU'RE TALKING ABOUT *PROJECT: PROMETHIUM*, AREN'T YA? YEAH, I GOT THE PLANS, AND IF YOU *WANT* 'EM... WELL, THEY'RE UP FOR *BID*.

DO NOT TRY OUR *PATIENCE*, TERMINATOR. YOU ARE WORK-ING FOR *THE H.I.V.E.*, AND WE DO NOT ABIDE *INSUB-ORDINATION.*

PALLY, I WORK FOR *MYSELF*. OUR CONTRACT CALLS FOR ME TO OFF THE TITANS --- *NOTHING ELSE.*

AND, IF YOU REALLY *WANT* THOSE PLANS ... I'LL SEE YOU AT THAT *AUCTION*-- *TOMORROW.*

MEANWHILE, SOARING ACROSS THE NEW YORK SKIES...

OKAY, SO MAYBE I *AM* DUCKING IT, BUT YOU KNOW HOW EASILY I COULD *SCREW* THINGS UP?

BY THE TIME WE FIND *STEVE DAYTON*, HE COULD GO FROM THE FIFTH RICHEST *GUY* IN AMERICA TO LOOKING FOR HANDOUTS FROM *BAG LADIES.*

SO, *UH-UH*... I'M NOT TAKING OVER DAYTON ENTERPRISES FOR *ANYTHING.*

SEEMS TO *ME* YOU JUST DON'T WANT TO GET *INVOLVED*. YOU'RE NOT *HALF* AS DUMB AS YOU *THINK* YOU ARE.

THANKS! I KNEW YOU'D UNDERSTAND... *SHEESH!* LOOK, YOU AND THE *OTHER* TITANS... YOU'RE ALL *OLDER* THAN I AM...

YOU WERE *TRAINED*... EVEN *BETTER-EDUCATED.* ME, I SORT OF GOOFED AROUND HERE AND THERE ...AND *NOW*, WELL...

...I JUST DON'T WANNA TAKE THE CHANCE I'LL DO SOMETHING *WRONG.*

14

YOU'RE GONNA *HAVE* TO TAKE THAT RISK *SOMETIME*, GAR. YOU CAN'T ALWAYS *PROTECT* YOURSELF AGAINST *FAILURE*.

SURE I CAN. JUST WATCH ME. 'SIDES, WHO CAN CONCENTRATE ON *BUSINESS* WHEN THERE ARE ALL THOSE GORGEOUS *GIRLS* OUT THERE JUST DYING TO MEET ME.?

GOTTA *ADMIT* IT, VIC -- THEY'RE A HECKUVA LOT *BETTER* TO CUDDLE UP WITH THAN BALANCE SHEETS AND YOUR TEXAS INSTRUMENTS COMPUTERS.

YOU DON'T HAVE A SERIOUS *BONE* IN THAT LETTUCE-GREEN *BODY* OF YOURS, *DO* YOU, LOGAN?

NOT IF I CAN GET AWAY *WITHOUT* ONE, STONEY.

IT'S ABOUT TIME *YOU TWO* SHOWED UP.

SORRY, WONDY-- BUT WE WERE STACKED UP OVER FIFTH AVENUE.

'SIDES, WHAT'S THE BIG *PROBLEM?* THIS IS JUST A REGULARLY SCHEDULED MEETING, ISN'T IT?

DON'T *BET* ON IT, STIFF-JOINTS. LOOK AT ROBBIE'S *FACE*. HE LOOKS LIKE HE JUST SWALLOWED A WHOLE *LEMON!*

EVERYWHERE I TURN-- *COMEDIANS!* SHEESH.!

GARFIELD, BE *SERIOUS!* THIS IS AN *EMERGENCY*.

YOU KNOW YOU'RE *STUNNING* WHEN YOU POUT? LET'S *SHUCK* THIS DIVE AND *BOOGIE*.

EYES *IN*, LOGAN ... WE'VE GOT *WORK*.

TWO ORDERS OF BUSINESS: FIRST, WALLY AND RAVEN WERE INVESTIGATING THE *THEFT* OF THE PROJECT: PROMETHIUM PLANS.

WE SEARCHED DAYTON INDUSTRIES, BUT I COULD SENSE *NOTHING* WHATSOEVER.

15

WHOEVER MADE OFF WITH THEM WAS *GOOD*... A *PRO*.

SECOND--AND I THINK THERE'S A *LINK* HERE--STARFIRE WAS ATTACKED BY *THE TERMINATOR* ON HER WAY HERE...

...AND A GOVERNMENT *FRIEND* OF MINE, *KING FARADAY*, TELLS ME THAT ABOUT ONE HUNDRED OF THE WORLD'S MOST FEARED *TERRORISTS* ARE HEADING FOR THIS COUNTRY...

SUDDENLY...

GREETINGS, OLD FRIENDS.

GREAT *HERA!* WHAT--?

THAT *VOICE*...IT'S COMING FROM *ME?*

DON'T YOU *RECOGNIZE* IT? THAT'S *THE TERMINATOR!*

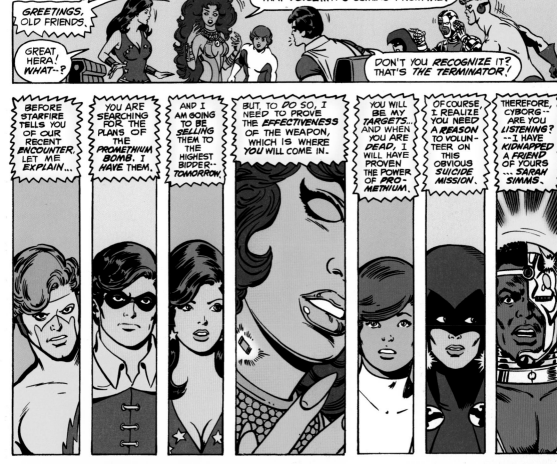

BEFORE STARFIRE TELLS YOU OF OUR RECENT *ENCOUNTER*, LET ME *EXPLAIN*...

YOU ARE *SEARCHING* FOR THE PLANS OF THE *PROMETHIUM BOMB*. I *HAVE* THEM.

AND I AM GOING TO BE *SELLING* THEM TO THE HIGHEST BIDDER-- *TOMORROW*.

BUT, TO *DO* SO, I NEED TO PROVE THE *EFFECTIVENESS* OF THE WEAPON, WHICH IS WHERE *YOU* WILL COME IN.

YOU WILL BE MY *TARGETS*...AND WHEN YOU ARE *DEAD*, I WILL HAVE PROVEN THE POWER OF *PRO-METHIUM*.

OF COURSE, I REALIZE YOU NEED A *REASON* TO VOLUN-TEER ON THIS OBVIOUS *SUICIDE MISSION*.

THEREFORE, CYBORG-- ARE YOU *LISTENING?*--I HAVE *KIDNAPPED* A *FRIEND* OF YOURS ...*SARAH SIMMS*.

WHAT? H-HE'S-- HE'S GOT *SARAH?*

I'LL *KILL* HIM! I SWEAR I'LL KILL HIM!!

IF YOU *FAIL* TO SHOW UP, I'M AFRAID HER PRETTY FEATURES WILL BE REDUCED TO *CINDER* AND *ASH*.

I *DO* TRUST YOU WILL ALL *ATTEND*. DIRECTIONS WILL ARRIVE IN THE MORNING. I'LL SEE YOU ALL *TOMORROW!*

16

HE'S GOING *CRAZY!* I CAN BARELY HOLD HIM *STILL!*

BE *CALM,* MY FRIEND... LET YOUR ANGER FADE IN-TO *ME...* FEEL CALM... QUIET...

AND, AS THE EMPATH'S GENTLE WORDS HAVE THEIR EFFECT...

...I -- I *LIKE* SARAH... SHE'S... THE FIRST *REAL* PERSON, WHO DIDN'T LOOK AT ME AN' *FLINCH*... DIDN'T BACK AWAY... LIKED ME *DESPITE* WHAT I'VE BECOME.

IT'S NOT LIKE WE'RE *LOVERS* OR SOMETHING... JUST *FRIENDS*... AND THAT SCUM TERMINATOR HAD NO RIGHT TO *INVOLVE* HER IN THIS.

I DON'T *LIKE* THIS... EITHER *SHE* DIES OR *WE* DO. IT'S JUST WHAT HAPPENED TO THE *DOOM PATROL!*

IT'S NOT *FAIR* THAT IT'S HAPPENING *AGAIN!*

FOR EIGHTEEN HOURS THEY WAIT; THEY PLAN. THEN AS SOON AS DIRECTIONS ARRIVE AT TITANS TOWER, THEY ARE OFF...

...WE CAN'T *GIVE IN* TO THESE DEMANDS. IF WE *DO,* ANY JOKER CAN KIDNAP SOME-ONE AND ORDER US AROUND.

THEIR SUPERSONIC T-JET RIPS ACROSS THE AMERICAN SKIES, AND, LESS THAN TWO HOURS LATER, THEY ARE SOARING OVER THE MAGNIFICENCE OF THE GRAND CANYON...

GREENIE, WE'RE *NOT* GIVIN' IN ... JUST *BUYING TIME.*

REMEMBER, WE KNOW THE *SECRET* OF *PROMETHIUM*... AND WE'VE *ALSO* FIGURED OUT THE SECRET OF HIS *BOMB.* SO AS CYBORG *SAID,* WE MAY BE *PLAYING* HIS GAME...

...BUT WE'RE PLAYING WITH *OUR RULES.*

YEAH, I *KNOW* IT, ROB -- BUT I STILL DON'T HAVE TO *LIKE* IT.

AND, AS THE TITANS EMERGE FROM THEIR JET...

SARAH! THANK GOD, YOU OKAY?

HE HASN'T *HURT* ME, VICTOR... BUT I *STILL* DON'T UNDERSTAND WHAT'S GOING ON!

WHAT'S *GOING ON,* BLONDIE, IS A LITTLE *TRADING.*

17

US FOR *YOU*, SARAH. SO, WE'RE *HERE*... LET HER *GO*.

FIRST, I WANT TO *CLEAR UP* A FEW THINGS... NO *GAMES*, NO *DOUBLE-CROSSES*. YOU BECOME *TARGETS* AT GROUND ZERO...

...OR MISS SIMMS HERE GETS A SECOND *MOUTH*.

WE'RE *HERE*. OBVIOUSLY, WE *AGREE*. LET HER *GO*, TERMINATOR.

SURE, SURE... *TAKE* HER.

H-HE GRABBED ME IN MY *APARTMENT*... BROUGHT ME *HERE*.

IT'S OKAY, BABE ...IT'S *OKAY*... YOU'LL BE *ALL RIGHT* NOW.

THEY MOVE AWAY FROM THE OTHERS, TOWARD THE *T-JET*, WHERE...

YOU STAY *HERE*, INSIDE THE *JET*. ANYONE COMES *AFTER* YOU, PRESS THE *RED CONTROL BUTTON*.

THE *AUTO-PILOT'LL* SCOOT YOU BACK TO *NEW YORK*.

BUT WHAT ABOUT *YOU*, VIC?

OH, VIC... THANK *GOD*.

I'LL BE *OKAY*... JUST DO AS I SAY. *PLEASE*.

THE GIRL IS *SAFE*. THERE IS NO LONGER ANY REASON TO *GO ALONG* WITH THIS FARCE.

WE'RE NOT *FIGHTING* HIM, KORY, WE GAVE OUR *WORD*.

SO? HE'S A *KILLER*. HE DOESN'T *DESERVE* COOPERATION.

PLEASE, KORY... THAT WILL BE *ENOUGH*.

EVENING, AND THE GRAND CANYON COMES *ALIVE* WITH THE SHIMMERING GLOW OF THE SETTING SUN...

... THAT'S *RIGHT*, FRIENDS AND BIDDERS: THE *PROMETHIUM BOMB*, BUILT FROM THE PLANS' OF *PROJECT: PROMETHIUM*.

WHERE *MOST* BOMBS EXPEND THEIR DESTRUCTIVE ENERGIES IN *SECONDS*, THIS ONE CONTINUES TO *BUILD* ITS FORCE... *EXPAND* ITS DESTRUCTIVE RANGE...UNTIL YOU *SHUT IT DOWN*.

YOU WANT *POWER* IN YOUR COUNTRY, THIS WILL *GIVE* IT TO YOU. NOW, *I* COULD USE IT, BUT I'M A *SIMPLE* SOUL...

TO *ME*, POWER COMES *SECOND*... AFTER *GOLD*, AND IT'S FOR *GOLD* THAT I'M *AUCTIONING* OFF THESE PLANS.

18

WELL, NOW DON'T GO *SHY* ON ME, GENTLEMEN ... SHALL WE HEAR THE *OPENING BID?*

TERMINATOR, WE HAVE ALL PREVIOUSLY *AGREED--* WE WANT *PROOF* OF THIS WEAPON'S POWER.

YOU PROMISED US A *DEMONSTRATION.*

AND THE *TERMINATOR* IS A MAN OF HIS WORD. *GROUND ZERO* HAS ALREADY BEEN *SELECTED* ...AND WE EVEN HAVE *HUMAN TARGETS* SO YOU CAN OBSERVE THE *EFFECTS.*

PLEASE *NOTE*, THEY ARE THE NEW *TEEN TITANS*, AND ONCE THEY ARE *DEAD*, MY CONTRACT WITH YOU *H.I.V.E.* PEOPLE WILL BE *COMPLETED.*

ANYWAY, GENTLEMEN, THE MOMENT YOU HAVE BEEN *WAITING* FOR IS *AT HAND.*

AND PLEASE REMEMBER, BIDDING MUST BE COMPLETED WITH GREAT *HASTE...*

"*THE AMERICAN AUTHORITIES WILL SURELY INVESTIGATE THE EXPLOSION. THUS WE HAVE LESS THAN FIFTEEN MINUTES IN WHICH TO CONCLUDE OUR BUSINESS.*

"*SETTLE BACK. THE FUN IS JUST BEGINNING. I DON'T KNOW ABOUT YOU...*

"*...BUT, FRANKLY I CAN'T WAIT!*"

OBSERVE, FOR IT HAPPENS ALL AT ONCE:

A GREAT GREY CLOUD RISES AMIDST A COLUMN OF LIVING FIRE.

THE DESERT SANDS, TOO, COME ALIVE, BLAZING WITH THE HEAT OF A HUNDRED SUNS.

THEN THE DEAFENING ROAR OF A THUNDER-CLAP; ONE MILLION DECIBELS OF EAR-SHATTERING AGONY.

THE IMPENETRABLE DARKNESS, THE INSUFFERABLE HEAT AND FIRE, THE MIND-NUMBING NOISE... IT MUST HAVE BEEN THIS WAY AT THE VERY DAWN OF CREATION...

BUT, CREATION CONTINUED AND EVOLVED. THIS, HOWEVER, WITHERS AND QUICKLY DIES...

...WITH ONLY THE RIPPLES OF A GLASSY DESERT TO MARK THAT IT HAD EVER BEEN.

KIND OF SHAKES YOUR *BOOTS*, DOESN'T IT?

NOW THEN, THE *BIDDING*?

THE *H.I.V.E.* OPENS THIS BID, TERMINATOR...

...WITH THE LIVES OF OUR *COMPETITORS!*

IF THERE ARE NOW NO *OTHER* BIDS, IT SEEMS WE HAVE *WON*.

YOU MAY KEEP THEIR *GOLD*, TERMINATOR... WE WILL KEEP THE *MONEY* WE BROUGHT WITH US.

WE BELIEVE THAT IS RATHER *EQUITABLE*, ISN'T IT?

20

NOW, TERMINATOR, GIVE US THE *PLANS*...

WAIT! H-HE'S G-GONE!

BUT NOT *FORGOTTEN!*

SO, YOU BOYS WANTED ME TO *GIVE IT* TO YOU, HUH?

SURE, FELLAS, I'D BE *GLAD* TO!

THIS WORKED OUT JUST *PERFECT.* Y'SEE, I KNEW YOU'D *DOUBLE-CROSS* THE OTHERS...

...WHICH WON'T EXACTLY ENDEAR *THE H.I.V.E.* TO THE CRIMINAL WORLD.

I ALSO WANTED *BACK* AT YOU FOR THE WAY YOU SUCKERED ME INTO THAT *CONTRACT.*

YOU CREEPS HELPED KILL OFF MY *KID.*

HE MAY'VE BEEN A *MORON,* BUT HE WAS *MY* MORON.*

*TEEN TITANS #2. --LEN.

WELL, NOW I GOT *YOUR* MONEY, TOO. NOT *BAD* FOR AN AFTERNOON'S WORK.

BUT HOW MUCH CAN YOU *SPEND* FROM BEHIND BARS, TERMINATOR?

WELL, WELL... I REALLY SHOULD BE *SURPRISED,* SHOULDN'T I?

REALLY SHOULD SHOUT OUT -- "THE TITANS-- *ALIVE!* BUT *HOW?"*

ONLY SOMEHOW I'M *NOT* SHOCKED. HOW'D YOU *DO* IT, BUDDIES?

IT WASN'T ALL THAT *DIFFICULT* ... ONCE DAYTON INDUSTRIES TOLD US THE *TRUTH* ABOUT PROMETHIUM.

WITH THAT AND SOME *OTHER* INFO WE HAD... WE WERE ABLE TO PIECE TOGETHER WHAT *REALLY* HAPPENED.

21

"WE WERE READY AS SOON AS THE BOMB WAS DROPPED.

"RAVEN CREATED CLOUD COVER WHILE KID FLASH USED HIS SUPER-SPEED TO ZOOM UPWARD TO THE BOMB. AT THE SAME TIME, STARFIRE USED HER STARBOLTS ... SETTING UP FLAMES WHICH SPREAD ACROSS THE DESERT.

"YOU SEE, WE WERE DUPLICATING THE EFFECTS OF THE BOMB... ONE BY ONE... SMOKE, FIRE...

"CYBORG USED ONE OF HIS HAND ATTACHMENTS TO CREATE A SONIC THUNDER-CLAP WHILE I DIRECTED ALL THE ACTIONS...

"SPECIFICALLY, KID FLASH. YOUR BOMB USED FISSIONABLE MATERIALS--IT EXPLODES ONLY WHEN THE MATERIALS MEET.

"KID FLASH'S VIBRA-TIONS PREVENTED THEIR COMING TOGETHER...

"TURNING A POTEN-TIALLY DANGEROUS DEVICE INTO A DUD WHICH WONDER GIRL WAS BRACED TO CATCH AS IT FELL.

"IT TOOK ALMOST ONE MINUTE FOR THE SMOKE TO CLEAR, BUT, BY THE TIME IT DID, WE HAD GONE.

"YOUR BIG MIS-TAKE, TERMINATOR, WAS STEALING THE PLANS FOR SOMETHING THAT HAD NOT BEEN PERFECTED.

WE KNEW YOUR PROMETHIUM BOMB WAS A PHONY... AND WE REASONED THAT IT WAS YOU WHO STOLE THAT NAVY ATOM BOMB.

AND ONCE WE KNEW THAT, WE KNEW HOW TO COUNTER YOUR ATTACK.

SO YOU KNEW MY WHOLE AUCTION GIMMICK WAS PHONY, EH? CLEVER ...BUT, FORTUNATELY, PAL, SO AM I.

SAY HELLO TO MY MERCENARY ARMY... THEY'RE JUST DYING TO KILL YOU!

SEE, PAL, I HAD 'EM READY... JUST FOR PROTECTION.

YOU NEVER LEARN, DO YOU?

TITANS--LET'S MOVE IT!

22

IT BEGINS WITH AN EXPLOSION OF VIOLENCE.

EACH TITAN MOVES INTO ACTION WITHIN SECONDS.

23

EACH TITAN KNOWS EXACTLY WHAT MUST BE DONE.

OOPS, TERMY'S TAKING IT ON THE LAM... GETTING OUT WHILE THE GETTING'S GOOD.

NO ONE ELSE SEEMS TO SEE HIM, SO I GUESS HE'S MINE.

WANNA PAY YA BACK ANYWAY FOR RECREATING THE PATROL'S FAREWELL.

'SIDES, YOU'LL PROBABLY SURVIVE MY GOING AFTER YA. IF CYBORG GOT YA, YOU'D BE INSTANT DOG MEAT!

WHICH IS A-OK WITH YOURS TRULY. HEY, UGLY... THE DANCE ISN'T OVER... IT'S NOT TIME TO LEAVE.

DON'T BELIEVE IT, SHAPE-CHANGER... I'M NOT THE BEST THERE IS BECAUSE OF MY LOOKS!

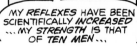

MY REFLEXES HAVE BEEN SCIENTIFICALLY INCREASED ...MY STRENGTH IS THAT OF TEN MEN...

WHILE, ELSEWHERE...

ANOTHER BATTLE ENDS AS WELL...

BUT ITS RESULTS ARE NOT NEARLY SO PLEASANT.

GAR LOGAN SCREAMS...

...AND WHEN THE SCREAMING STOPS, HE FALLS.

FIVE HUNDRED JERKS AGAINST THE SEVEN OF US.

THEY SHOULD'A KNOWN WE OUTNUMBERED 'EM.

HOLD!...I ...I SENSE... GREAT AZAR! IT'S GARFIELD!

LOGAN? WHAT ARE YOU TALKIN' ABOUT? WHERE IS HE? WHAT HAPPENED TO HIM?

C'MON, WITCH, WHAT'S GOIN' ON?

CYBORG, DON'T GRAB RAVEN LIKE THAT... YOU'LL HURT HER.

NO, ROBIN... DO NOT WORRY ABOUT ME. BUT... GARFIELD...

I CAN SENSE WHAT HAPPENED. HE RAN AFTER THE TERMINATOR...

...BARELY BREATHING.

N...NO! GOD, I...IT'S TOO LATE... TOO LATE.

THERE WAS A FIGHT... TERMINATOR SHOT GARFIELD WITH... SOMETHING...

GARFIELD LOGAN...THE CHANGELING... HE'S--DEAD!!

OH, GREAT AZAR HELP US... I... I SENSE GARFIELD LYING THERE... HIS PULSE RATE... SLOWING...

DO WE REALLY HAVE TO SAY IT? TO BE CONTINUED!

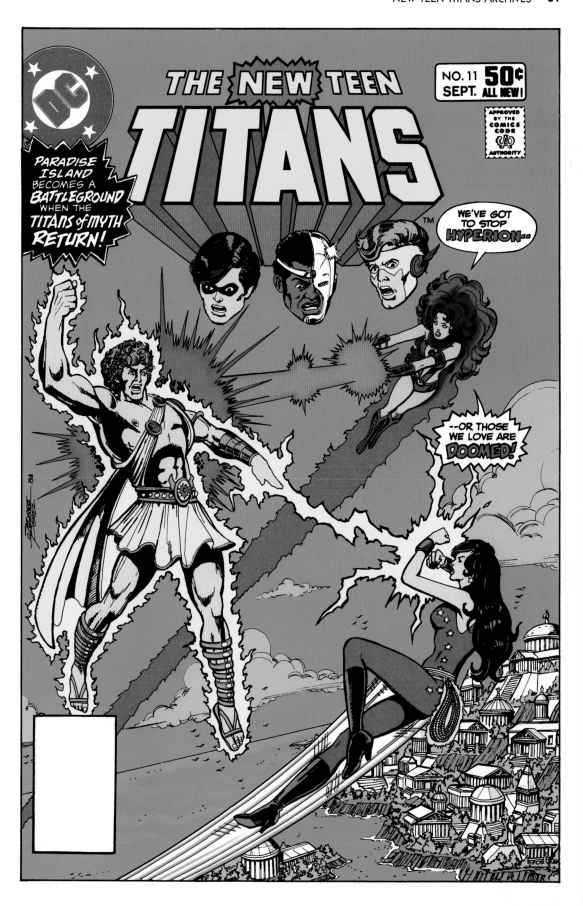

MARV WOLFMAN & GEORGE PÉREZ . ROMEO TANGHAL . COSTANZA . ADRIENNE ROY . LEN WEIN
writer-co-creators-artist   embellisher   letterer   colorist   editor

VIC'S FALLING TO PIECES BACK THERE. I DIDN'T KNOW HE AND GAR WERE SO *CLOSE.* THEY SEEM LIKE SUCH *OPPOSITES!*

THEY ARE, AND MAYBE THAT'S *WHY.* THEY *COMPLEMENT* EACH OTHER. EACH ONE'S WEAKNESSES ARE THE OTHER'S STRENGTHS!

BESIDES, WHAT IS IT THEY SAY ABOUT OPPOSITES *ATTRACTING...?*

...YOU'RE *SURE* OF THAT, RAVEN? HE'S STILL ALIVE?

HIS *HEART* DOESN'T BEAT, BUT HIS *BRAIN* STILL PULSES WITH LIFE.

AND HE'LL *STAY* THAT WAY, VIC-- IN THIS *SUS-PENDED ANIMATION CHAMBER* WE BORROWED FROM *S.T.A.R. LABS.*

BUT IF HIS HEART'S STOPPED, HOW CAN WE BRING 'IM *BACK?*

GOD, I NEVER REALLY THOUGHT ABOUT ONE OF US ACTUALLY *DYIN'!* NEVER THOUGHT US *SUPER-HERO* TYPES HAD ANY PROBLEMS LIKE THAT!

OUR ONE CHANCE, VIC-- IS THE AMAZONS' *PURPLE RAY...* IT WAS FIRST CREATED BY *WONDER WOMAN* HERSELF, * THEN MODIFIED, IMPROVED UPON BY PAULA VON GUNTHER, THE AMAZONS' GREATEST *SCIENTIST.*

"PURPLE RAY"? IT SOUNDS LIKE SOMETHIN' OUTTA *STAR TREK!*

BUT IT'S NOT *FICTION,* VIC, AND IT'S NOT A *PANACEA.* THE RAY'S *FAILED* AS OFTEN AS IT'S *WORKED.*

IT COMES DOWN TO *THIS,* VIC-- IT'S OUR ONLY *HOPE...* AND FOR IT TO WORK, WE'VE GOT TO *PRAY!*

* FIRST SHOWN IN *WONDER WOMAN #1.* --LEARNED LEN.

2

WHAT REALLY RUBS ME *WRONG* IS THAT THE TERMINA-TOR *ESCAPED* US AFTER SHOOTING GAR.

DON'T WORRY, WALLY. WHEN THIS IS *OVER*, WE'LL *FIND* HIM!

HOLD IT, DICK-- LOOK *AHEAD!* THAT STRANGE *CLOUD-BANK*--

AND NOW MY INSTRUMENTS HAVE GONE DEAD! *DONNA?*

DON'T *WORRY* ABOUT IT, DICK... THIS IS THE WAY THROUGH THE *BERMUDA TRIANGLE* TO PARADISE ISLAND. WE'LL BE PERFECTLY *SAFE.*

THE CLOUDS WERE PUT HERE BY THE GODDESS ATHENA TO PROTECT THE AMAZONS FROM *MAN'S WORLD!*

"MAN'S WORLD"? YOU GIRLS GOT A *HATE* ON FOR MEN, OR SOMETHIN'?

NOT *HATE*, VICTOR-- *FEAR!* MEN *ENSLAVED* THEIR WOMEN FOR TOO MANY YEARS.

PARADISE ISLAND IS A PLACE WHERE THE AMAZONS CAN LIVE *WITHOUT* MEN...AND LIVE IN *PEACE!*

A PLACE WHERE *SCIENCE* IS DEDICATED TO *LIFE*, NOT TO *WAR!*

WE'RE COMING THROUGH THE *CLOUDS* NOW... AND MY INSTRUMENTATION IS *RETURNING!*

IT'S BEEN SO LONG SINCE I'VE BEEN HERE, BUT ALREADY I FEEL *EXCITED!*

THERE-- DO YOU *SEE* IT-- *HOME!*

HOME--? THAT AIN'T NO *HOME*, GIRL! THAT'S *DISNEYLAND GONE MAD!*

THIS IS *INCREDIBLE*, DONNA. THE SKIES ARE SO *BLUE* HERE, THE AIR--EVEN THROUGH THE TITANS' JET-- FEELS SO *WARM!*

NOT SINCE I WAS TAKEN FROM *TAMARAN* HAVE I SEEN ANYTHING THAT COMES SO CLOSE TO *PARADISE* ITSELF!

3

PRETTY OR NOT, GIRL-- I DON'T LIKE LEAVIN' GAR *BEHIND.*

I'VE TOLD YOU, VICTOR, *MEN* CANNOT SET FOOT UPON PARADISE ISLAND--NOT WITHOUT ALL THE AMAZONS INSTANTLY *LOSING* THEIR POWERS AND IMMORTALITY.

THAT WAS THE DECREE OF THE *GODS*... AND IT CAN-NOT BE *DISOBEYED!*

YOU'LL TAKE CARE OF HIM, WON'T YOU?

DO YOU *REALLY* HAVE TO *ASK?*

HE MAY GET ON MY *NERVES* AT TIMES, BUT I *LIKE* GAR VERY MUCH.

HE'S A FRIEND, A *GOOD* FRIEND, AND I'LL DO EVERYTHING I *CAN.*

KORY, YOU TAKE GAR AND *FLY* HIM DOWN... MAKE CERTAIN HE DOESN'T TOUCH THE *GROUND.*

I UNDERSTAND, DONNA.

LET'S GO THEN. THE FASTER WE *MOVE,* THE BETTER OUR CHANCE FOR *SUCCESS!*

DONNA TROY, *WONDER GIRL,* GLIDES ON THE AIR CURRENTS CROSSING PARADISE ISLAND--WHILE STARFIRE, PROPELLED BY SOLAR POWER, FLIES OF HER OWN ACCORD...

As for Raven, she moves as only a mystic can...

HOLA, DAUGHTER!

IT HAS BEEN *TOO* LONG!

I MISS YOU *ALWAYS,* MOTHER, BUT--

I KNOW... YOU BELONG IN *MAN'S* WORLD. ONCE, THOUGH, I WISH ONE OF MY DAUGHTERS WOULD *STAY* HERE, THERE ARE TIMES I GROW *LONELY.*

MOTHER... IS PAULA *READY* FOR US?

SHE *IS!*

OF COURSE, THERE CAN BE NO *DELAY.* COME...EVERYTHING HAS BEEN *PREPARED.*

THERE THEY *GO,* AND HERE WE STAY. MAN, I FEEL SO BLASTED *USELESS!*

IF ANYTHIN' *HAPPENS* TO THAT WALKIN' *SALAD...*

YOU KNOW THEY'LL DO WHAT THEY *CAN,* VIC...JUST AS WE'VE GOT *OUR* WORK TO DO.

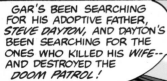

GAR'S BEEN SEARCHING FOR HIS ADOPTIVE FATHER, *STEVE DAYTON,* AND DAYTON'S BEEN SEARCHING FOR THE ONES WHO KILLED HIS *WIFE*-- AND DESTROYED THE *DOOM PATROL!*

IT'S ABOUT TIME WE *HELPED* GAR...AND IT'S ABOUT TIME WE DID SOMETHING TO *FIND* THOSE KILLERS!

BESIDES, SUPERGIRL'S *ALSO* WORKING OUT OF NEW YORK THESE DAYS-- SO, THE CITY SHOULD DO WELL ENOUGH WITHOUT *US* AROUND.

THE T-JET ROCKETS OFF TOWARD AFRICA...

WHILE... FAR *BELOW* THE MYSTICALLY-ENSHROUDED LAND OF *PARADISE ISLAND,* THERE IS A WORLD MORE *STRANGE* THAN ANY WORLD EVER *SPECULATED* UPON BY MAN...

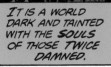

IT IS A WORLD DARK AND TAINTED WITH THE SOULS OF THOSE TWICE DAMNED.

A WORLD OF INCALCULABLE MADNESS, A WORLD OF IMPOSSIBLE EVIL. IT IS A PURGATORY BEYOND ALL PURGATORIES...THE GREATEST HELL OF ALL.

THIS IS A WORLD OF BURNING BRIMSTONE AND SULPHUR, SPOKEN OF ONLY IN MUTED WHISPERS-- EVEN BY THE GODS THEMSELVES.

THIS IS TARTARUS... A LAND FEARED EVEN BY THE DEAD!!

5

I LIVE, YES... BUT HOW *USEFUL* AM I WHEN I AM SO TERRIBLY *WEAK?*

I NEED *STRENGTH!* I NEED MY POWER *RENEWED!*

I, WHO AM THE LIVING *PERSONIFICATION* OF THE SUN ITSELF MUST BATHE ANEW IN ITS LIFE-GIVING *RAYS.*

I MUST LET ITS WARMTH *REKINDLE* MY BEING.

GAEA, MY MOTHER, YOUR MIGHTY SON RETURNS TO THE *SKIES!* OH, HOW I FEEL *RE-NEWED!* OH, HOW MY *POWER* RUSHES TO ME ONCE MORE!

CHAOS BE *PRAISED!* GAEA AND URANUS BE *LOVED!* THE SWEET BREATH OF *LIFE* THAT YOU BESTOWED UPON THIS GRAND WORLD EARTH IS *MINE* AGAIN!

AND THE AIR IS STILL AS SWEET, STILL AS FULL OF *HOPE!*

BEHOLD, ALL WHO CAN SEE MY *FORM* AND HEAR MY WORDS-- *BEHOLD!* HYPERION IS *FREE,* AND HYPERION IS ONCE MORE A GOD AMONGST *GODS!*

7

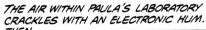

THE AIR WITHIN PAULA'S LABORATORY CRACKLES WITH AN ELECTRONIC HUM. THEN...

YOUR *PURPLE RAY*, PAULA... IT SHUT ITSELF *OFF!*

WHAT'S *GOING ON* HERE?

QUEEN HIPPOLYTE, PLEASE COME HERE--*LOOK!*

OUR PURPLE RAY IS *SOLAR-POWERED*... AND SOMETHING IS DISTURBING... NO, *INTERCEPTING* THE SOLAR COLLECTORS.

INTERCEPTING? OUT THERE, BUT-- *HOLD!* DO YOU SEE IT, DAUGHTER?

I *DO*, MOTHER, ALTHOUGH IT'S SO *FAINT*. IT'S A *SILHOUETTE*-- OF A *MAN?*-- FLYING BEFORE THE *SUN?*

IS IT *POSSIBLE?*

IT IS *THERE!*

THEN THERE IS ONLY ONE THING I CAN *DO*-- AND THAT'S *INVESTIGATE!*

IF WHOEVER THAT IS *FRIENDLY*, I'LL ASK HIM TO *MOVE!*

IF HE PROVES A *THREAT*, HE'LL RUE THE DAY HE ENTERED OUR *SKIES!*

IT *IS* A MAN...OBLIVIOUS TO MY *PRESENCE* HERE.

BUT NOT FOR *LONG!*

EH? WHAT'S *THIS?*

A *LASSO* FORGED FROM THE FINEST GOLD LINKS?

8

AND *THERE*... THE ONE WHO *WIELDS* IT!

CHAOS BE *PRAISED!* SHE'S A *WOMAN*, AND A *BEAUTIFUL* ONE AT THAT!

WELL, YOU'VE *SNARED* YOURSELF A *GOD*, MY DEAR...

AND NOW THAT YOU *HAVE* ME...

...DO YOU INTEND TO *HAVE YOUR WAY* WITH YOUR PRIZE?

HERA HELP ME! I SHOULD BE *CONTROLLING* YOU--HOW COULD...

HERA? YOU CALL UPON THAT UPSTART *CHILD* FOR HELP? WHY, YOU DON'T NEED THAT *TRAITRESS*...

NOT WHEN YOU CAN HAVE *HYPERION* HIMSELF!

MFMMFM FFMM

SHE IS *STARTLED*, THIS AMAZON...

BUT, BECAUSE SHE *IS* AN *AMAZON*, TRAINED FROM CHILDHOOD IN THE ART OF WARFARE, SHE REACTS...

...INSTANTLY, *TERRIBLY!*

GET YOUR HANDS *OFF* ME!

WHOMP!

OH, NO-- HE'S *FALLING* TO THE *ISLAND*... BUT, IF HE TOUCHES *GROUND*...

I CAN'T LET HIM FALL... I'VE GOT TO *SAVE* HIM!

WHAT? HIS EYES ARE *OPEN*...

AND THEY ARE ONLY FOR *YOU*, MY MAGNIFI-CENT MORTAL!

WHEN A *GOD* FEELS LOVE, THE WORLD BURNS BRIGHTER THAN THE *SUN* ITSELF!

GREAT ZEUS! HE'S GLOWING SO BRIGHTLY... *CAN'T SEE!*

9

THROUGHOUT TIME THE GODS HAVE TAKEN *MORTALS* TO LOVE, MORTALS WHOSE *BEAUTY* TRANSCENDS THE BOUNDARIES 'TWEEN GOD AND MAN.

AND ALWAYS HAVE THE MORTALS RESPONDED *IN KIND...*

FOR WHO CAN DENY A *GOD?*

WHO CAN RESIST THE *INNER LIGHT* THAT MAKES US SO MUCH *MORE* THAN MAN?

WE ARE *GODS.* INDEED, I AM A GOD *ABOVE* GODS... AND I CALL FOR *YOU...*

AND I *WANT* YOU...

AND, I WILL NOT BE *CONTENT* SO LONG AS A CREATURE AS *BEAUTIFUL* AS YOU, AS *MAGNIFICENT* AS YOU, IS NOT TOTALLY MINE TO *POSSESS.*

COME TO ME, JOIN WITH ME, TAKE MY HAND AND *KNOW* SUCH THINGS AS FEW *OTHER* MORTALS HAVE BEEN FORTUNATE ENOUGH TO *SHARE.*

YOU WILL BE *FULFILLED* IN WAYS NO MERE MORTAL COULD ASPIRE TO.

SHE IS ENTHRALLED, IS WONDER GIRL, ENTHRALLED BY AN ETERNAL POWER AND MAGNIFICENCE BEYOND ANY SHE HAS EVER KNOWN.

AND SHE FINDS SHE CANNOT *DENY* HER EMOTIONS, OR DENY WHAT SUDDENLY MEANS SO VERY MUCH TO HER.

WHILE... LOOK...DONNA IS IN *TROUBLE.* KORIAND'R--?

TROUBLE? IT LOOKS TO ME LIKE THEY'RE IN *LOVE!*

10

STUNNED, STAR-FIRE FALLS LIKE A LEADEN WEIGHT...

WHILE ON THE SHORES OF PARADISE ISLAND, AMAZONS AT THE READY MOVE QUICKLY INTO ACTION...

CYRENE, LEDA-- YOU RESCUE THE OUT-WORLDER! TARPEIA, YOU ALERT OUR QUEEN!

ATHENA PRESERVE US, CHRYSE! LOOK! THE AIR-WALKER IS PREPARING FOR BATTLE!

HYPERION, IF THAT IS TRULY YOUR NAME-- RELEASE YOUR MENTAL HOLD ON THAT GIRL! SHE BELONGS TO US!

DOES SHE NOW? DO YOU HAVE OWNERSHIP PAPERS, WRAITH?

CAN YOU PROVE SHE IS YOUR SLAVE?

AND, EVEN IF YOU COULD, DO YOU BELIEVE A TITAN ACCEPTS MEANING-LESS CONTRACTS BETWEEN MORTALS AS GOSPEL?

HIS EYES GLOW WITH GOLDEN LIGHT; GREAT BEAMS SHIMMER FORTH...

AND, IN SECONDS, THEY DO THEIR AWFUL WORK...

ARGHHH!

WHAT DID YOU DO TO HER, HYPERION? SHE WAS MY FRIEND.

SHE IS NOT HURT, AT LEAST NOT PERMANENTLY ...BUT IT WILL BE A LONG WHILE BEFORE SHE ATTACKS ME AGAIN, EH?

BUT FORGET HER--AND FORGET YOUR MORTAL PAST. FOR NOW, YOU WALK WITH HYPERION...

NOW YOU WALK WITH THE GODS!

MY STRENGTH IS FULL ONCE MORE, AND I HAVE MY MISSION BEFORE ME. COME, AND TOGETHER WE SHALL FIND GLORY!

IT IS AN ALL-ENVELOPING FLAME WHICH CONSUMES THEM. A FLAME WHICH BURNS BRIGHTLY FOR A MOMENT, HOLDS A MOMENT MORE, THEN IS GONE, TAKING WITH IT WONDER GIRL AND THE MAN-GOD CALLED HYPERION!

12

BUT, FAR BELOW...

UNHHH! NEVER HAVE I *FELT* ANYTHING LIKE THIS BEFORE!

TO SUMMON MY SHATTERED *SOUL-SELF* IS PURE *AGONY!*

KORIAND'R, ARE YOU ALL RIGHT?

MY INSIDES FEEL AS IF THEY ARE *BURNING.*

WHILE...

CAN HE TRULY BE *HYPERION* AS HE CLAIMS?

A *TITAN* RETURNED TO EARTH? IF THAT IS SO, PANTHIA, THEN I FEAR THE HORRORS WE HAVE JUST *SEEN*...

...WILL *PALE* BEFORE WHAT IS *YET TO COME!*

THE WARMTH OF PARADISE ISLAND FADES HERE DEEP IN THESE SHADOW-SHROUDED PITS. INDEED, ANY WARMTH THAT IS FELT AT ALL COMES NOT FROM THE SUN ABOVE, BUT FROM THE STYGIAN PURGATORY THAT AWAITS THESE TWO FAR, FAR BELOW...

YOU REALLY *ARE* HYPERION? YOU'RE ONE OF THE ORIGINAL *TITANS!?*

INDEED, MY DEAREST ONE...ONE OF *TWELVE,* I AM.

TITANS...! MY FRIENDS AND I-- WE TOOK OUR *NAME* FROM YOU!

BUT, ACCORDING TO ALL THE *MYTHS,* YOU WERE *DESTROYED,* SENT TO THE HELL KNOWN AS *TARTARUS!*

INDEED, TARTARUS HAS BEEN OUR *PRISON* FOR THIRTY THOUSAND OF YOUR YEARS...BUT *DEAD?* NAY, A TITAN CAN-NOT BE *SLAIN*--

--NOT EVEN BY THOSE TRAITOR GODS WHO WERE OUR *CHILDREN!*

BUT, AT LAST, I WAS *FREED,* AND NOW YOU AND I WILL FREE MY BROTHER AND SISTER *TITANS!*

THEN, TOGETHER, WE WILL MARCH INTO *OLYMPUS* AND TAKE THAT REALM AS *OUR OWN!*

AND YOU, MY BEAUTIFUL, MY MAGNIFICENT CREATURE --YOU WILL STAND AT MY SIDE AS AN *IMMORTAL REBORN!*

SHE WILL BE *DEAD,* SUN GOD! AS WILL *YOU!*

GREAT GAEA!

13

THOUGH HYPERION, IT APPEARS, HAS NO INTENTION OF ALLOWING THAT TO HAPPEN.

DOG! HOW DARE YOU PRESUME TO STAND IN THE WAY OF A *TITAN BORN?*

MY PATH WILL NOT BE BARRED BY ANY HELL-BORN CREATURE WHOSE *STINK* IS AS FOUL TO MY *NOSE* AS HIS DISGUSTING VISAGE IS TO MY *EYES!*

BRONTES!

YAGGHHH!

ZEUS PROTECT US!

BRONTES HAS BEEN *CONSUMED* IN A SINGLE, SEARING *FIREBALL!*

AS WILL YOU TWO SNIVELING *SYCOPHANTS* IF YOU STILL STAND IN MY *WAY!*

MOVE *NOW,* MAGGOTS! HYPERION *COMMANDS* IT!

NO! NEVER!!

SKRAKK

YOUR BONES WILL *FRY* IN TARTARUS BEFORE WE FAIL THE TASK GIVEN US!

HY-- HYPERION?

WHAT HAVE YOU *DONE* TO HIM?

HERA HELP HIM... IF HE'S *DEAD,* IF YOU'VE KILLED HIM--

BTAM!

--YOU'LL SORELY REGRET CONFRONTING THE POWER OF AN *AMAZON* ENRAGED!

15

STEROPES--? IS HE DEAD, GIRL?

HE TRIED *KILLING* THE MAN I...*LOVE.*

SHE *HESITATES* ON THAT SINGLE WORD...IT IS A WORD *UNSPOKEN* TILL NOW...

BUT, SPOKEN AT LAST, SHE ALLOWS THE SUD-DEN EMOTION TO WARM HER TREMBLING HEART. THEN...

STAND BACK, MY *BEAUTIFUL* AMAZON... THERE IS NO NEED TO *SOIL* YOUR SWEET HANDS ON THAT VERMIN.

IT APPEARS SUDDENLY, THIS GLOWING, GROWING FIREBALL...

...AND WHEN IT ABRUPTLY *CONSUMES* ITSELF, IT CONSUMES ARGES AS WELL...

Y-YOU'RE *ALIVE?* THANK *HERA!* WHEN I THOUGHT YOU HAD *DIED,* MY RAGE COULD NOT BE CONTROLLED!

THEN *CALM* YOURSELF, MY *LOVE.* STEROPES' *LIGHTNING* COULD NO MORE KILL AN IMMORTAL THAN *ZEUS* HIMSELF WILL STAY MY HAND FROM *DESTROYING* HIM AND HIS *RENEGADE* GODS!

I'M SO *AFRAID,* HYPERION... AND SO UNCERTAIN... I DON'T KNOW WHAT'S *HAPPENING* TO ME...

YOU WANT *ANSWERS?* WELL, THEN, YOU SHALL *HAVE* THEM!

THEN YOU WILL UNDER-STAND WHY I HAVE *RETURNED* TO THIS WORLD, AND WHY THERE SHALL SOON COME A *WAR* THAT WILL SHAKE THE VERY *COSMOS!* 16

TO MARCH INTO HELL, WHERE EVEN NOW A GRIM-FACED HYPERION BEGINS HIS RECOUNTING...

BEFORE MAN, EVEN BEFORE THE BIRTH OF THE FIRST PLANET, THERE IS *CHAOS*...THE ENDLESS GULF OF NOTHINGNESS.

THEN, BORN FROM CHAOS WAS THE FIRST LIFE, SHE WHO WOULD BE MOTHER TO US ALL, SHE WHO WAS CALLED *GAEA!*

THERE IS MUCH TO *UNDERSTAND* HERE. THERE IS THE *PAST* AND, AS ALWAYS, THE PAST IS BUT *PROLOGUE* TO ALL THAT IS TO COME.

CHAOS, ROILING, TROUBLED, GROWING MORE AND MORE FURIOUS.

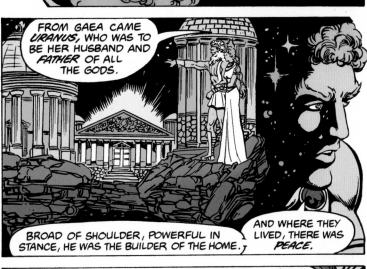

FROM GAEA CAME *URANUS*, WHO WAS TO BE HER HUSBAND AND *FATHER* OF ALL THE GODS.

BROAD OF SHOULDER, POWERFUL IN STANCE, HE WAS THE BUILDER OF THE HOME.

AND WHERE THEY LIVED, THERE WAS *PEACE*.

BUT THEN, FROM GAEA WERE BORN THE FIRST *GODS*-- MY BROTHERS AND SISTERS--

--WE WHO ARE CALLED *THE TITANS!* FOR LIKE GREAT TITANS WE STRODE THE UNIVERSAL SEAS, RULING ALL THAT WE SURVEYED!

IN ALL, THERE WERE *TWELVE* OF US!

18

"TO GAEA WERE ALSO BORN THE THREE CYCLOPES, AND OTHER HIDEOUS MONSTERS BEYOND MORTAL COMPREHENSION.

"BUT THESE BIRTHS UPSET URANUS, AND HE BANISHED ALL TO THE PITS OF TARTARUS.

"HE INTENDED TO KILL BOTH MONSTER AND TITAN ALIKE...

"...BUT GAEA HAD OTHER PLANS FOR HER CHILDREN.

"SHE ENLISTED ONE OF HER SONS, MY BROTHER, CRONUS, THE EARTH GOD-- AND CRONUS SLEW OUR FATHER WITH ONE BLOODY STROKE OF HIS SWORD.

"FROM THEN ON THERE WAS PARADISE ON EARTH, PARADISE FOR ALL.

"MAN AND WOMAN WERE BORN TO EARTH, AND FOR UNTOLD AGES MAN AND GOD WALKED IN PEACE AND HARMONY.

"THIS, THEN, WAS THE GOLDEN AGE, AND AN AGE OF MAGNIFICENCE UNRIVALED, TO THIS DAY.

"BUT CRONUS WAS TOLD BY ORACLE THAT ONE OF HIS OWN CHILDREN WOULD END HIS REIGN...

"SO HE WHO HAD KILLED HIS OWN FATHER NOW SWALLOWED HIS CHILDREN...

"ALL BUT ZEUS, HIS ELDEST BORN.

"ZEUS, WHO WAS TAKEN INTO HIDING BY RHEA, CRONUS' WIFE AND SISTER BOTH,

"AND THUS, IN HIDING, ZEUS GREW IN POWER...

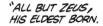

"...AND RETURNED TO DEFEAT US TITANS IN BATTLE...

"...THEN CAST US INTO THE PITS OF TARTARUS WHERE WE WERE TO STAY FOR ALL THESE MANY YEARS!

19

WE WERE *BANISHED*, ALL TWELVE OF US INCLUDING THIA, MY SISTER AND WIFE, FORMED INTO *STONE COLUMNS...*

BUT, EVEN CAST IN STONE, I SENSED THIA HAD *VANISHED* DURING OUR BANISHMENT...SHE WAS GONE, LEAVING ME ALONE WITH NOTHING MORE THAN MY *THOUGHTS* TO KEEP ME COMPANY...

"*BUT THOUGHTS SERVED ME WELL, MY DARLING. FOR AS I STOOD SILENT, THANATOS, HE WHO IS DEATH HIMSELF, LED THOSE NEWLY DEAD PAST MY PRESENCE...*

"*...AND I REACHED INTO THEIR HEARTS, AND PLUCKED THE DYING EMBERS OF SUNLIGHT I FOUND THERE AND TOOK THEM TO MY BOSOM.*

SO MANY *YEARS* IT TOOK, EACH HEART ADDING TO THE LAST, THEN, AT LAST, I HAD *REGAINED* ENOUGH OF MY POWER--

--AND I BURST *FREE*, FREE TO GREET THE WORLD *ANEW!*

AND FREE TO FIND YOU-- WHOSE BEAUTY FILLS ME WITH *LOVE.*

BUT NOW I MEAN TO FREE MY *FELLOW* TITANS, AND TOGETHER BANISH ZEUS AND HIS ILK. THEN, MY DEAREST, MY *DARLING--*

--THEN WE WILL CREATE *PEACE* AGAIN ON EARTH.

THERE SHALL COME A NEW GOLDEN AGE...BRIMMING WITH *LOVE...*

...LIKE THE LOVE THAT BINDS US *NOW!*

SHE IS AN AMAZON, TRAINED FROM CHILD-HOOD IN THE WAYS OF WAR.

BUT, NOW, SHE IS ONLY A *WOMAN*...A WOMAN HELD TIGHTLY IN THE ARMS OF AN IMPOS-SIBLE *LOVE.* ⓩ

BUT AS WONDER GIRL EMBRACES THE SUNGOD, FAR ABOVE, AT THE ENTRANCE TO THESE DARKENED PITS...

THERE, MY SISTERS --THE FIRST OF OUR FOES LIES AHEAD!

FORWARD --TO VICTORY!

BUT, WHAT MANNER OF VICTORY IS POSSIBLE AGAINST THIS MONSTROUS DEFORMITY THAT ALSO CALLS ITSELF THE SON OF GAEA... FIFTY HEADS IT BOASTS... ONE HUNDRED POWERFUL ARMS...

ALREADY FIVE AMAZONS LIE DEAD, AND MORE WILL DIE, UNLESS I CAN STOP IT!

NO, KORIAND'R -- DON'T! THERE IS ANOTHER WAY!

RAVEN, I WON'T HIDE NOW... AND I WON'T HOLD BACK MY FULL POWER.

I DO NOT ASK YOU TO, BUT THE CREATURE CANNOT BE SLAIN... SO LISTEN.

IN HURRIED WHISPERS, THE MYSTIC MISTRESS EXPLAINS TO THE GRIM, ALIEN PRINCESS, THEN...

THE GAMES OF AVOIDING BATTLE ARE BEGINNING TO GRATE AT ME, RAVEN! I WANT TO LASH OUT WITH ALL MY POWER... JUST ONCE.

BUT ALL THAT I WAS TAUGHT BY THE OKAARAN WARLORDS TELLS ME THAT THIS TIME AT LEAST YOUR PATH IS BEST!

KORIAND'R'S STARBOLTS CREATE A WALL OF SOLID FLAME, A WALL THROUGH WHICH EVEN THIS MANY-HEADED MONSTER FEARS TO PASS...

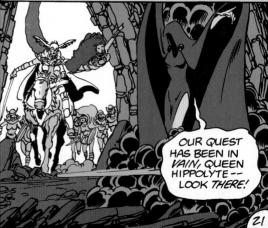

HIPPOLYTE LEADS HER ANXIOUS ARMY ONWARD, DOWN THROUGH CAVERNS AS DARK AS INFINITE SPACE, TO A POINT WHERE ALL REALITY SEEMINGLY ENDS. TWO DAYS PASS IN THE INTERIM...

OUR QUEST HAS BEEN IN VAIN, QUEEN HIPPOLYTE -- LOOK THERE!

21

PHILEGETHON! THE RIVER OF FIRE!

AND *BEYOND* THAT, QUEEN, A WALL OF *SOLID DIAMOND!*

NOT EVEN MY SOUL-SELF CAN *PENETRATE* IT!

AND MY DIMENSION-SPANNING *TELEPORTATIONAL* POWERS CANNOT GET ME THROUGH. I'VE TRIED A DOZEN TIMES AND *MORE...*

...AND I HAVE *FAILED* IN MY *EVERY* EFFORT.

BUT WE CAN'T HAVE COME ALL THIS WAY FOR *NOTHING.*

THAT WOULDN'T BE *FAIR!*

PERHAPS *YOUR* POWERS CANNOT HELP US, RAVEN, BUT WE ARE STILL FAR FROM *HELPLESS!*

THIS SWORD, GIVEN TO ME THREE THOU-SAND YEARS AGO BY *ATHENA,* GODDESS OF WISDOM--

-- CAN ONLY BE USED *ONCE* BEFORE THE SWORD FOREVER RETURNS TO ITS SCABBARD ON *MOUNT OLYMPUS!*

BUT *ONCE* IS ALL I *NEED!*

I MUST HAVE MY *DAUGHTER* BACK!

SKR KRAK

WHILE FAR BEYOND THE DIAMOND BARRIER...

HOW MUCH *LONGER,* HYPERION? IT'S BEEN *DAYS!*

TO BREAK THE SPELLS AND MAGIC OF ZEUS REQUIRES *TIME...* BUT VERY *SOON* NOW THEY WILL BE FREE. HAVE *PATIENCE,* MY DARLING.

SHE WATCHES, FOR-GETTING ALL BUT THIS ONE BEING.

SHE FEELS A SUBLIME THRILL AS HYPERION'S *MIGHTY* POWERS INSINUATE THE *LIVING STONE...*

22

AND SHE IS OVERWHELMED IN WHAT SHE SEES NEXT. THERE IS A BURST OF RADIANT LIGHT, AND BEFORE HER SUDDENLY STANDS NOT ONE, BUT ELEVEN MAGNIFICENT TITANS!

IAPETUS AND THEMIS, GODS OF JUSTICE!

CRIUS AND MNEMOSYNE, GODS OF MEMORY!

COEUS AND PHOEBE, THE MOON GODS!

CRONUS AND RHEA, THE EARTH GODS!

OCEANUS AND TETHYS, THE SEA GODS!

AS ONE, THE RAISE THEIR HANDS HEAVEN-WARD, AS IF THEY OWNED ALL THEY CAN TOUCH, AND SUDDENLY THE TRUTH BECOMES ASTONISHING-LY CLEAR...

AFTER THIRTY THOUSAND YEARS, THE TITANS WALK THE EARTH!!

GAEA BE PRAISED, HYPERION... YOU'VE *FREED* US!

WE HAVE WAITED *LONG* -- EH, OCEANUS?

TOO LONG, BUT THERE IS NOW TIME TO MAKE IT ALL UP!

OH, BLESS CHAOS FOR OUR *FREEDOM* AT LAST!

THERE WILL BE TIME ENOUGH TO FROLIC LIKE *CHILDREN.*

RIGHT NOW THERE IS *WORK* THAT NEEDS TO BE DONE!

GIVE US A MOMENT TO *REJOICE,* CRONUS ...SURELY *THAT* COULD NOT HURT...

IT *CAN,* MY WIFE... FOR THE *GOD* YOU SAVED, THE CHILD I WISHED *DEAD,* WILL DO *ANYTHING* TO KEEP US FROM *USURPING* HIS JEWELED THRONE!

TO SUCCEED, WE MUST *PLAN!*

23

BUT...

THAT *NOISE*...? HAS ZEUS DISCOVERED US *ALREADY?*

WE ARE NOT YET *READY* TO FIGHT! OUR POWERS MUST BE RE-NEWED!

THERE'S *NO TIME* FOR THAT NOW... WE DEMAND WHAT YOU'VE *TAKEN* FROM US.

GIVE US BACK OUR *TEAMMATE* OR BE READY TO *FIGHT!*

HMMM. THESE WARRIORS ARE ALL *WOMEN.* THEY CANNOT COME FROM *OLYMPUS.* MY SON, *ZEUS,* IS TOO MUCH THE *MISOGYNIST* TO CREATE A FEMALE FIGHTING FORCE!

THEY ARE *MORTALS!* THEY WILL PROVE *EASY* TO KILL!

YOU'LL *TALK* INSTEAD OF *BATTLE* WITH YOUR DAUGHTER'S KIDNAPPERS? *SLAY* THEM, HIPPOLYTE-- DON'T MAKE *SPEECHES!*

NO, CRONUS... WE HAVEN'T COME TO *FIGHT*... NOT IF YOU RETURN MY *DAUGHTER* TO US. SHE IS *ALL* WE SEEK, NOTHING *MORE.*

BUT THEY AREN'T HOLDING ME *AGAINST MY WILL,* KORIAND'R.

IN FACT, I'VE WILLINGLY *JOINED* WITH THEM, NOT ONLY WITH MY *SOUL*.... BUT WITH MY *HEART!*

PLEASE TRY TO *UNDERSTAND* ME, MOTHER... FRIENDS. THIS IS WHAT I *WANT.*

24

THEY'VE *DONE* SOMETHING TO HER!

THE GODS HAVE THEIR WAYS TO *MESMERIZE* A WOMAN. LONG AGO EVEN *I* BELIEVED ONE LOVED ME...

...UNTIL HE *STOLE* WHAT WAS RIGHTFULLY *MINE!*

THINK WHAT YOU *WANT* TO, MOTHER--IT DOESN'T *MATTER,* I'VE MADE MY *DECISION.*

I'M NOT *TRULY* AN AMAZON... I DON'T EVEN KNOW *WHO* I AM,... OR ANYTHING OF MY *PAST.*

BUT I KNOW MY *FUTURE,* AND IT'S TO WALK WITH THE *GODS!*

LET THAT BE THE *END* OF IT, AMAZONS!

WE HAVE SPENT *ENOUGH* TIME IN THESE CURSED PITS. OUR DESTINY LIES IN *OLYMPUS*... AND THAT IS WHERE WE *MUST BE!*

THE UNEARTHLY AMBER GLOW *SURROUNDS* THEM, HOLDS THEM IN COILS OF SCINTILLATING ENERGIES...

FOR A MOMENT THEY SHIMMER LIKE SOME DESERT MIRAGE...

THEN, LIKE ALL *TOO* MANY MIRAGES, THEY ARE *GONE!*

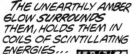

WHAT *HAPPENED* TO THEM? WHERE *ARE* THEY?

NO, HIPPOLYTE, ALL IS *NOT* HOPELESS OR I WOULD NOT HAVE TRAVELED SO FAR TO *FIND* YOU.

--BUT *SAVE* IT FROM THE *TITANS* THEMSELVES!

WHERE THEY HAVE *GONE,* MY FRIEND, WE CANNOT *FOLLOW.* MY DAUGHTER IS *LOST* TO US FOREVER.

WE NEED YOU AND YOUR ARMIES ...NEED YOU TO WAGE A WAR THAT WILL NOT *DESTROY* MANKIND--

YOU? OF COURSE! IT COULD *ONLY* BE YOU!

NEXT ISSUE: WHO IS HIPPOLYTE STARING AT? WHAT HAS HAPPENED TO THE TITANS? FOR THE ANSWER YOU MUST READ...

CLASH OF THE *TITANS!*

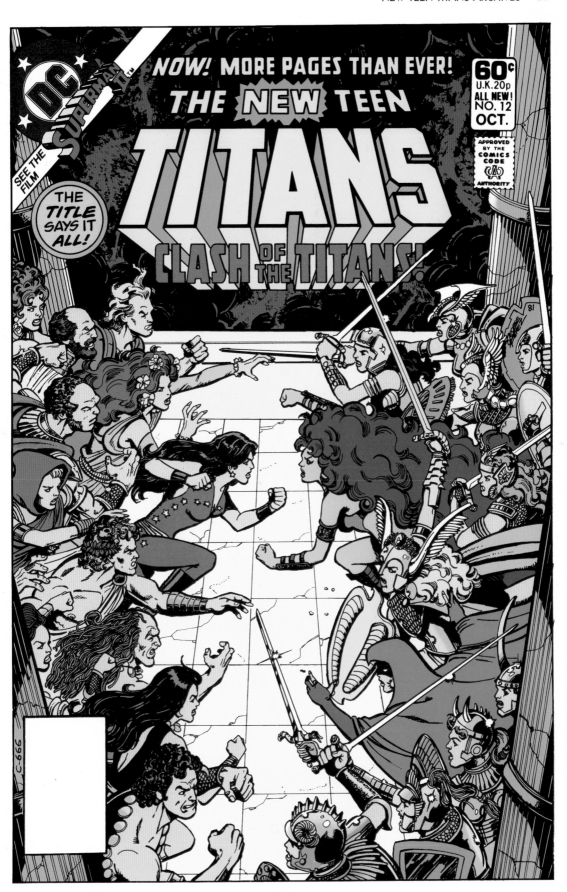

ATHENA, FOR A THOUSAND YEARS OR MORE HAVE WE LIVED BY YOUR WORD, BUT *CRONUS,* LEADER OF THOSE TITANS, SWEARS THERE CAN BE A NEW *GOLDEN AGE* ON EARTH.'

THE BEAUTY AND SERENITY THAT *ONCE* WAS COULD AGAIN BE HAD BY *ALL!*

NO, HIPPOLYTA, THERE CAN BE *NO SECOND* GOLDEN AGE...

FOR, SHOULD WELL-MEANING CRONUS EVER *SIT* ON THE THRONE OF OLYMPUS, WHAT SHALL THEN EXIST WILL MERELY BE--*CHAOS UNLEASHED!*

FOR THE SAFETY OF ALL, WE OLYMPIANS MUST *SLAY* THESE TITANS WHO ARE OUR PARENTS, AS THEY DID *THEIR* PROGENITORS!

MUST IT *ALWAYS* BE THAT WAY, ATHENA? PARENT AGAINST CHILD?

MUST *ALL* GENERATIONS EVER BE AT *WAR* WITH EACH OTHER?

MYSELF AGAINST *TRIGON?* YOU AGAINST *CRONUS* AND THE OTHERS...?

WHAT INTERESTS *ME,* ATHENA-- IS WHAT CAN *YOU* OFFER US? THEY PROMISE ETERNAL *PEACE...*

...AND EVEN WE WARRIORS OF TAMARAN PREFER EMBRACING PEACE TO BATTLE!

I CAN OFFER NOTHING THAT HAS NOT ALREADY *BEEN.* I OFFER NO PARADISE, OR PEACE OR EVERLASTING *HOPE.*

BUT *LISTEN* PLEASE BEFORE YOU TAKE SIDES AND I PROMISE THAT YOU WILL *UNDERSTAND!*

2

BUT NOW WE MUST TAKE *LEAVE* OF THIS DEEPEST OF ALL STYGIAN PITS AND RISE TO THE HIGHEST OF ALL SUMMITS: THE PEAK OF *MOUNT OLYMPUS* --

--LEGENDARY *HOME* OF THE GODS!

THERE, RHEA, MY WIFE -- OUR *GOAL* NOW STANDS BEFORE US!

AND *YOU,* CRONUS, SHALL AGAIN *RULE* AS IS YOUR RIGHT!

AHHH, MY LOVE, THE *GRANDEUR* OF OUR DIVINE MISSION FILLS ME WITH THE WARMTH OF THE LIVING *SUN!*

AS LONG AS I STAND WITH *YOU,* HYPERION, I *SHARE* YOUR WARMTH.... AND YOUR *LOVE*...

WE STAND *TOGETHER,* AND TOGETHER WE SHALL *TOPPLE* THE GODS!

YET, IN THE FURTHEST REACHES OF WONDER GIRL'S MIND, THERE REMAIN THE SLIGHTEST VESTIGES OF NAGGING *DOUBT*...

...DOUBT SHARED BY ANOTHER OF THESE ELDER GODS WHO CALL THEMSELVES *THE TITANS!*

TETHYS, MY LOVE, WE BELONG IN OUR UNDERSEA HOMES, NOT HERE IN THESE WIND-SWEPT SKIES.

I WANT *NOTHING* OF THIS BATTLE!

YET, OCEANUS-- WE MUST OBEY CRONUS' *COMMAND!* HE IS OUR *LEADER!*

AT LAST--*OLYMPUS!* IT HAS BEEN A *LONG* TIME, EH, CRIUS?

BUT NOT LONG ENOUGH TO *ERASE* THE FOUL PAST FROM THE GODS OF MEMORY, IS IT, MNEMOSYNE?

I WILL FOREVER REMEMBER OUR HATED *IMPRISONMENT* IN TARTARUS!

3

CRONUS, LOOK BEYOND THE MISTS, GUARDING THE OLYMPIAN GATES -- *THE THREE SEASONS!*

THEN QUICKLY, WE MUST *SUBDUE THEM!*

THEY ARE MY CHILDREN AS WELL AS ZEUS'-- THEIR POWER IS *TERRIBLE!*

THEN CONSIDER THEM *STOPPED,* THEMIS.

BUT... EIRENE! EUNOMIA! IT IS AS ATHENA *PREDICTED.* THE TITANS *RETURN!*

YOU *BATTLE* THEM! I MUST WARN OUR *FATHER!*

NO, DIKE, ZEUS MAY INDEED *HEAR* OF OUR COMING, BUT HE WILL NOT LEARN OF IT FROM *YOU!*

THAT THE MOON GODS *SWEAR!*

THE *SLEEP OF NIGHT* WILL OVERTAKE YOU... YOU'LL REST *UNHARMED* AS A GIFT TO THEMIS, YOUR MOTHER.

HYPERION, WE ARE *THROUGH!* ONLY THE *GATES* STAND BETWEEN US AND THE SHATTERING OF THAT ORACLE'S *CURSE!*

WELL, WHAT DO YOU *WAIT* FOR, CRONUS?

PATIENCE, BROTHER... LET US *SAVOR* THIS MOMENT, FOR OUR *DESTINY* AWAITS BEHIND THIS FRAGILE DOOR.

DESTINY--AND THE *POWER INFINITE!*

CRONUS BREATHES IN DEEPLY AS HE RAISES HIS SCYTHE HAND HIGH...

BUT LET US MOVE AHEAD OF CRONUS AND *BRIDGE* THE GULF THAT SEPARATES HIM FROM THE MAGNIFICENCE OF OLYMPUS!

OH, IT HAS BEEN SPOKEN OF IN *MYTH*, BUT NO MERE LEGEND CAN EXAGGERATE ITS MAGNIFICENT *REALITY*.

IT IS *GLORIOUS*, THE CENTER OF ALL THAT IS! IT IS *POWER*, AND THE POWER IS WITHOUT EQUAL!

AND, STANDING AT ITS THRESHOLD, ITS GOD SUPREME-- *ZEUS*, HE WHO WIELDS THE THUNDERBOLT COSMIC!

HEAR ME, OLYMPIANS-- WE ARE READY FOR *WAR*, AND WE ARE READY FOR *VICTORY*!

PLEASE, MY HUSBAND, DO NOT *DESTROY* THEM.

WHAT? YOU DARE BEG FOR *LENIENCY* WHEN THEY COME TO DESTROY *US?* HAVE YOU GONE *MAD*, HERA?

BUT CRONUS IS YOUR *FATHER*. DOES THAT MEAN *NOTHING* TO YOU?

IT *DOES*, AND I DO NOT FORGET THAT WHEN I WAS BUT A *CHILD* HE ORDERED *ME* DESTROYED.

ONLY MY BELOVED MOTHER, *RHEA*, PROTECTED ME UNTIL THE *ORACLE'S* PREDICTION COULD COME TRUE.

AYE, FATHER-- EVEN I REMEMBER-- HE SAID "THE SON WOULD RISE AND BANISH THE FATHER." HE SAID "THE CHILD SHALL RULE AND THE FATHER WOULD *DIE!*"

SO, YOU SEE-- IT IS MY *DESTINY*, HERA, AND, BY THE POWER OF MY THUNDERBOLT, OUR PARENTS, THESE ELDER GODS, THESE SELF-PROCLAIMED *TITANS*--

-- MUST ALL *PERISH* LEST WE OLYMPIANS DIE IN THEIR STEAD!

6

WITH A HEAVY CRUNCH, CRONUS' SCYTHE CLEAVES THE GLIMMERING GATES AS IF THEY WERE WIND-BLOWN STRAW...

... AND OLYMPUS SUDDENLY STANDS OPEN AND UNGUARDED...

...OR SO IT WOULD SEEM TO THE NAKED EYE.

NO ARMIES AWAIT US FOR BATTLE? THIS IS *UNLIKE* OUR CHILDREN.

TAKE CARE, MY BROTHERS AND SISTERS--SOMETHING IS *WRONG.*

STEP *CAREFULLY,* ALL.

I FEAR THE VERY *GROUND* WE TREAD UPON MAY BE ALIVE WITH *TRAPS* SET BY THAT DEVIOUS SON OF MY BLOOD!

WHAT?

MMMMMMMMMM!

BY THE CHAOS THAT SPAWNED US ALL!!

NOW THE FIGHT *BEGINS!*

THE FURIES! DAMN THEIR SOULLESS, SERPENTINE HIDES!

TO MY *SIDE!* THE BATTLE LINE HAS BEEN DRAWN!

7

BUT STILL SHE MOVES LIKE THE SWIFT-LEGGED *PANTHER*, AND HER STRENGTH, WHICH RIVALS THAT OF *HERACLES* HIMSELF, IS SAVAGE AND MIGHTY BEYOND HUMAN BELIEF.

IN AN INSTANT, MIGHTY ARES, WAR GOD, FALLS!

WONDER GIRL GLANCES AT HER SIDE, FEELING FLESH POUNDING GODLY FLESH, AND STEEL GLANCING OFF UNSHATTERABLE STEEL...

BUT, FAR OFF, IN THE SEAS WHICH FOREVER ENCIRCLE OLYMPUS, *POSEIDON*, GOD OF THE OCEANS, CONFRONTS HIS PARENTS, OCEANUS AND TETHYS.

GET *AWAY,* BOTH OF YOU-- BEFORE I AM FORCED TO *KILL!*

ZEUS HAS GIVEN ME HIS COMMAND, AND EVEN *I* CANNOT DENY HIM.

YOU WILL NOT *HAVE* TO, ERRANT SON, FOR YOURS IS STILL THE POWER OF A *CHILD* WHEN COMPARED WITH THAT OF A *TITAN BORN.*

YOU CANNOT *FIGHT* US, MY SON...FOR YOUR OWN FISH'S TAIL SHALL CRUSH THE *BREATH* FROM YOUR HEAVING LUNGS.

12

BUT, EVEN AS THE HORRORS OF WAR OVERTAKE OLYMPUS, WONDER GIRL BATTLES ON 'TWEEN THE LIGHTNING AND THE THUNDER WHICH ROCK WHAT WAS ONCE A PALACE OF PEACE.

SHE BATTLES BECAUSE SHE MUST, FOR HYPERION'S GOLDEN GLOW STILL HOLDS HER MIND, AND MORE-- HER HEART.

SHE BATTLES THOUGH DOUBTS PLAGUE HER. YET, WHAT CAN SHE, A MERE MORTAL, DO, WHEN ENTHRALLED BY THE GOD OF THE SUN?

WATER STORMS FALL FROM THE SKY AND SHE SEES APOLLO AND HEPHAESTUS BOTH RESIST WITH ALL THEIR GODLY POWER.

EPIC STRUGGLES 'TWEEN LIGHT AND DARK BEGIN TO RIP AT HER WILL...

...AS ALL HER DOUBTS RUSH FORWARD LIKE THE RAGING TIDE.

AND SHE, WHO HAS SPENT MOST OF HER LIFE WITHOUT KNOWING FEAR, TREMBLES AS COLD DARKNESS GRIPS THE SKY-TOWERING SPIRES OF THIS HOME OF THE ALL-KNOWING GODS.

13

BUT THEN THE DOUBT DROWNING HER MIND IS SUDDENLY GONE -- FOR THE MOMENT, AT LEAST-- AS IAPETUS, TITAN-GOD OF JUSTICE, SCREAMS...

ZEUS SENT THIS BEAST TO *SLAY* YOU? WELL, BY HERA -- HE WON'T GET THE *CHANCE!*

... AND AS LION-HEADED, GOAT-BODIED, DRAGON-TAILED CHIMERA SLASHES FORWARD WITH RAZOR-SHARP TALONS, AND STREAMS OF FIERY BREATH...

"BY HERA"? I STILL *SWEAR* BY THE NAMES OF THOSE GODS I NOW *FIGHT.*

BY *WHY?* WHY AM I *DOING* THIS?

WHY? WHY? WHY?

THIS ISN'T *MY* BATTLE! THIS ISN'T MY *WAR!* YET I FIGHT AND I CANNOT *STOP!*

WHILE...

HOW MANY TIMES MUST I *SLAY* YOU, FATHER?

WHEN WILL YOU FINALLY REALIZE YOUR DAYS ARE *OVER?*

YOU CALL ME A *FOOL*, ZEUS-- BUT YOU ARE *MORE* THAN FOOLISH!

WITH YOUR POWER YOU COULD HAVE MADE A *PARADISE* OF THIS UNIVERSE...

...YOU COULD HAVE CREATED AN EVERLASTING *PEACE* THROUGHOUT ALL THE WORLDS BOTH KNOWN AND NOT.

14

IT IS *OVER,* MY LOVE... WE HAVE *WON!*

OLYMPUS IS *OURS!!* THE GODS ARE *HELPLESS* NOW...

ENCASED IN *STONE* EVEN AS *WE* WERE FOR ALL THOSE MANY YEARS.

BUT, LET US NOT MAKE *THEIR* MISTAKE, MY BROTHERS.

THEY MERELY *BANISHED* US TO THE HELLPITS OF TARTARUS--

--LET US *DESTROY* THESE UPSTARTS WHILE WE STILL HAVE *CONTROL.*

DESTROY? NO, CRONUS, THAT'S AGAINST EVERY-THING WE WERE FIGHTING FOR.

YOU PROMISED ALL *PEACE.* HOW CAN YOU *BEGIN* BY CAUSING *DEATH?*

HOW CAN YOU SPREAD *LOVE* IF THERE IS ONLY *HATE* IN YOUR HEART?

DONNA, THAT IS *ENOUGH!* CRONUS IS OUR *LEADER!*

YOUR WORDS *STING,* MORTAL! WHAT YOU SAY HAS *MERIT,* BUT JUST CANNOT *BE.*

YOU *LIE* TO YOURSELF IF YOU BELIEVE THAT, CRONUS. YOU DO IT FOR *YOURSELF* AND NO OTHER.

YES, MY DAUGHTER... ATHENA'S WISDOM HAS *GUIDED* US ON OUR JOURNEY TO OLYMPUS.

AND IT APPEARS WE HAVE ARRIVED JUST *IN TIME.*

BECAUSE YOU CANNOT SEEM TO *REALIZE*--

I *DO* BELIEVE IN LOVE AND PEACE, BUT IF WE FAIL TO *DESTROY* THESE CHILD-GODS, THEY WILL SOME DAY RETURN TO DESTROY US! WHAT WE MUST DO WE DO FOR THE *WORLDS* THAT WILL REALIZE SALVATION.

YOU?!?

-- YOUR DREAMS OF THIS NEW GOLDEN AGE WOULD ONLY *DESTROY* THE VERY ONES YOU CLAIM TO WISH TO *HELP.*

16

HIPPOLYTA SPEAKS THE *TRUTH*, CRONUS. *ABANDON* THIS FRUITLESS BATTLE WITH YOUR CHILDREN.

RETURN TO THE PITS OF *TARTARUS* AND CARVE FROM ITS WALLS OF FIRE AND BRIMSTONE A *PALACE* FIT FOR THE ELDER GODS!

THEY *WON'T* STOP THEIR FIGHT, MOTHER --THEY *BELIEVE* THEIR WAY IS RIGHT, AND SO DO I.

IT GRIEVES ME TO HEAR YOU *SAY* THAT, DAUGHTER --FOR IT MEANS THERE MUST BE *WAR.*

BUT WHY, MOTHER? *WHY?* WE ALL SEEK THE SAME *PEACE.*

NONE OF US *WANT* TO FIGHT, DO WE?

ALL OF THIS IS SO *STRANGE* TO ME, AND IT *BOTHERS* ME...

I....I DON'T FEEL IN *CONTROL* OF MYSELF ...OR OF ANYTHING *AROUND* ME.

CAN YOU *TELL* ME, MOTHER -- WHAT'S *HAPPENING* HERE? WHAT'S GOING ON?

YOU SENSE THE *TRUTH*, DONNA -- EVEN THOUGH PART OF YOU *REJECTS* IT.

THERE YOU ARE *WRONG*, GODDESS. SHE KNOWS THE TRUTH IS IN WHAT WE *TITANS* WANT.

SHE KNOWS *THAT* AS WELL AS SHE KNOWS THE TRUTH OF OUR *LOVE!*

THE LOVE I FELT THE MOMENT I FIRST SET *EYES* UPON HER.

EVEN *THAT*, HYPERION ....IT HAPPENED SO *QUICKLY*...

I DON'T EVEN UNDER-STAND *WHY* IT HAPPENED, OR *HOW.*

DONNA, WE HAVE *HEARD* ATHENA'S WORDS, AND THEY ARE *WISE.* LISTEN TO THEM BEFORE CHOOSING SIDES.... *PLEASE!*

17

YOU SEE THE EARTH AS IT WOULD BE IF *CRONUS'S* RULE HELD SWAY.

YOU SEE *PEACE,* YOU FEEL THE *TRANQUILITY* THAT PERVADES ALL.

THEN YOUR OWN WORDS PROVE US *RIGHT,* OLYMPIAN.

IT'S *BEAUTIFUL,* ATHENA... IT'S WHAT MAN-KIND'S ALWAYS *DREAMED* OF.

I WILL HAVE GIVEN THE WORLD *LOVE...*

...AND THAT IS MORE THAN *ZEUS* HAS EVER DONE!

THE VISION CONTINUES, CRONUS... *WATCH,* THEN SPEAK LATER.

"YOUR VERY OWN WORDS BE-TRAY YOU, CRONUS. YOU DON'T BELIEVE MAN IS *EQUAL* TO THE GODS...

"YOU SEE THEM AS *WORSHIPPING* YOU.

"YOU SEE THEM AS *SHEEP,* TO PROTECT AS YOU WOULD YOUR FLOCK.

"YES, THERE WOULD BE PEACE AND TRANQUILITY, BUT MANKIND'S WILL WOULD BE DESTROYED.

"YOUR NEW GOLDEN AGE WOULD BRING BEAUTY, BUT AT WHAT COST?

"THE ANSWER, CRONUS -- IS MAN'S *FREEDOM!*

"THEY HAVE A *DIVINE RIGHT* TO BE FREE, NOT TO BEND TO *YOUR* THINKING, TITAN."

IF THEY WANT PEACE, THAT IS THEIR *RIGHT.* IF THEY ARE FOOLISH ENOUGH TO DEMAND *BLOOD,* THAT TOO SHOULD BE THEIRS TO DECIDE.

LONG AGO ZEUS *UNDERSTOOD* THAT TRUTH. MAN HAS FREE WILL TO DO AS HE WISHES...

AND THE GODS MUST BE FOREVER RESTRICTED FROM *INTERFERING* WITH THOSE WHOM THEY HAVE CREATED.

CAN YOU *DENY* THIS, CRONUS? *CAN* YOU, GOD OF GODS?

PLEASE, CRONUS... *ANSWER* HER!

18

YOU *TELL* ME, HYPERION. IS THIS WHAT WILL *HAPPEN* IF CRONUS RECREATES HIS GOLDEN AGE?

DONNA, I--

DONNA, HYPERION HOLDS YOU UNDER *HIS* SWAY. HIS SUN POWERS CONTROL YOUR *HEART.*

CAN YOU BELIEVE *CRONUS* WOULD PROVE ANY DIFFERENT?

IS SHE *RIGHT?* HYPERION? DID YOU *MAKE* ME LOVE YOU?

FOR HEAVEN'S SAKE, HYPERION, *DID YOU DO THIS TO ME?!?*

WE ARGUE TOO LONG, AND THE TIME FOR *TALK* IS DONE!

WE TITANS HAVE *WON* OUR BATTLE WITH THE GODS OF OLYMPUS!

YOU MORTALS SHALL NOT TALK US OUT OF OUR RIGHTFUL *VICTORY!*

THEN, WE'LL TURN THAT VICTORY *AGAINST* YOU, CRONUS--

--FOR YOU'RE NO GOD OF *MINE!*

AND NOT EVEN THE LIVING *GOD,* X'HAL HERSELF, DEMANDS SUCH MINDLESS SUBSERVIENCE!

THEN THIS X'HAL OF YOURS IS A *FOOL!*

WHAT *USE* IS POWER UNLESS ONE *WIELDS* IT?

THEN THE DIE HAS BEEN *CAST!*

THERE MUST BE WAR!

19

BROTHERS AND SISTERS, LET US *UNITE* OUR POWERS... LET US SHARE OUR *STRENGTHS*.

ONE FINAL BATTLE, AND THE WORLD IS *OURS!*

BY HERA! THEY SHATTER THE VERY *GROUND* BENEATH OUR FEET!

BUT NOT EVEN THE WILL OF THE *TITANS* SHALL STOP US!

OVER SHIFTING ROCK OR GUSHING WAVE--WE AMAZONS FIGHT TO THE *END!*

KORIAND'R, THE AMAZONS TAKE ON THE TITANS...IT IS UP TO US TO *FREE* THE ONE WHO CAN HELP US GAIN VICTORY.

A MOMENT, RAVEN...THAT BLAST WAS *POWERFUL.*

AND AGAIN I HAVE BEEN *DEFEATED* WITH FAR TOO MUCH *EASE.*

IF WE *SURVIVE* THIS WAR, RAVEN, I MUST RETURN TO THE TRAINING OF THE *OKAARAN WARLORDS!*

DO WHAT YOU WILL IF WE *LIVE...*

...BUT FOR NOW, ZEUS MUST BE *FREED!*

HE LIVES ...I CAN *SENSE* HIS SOUL...

THEN *STAND BACK,* RAVEN -- I'LL FREE HIM WITH A *STARBOLT!*

NO, GIRL, MY *HUSBAND* PLACED THE OLYMPIAN THERE ...AND THERE SHALL HE *REMAIN!*

RHEA! YOU ABOVE ALL KNOW THE *FOLLY* OF THIS FIGHT. YOU RISKED YOUR HUSBAND'S WRATH BEFORE IN *SAVING* ZEUS FROM CRONUS' RAGE.

BUT... I CANNOT *DEFY* HIM AGAIN... I *CAN'T!*

20

THEN I *TOO* MUST DO WHAT MUST BE DONE!

I, WHO *ABHOR* VIOLENCE, MUST LASH OUT, OR THERE WILL BE *BLOOD* STAINING THE GROUNDS OF OLYMPUS AND EARTH ALIKE!

THIS WILL NOT *HURT* YOU, RHEA... MY SOUL-SELF' WILL MERELY *EASE* YOUR ANGER, *SUBDUE* YOUR NEED FOR WAR.

YOU WILL SLEEP AWAY THIS BATTLE IN *PEACE*, AND PRAY I CAN DO THE SAME FOR YOUR BLOODTHIRSTY *FELLOWS!*

KORIAND'R, HAVE YOU FOUND A WAY TO *FREE* THE OLYMPIAN?

I'M *TRYING*, RAVEN, BUT NOT EVEN MY *STARBOLTS* CAN SMASH CRONUS' WALL OF STONE.

DO YOU KNOW HOW *FRUSTRATING* IT IS? BEING SO *POWERLESS* WHILE POSSESSING SO MUCH *POWER?*

WHILE...

IT IS *YOUR* FAULT, WOMAN-- YOU WHO ARE MY LOVE'S *MOTHER!* YOU SET HER *AGAINST* ME.

YOU'LL *DIE* FOR THAT-- AS MY *PARENTS* HAD TO DIE THAT WE TITANS WOULD LIVE.

NO, HYPERION-- *STOP!*

WHATEVER *HATRED* EXISTS BETWEEN YOU AND YOUR ELDERS...OR YOU AND YOUR CHILDREN--

--THAT HATRED DOES NOT EXIST IN *ME.*

I *LOVE* MY MOTHER, AND IF YOU *HURT* HER, OR EVEN *TRY*--

--SO HELP ME, HYPERION-- GOD, OR TITAN, OR WHAT-EVER YOU ARE-- *I WILL MAKE YOU SUFFER!*

DONNA... DAUGHTER...

AT LAST, RAVEN, I'VE CREATED A *FISSURE*...THE ROCK WILL *BREAK* NOW.

STAND BACK, RAVEN, AND, BY X'HAL--

21

--THE OLYMPIAN WILL BE FREE!

BY THE CHAOS!

NO...NOT AGAIN...HOW MANY *LIVES* DOES THIS ZEUS *POSSESS*?

MORE THAN ENOUGH, MY FATHER!

AND *WISDOM* ENOUGH TO KNOW HOW TO *USE* SUCH LIVES.

AGAIN WE STAND AT EACH OTHER'S THROATS --READY TO KILL OR *BE* KILLED.

BUT, THERE IS NO *REASON* FOR THIS FOLLY. YOU MUST REMEMBER THE WORDS OF THE *ORACLE*.

I *REMEMBER* HIM, DAMN YOU! I REMEMBER HIM SAYING THE *CHILD* SHALL LIVE ON, THE PARENT SHALL *PASS ON*!

BUT *THIS* TIME HIS WORDS NEED NOT COME *TRUE*.

THERE IS NO OTHER *WAY*, CRONUS ...AND YOU MUST *KNOW* THAT NOW.

FROM PARENT TO CHILD, THE MANTLE IS *ALWAYS* PASSED ON.

22

"I WAS BORN OF YOUR SON'S *BROW*-- AND I, *ATHENA*, AM *GODDESS* OF WISDOM. I SEE CLEARLY WHAT OTHERS *CANNOT*."

"...AND I KNOW THAT, AS GAEA AND URANUS PASSED THE POWER UNTO *YOU*, AND YOU TO *US*, SOME DAY WE WILL PASS ON *OUR* POWER AS WELL."

"THAT IS THE WAY OF THE *UNIVERSE*. NEITHER MAN NOR GOD MAY *CHANGE* THAT ONE ETERNAL *TRUTH*."

"YOU DEMAND OUR *DEATHS*?"

"NO!"

"YET WE CANNOT LIVE *HERE*...SUCH IS NOT OUR *WAY*, ATHENA."

"ONLY *YOU*, OCEANUS, FOUGHT OUR *WAGING* THIS WAR. WHAT SAY YOU *NOW*?"

"THERE IS BUT ONE PLACE WE CAN GO, CRONUS -- *TARTARUS*!"

"RETURN TO THAT *HELL*? HOW CAN ONE FORGET ITS *HORRORS*? THERE MUST BE *ANOTHER* PLACE, CRONUS."

"THERE IS *NONE*, MNEMOSYNE, AND WE HAVE NO PLACE *HERE*."

"I FEAR ATHENA'S WORDS ARE *TRUE* ...WHAT WE WISH FOR MAN, AS NOBLE AS OUR ASPIRATIONS MAY BE--"

"--ITS *RESULT* WOULD BE MORE THAN FOLLY--'TWOULD BE *DISASTER*!"

"TARTARUS *NEEDN'T* BE A HELL. YOU CAN MAKE IT *MORE*."

"*FIGHT* TO MAKE IT THE *PARADISE* YOU SEEK."

"SHE IS *CORRECT*, CRONUS."

"OUR *TIME* HERE, OUR *PLACE* HERE, IS NO MORE. LET THOSE WHO HAVE COME AFTER US *INHERIT* WHAT IS NOW RIGHTFULLY THEIRS."

23

CRONUS--*NO!* WE MUST NOT ABANDON OUR *IDEALS.*

THEY ARE ALL *WRONG.* WE *CAN* REMAKE THIS WORLD AS YOU SEE IT!

WE CAN *AVOID* THE PROBLEMS THEY PREDICT.

HYPERION, IT IS *OVER...* THE OLYMPIANS, OUR CHILDREN, ARE *CORRECT.*

THEN WHAT AM I TO *DO?* I HAVE ALREADY LOST MY *FIRST* LOVE, THIA--

--MUST I LOSE THIS *SECOND* LOVE AS WELL?

THERE WASN'T *LOVE* BETWEEN US, HYPERION ...NO *TRUE* LOVE.

NO, YOU CANNOT *SAY* THAT. I *LOVED* YOU... I *DID.*

YES, I USED MY POWERS TO *MAKE* YOU LOVE ME, BUT THAT WAS FOR *US...*

AND THINK-- SOON YOU CAN BE A *GODDESS*... AN *IMMORTAL.*

NO, BROTHER, SHE CAN *NEVER* BE A GODDESS.

SHE IS A *MORTAL...*

...AND THAT IS WHAT SHE MUST FOREVER *REMAIN.*

YOU SOUGHT TO POSSESS *HER* AS I SOUGHT TO POSSESS A *WORLD.* IT IS *WRONG.*

NO...NO ...IT IS NOT *FAIR,* CRONUS ...TO HAVE SO MUCH--

I AM A GOD OF THE *SUN* ...I TOUCHED THE *LIGHT* ...AND NOW... NOW YOU WANT TO PLUNGE ME INTO *DARKNESS* FOREVER

IT... IT IS NOT *FAIR...* NOT FAIR *AT* ALL...

WHY... WHY MUST I *SUFFER* SO?

IN SOME WAY, TO SOME MEASURE, HYPERION, WE *ALL* SUFFER-- AND ALL WE CAN HOPE FOR IS TO *GROW.*

THAT'S *ALL* WE CAN HOPE FOR...

...THAT'S *ALL...*

--NOT FAIR TO LOSE IT ALL, AND TO *WANT* SO MUCH *MORE.*

24

THERE IS STILL ONE LAST *ITEM* TO ATTEND TO, MY HUSBAND.

THE OLYMPIANS!

OUR SON *ZEUS* COULD FREE THEM NOW, BUT LET THE ENMITY BETWEEN PARENT AND CHILD *END.*

WE WHO GAVE YOU LIFE AN *AGE AGONE*...

...NOW RETURN TO YOU ITS *FREEDOM* AS YOU DESERVE.

IT IS *OVER* NOW.

AND WE ARE *READY.*

TARTARUS *AWAITS* US... BUT THIS TIME WE GO NOT AS *DEFEATED* TITANS...

WE TRAVEL NOT TO SOME *PRISON*...

...BUT TO OUR *HOME,*

FOR WE *TOO* HAVE GAINED OUR FREEDOM... AND HOPEFULLY, GAINED EVEN *MORE.*

ALL OF YOU BUT *I*... I HAVE *LOST*... LOST *HOPE*... LOST *LOVE*...

YOU *FOUND* LOVE, HYPERION... YOU EVEN *INSPIRED* LOVE... I *CARED*...

...AND EVEN *NOW,* I CARE ...FOR THE *GOODNESS* THAT IS IN YOU.

FAREWELL, MY PARENTS... YOU GO NOT TO *HELL* --

--BUT TO *HEAVEN.*

AND ONE DAY, WE, YOUR CHILDREN, SHALL WALK *BESIDE* YOU AGAIN.

AND ON THAT BRIGHT DAY, WE SHALL WALK TOGETHER IN *LOVE.*

25

EPILOGUE ONE:

PARADISE ISLAND: AS A PLANE SWOOPS HIGH AND AWAY FROM THIS ISLE OF PEACE AND HOPE.

SOON, IT WILL BE GONE.

I DO NOT *UNDERSTAND.* WHY DID DONNA LEAVE WITHOUT EVEN A WORD?

I READ HER *SOUL,* KORIAND'R... AND HER *HEART.*

AND PERHAPS *I,* ABOVE ALL, KNOW WHAT HAPPENED TO HER.

FOR *LIKE* HYPERION, I TOO HAVE MANIPULATED THAT EMOTION CALLED *LOVE...*

...AND I KNOW HOW TERRIBLY *CRUSHED* DONNA NOW FEELS.

FOR EVEN THAT ARTIFICIALLY CREATED LOVE IS FELT BY BOTH MAN AND WOMAN -- AND IT IS A PAIN I HAVE YET TO *ERASE.*

MY HEART *REACHES OUT* FOR HER...

...FOR I *TOO* LOVED A GOD WITH ALL MY HEART AND ALL MY SOUL...

...AND I... I HAVE NEVER LOVED *ANOTHER* MAN SINCE.

I CAN ONLY PRAY THAT *MY* FATE AND MY *SUFFERING* IS NOT SHARED BY THE DAUGHTER I LOVE.

EPILOGUE TWO:

THE LABORATORY OF PAULA VON GUNTHER...

THE MALE RESPONDS WELL TO THE *PURPLE RAY.*

HE WILL *NOT* DIE AFTER ALL.

COME, HESTIA, PAULA AND THE OTHERS WILL WANT TO *KNOW.*

THE AMAZONS LEAVE TO SPREAD THE JOYOUS WORD THAT *GARFIELD LOGAN,* WHO HOVERED ON THE VERY BRINK OF DEATH, NOW *LIVES...*

BUT SOON, THEY WILL ALL RETURN TO *DISCOVER...*

...THIS IS NOT QUITE THE SAME GARFIELD LOGAN THEY HAD ONCE KNOWN.

I... I LIVE AGAIN... AND I LIVE -- TO KILL!!

26

EPILOGUE THREE:

NEW YORK CITY STANDS TALL, PROUND, AND SEEMINGLY ETERNAL...

AND, IN THE APARTMENT OF ONE TERRY LONG, AGE 29, PROFESSOR OF HISTORY AT MANHATTAN UNIVERSITY...

HUH? WHO CAN *THAT* BE?

IF THAT'S *McREADY*... I PAID THE BLASTED *RENT* LAST--EH?

DONNA?

TERRY, PLEASE-- OPEN THE *DOOR*...

DONNA, *WHA--?*

DON'T, TERRY-- PLEASE DON'T *TALK* NOW...

...AND PLEASE DON'T ASK ME WHAT *HAPPENED.*

JUST *HOLD* ME...

...AND DON'T LET ME *GO*... NOT FOR A VERY LONG TIME.

BELIEVE ME, DONNA, I *WON'T*...

...I *LOVE* YOU.

I TRULY LOVE *YOU.*

AND DAY PASSES INTO NIGHT, AND NIGHT TO DAY...

...AND THE FAINT LIGHT OF HOPE BEGINS TO GLOW, AND THE DOUBTS, THOUGH NEVER GONE, RECEDE FAR, FAR AWAY...

NEXT ISSUE: WONDER GIRL IN NEW YORK! RAVEN AND STARFIRE ON PARADISE ISLAND! BUT, WHAT OF THE GUYS?

TITANS-- TOGETHER!

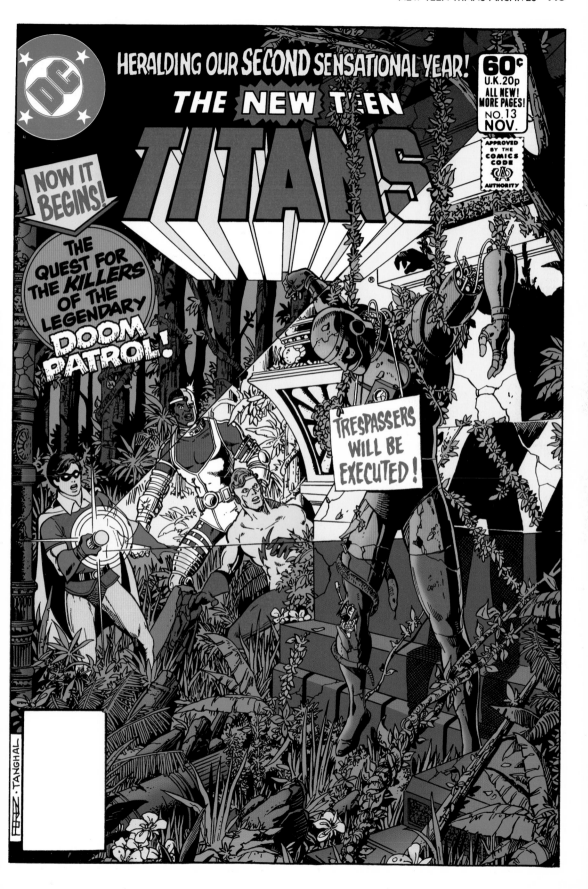

OH, MAN-- SHE'S PICKIN' UP THAT FORK-LIFT LIKE IT'S A *TOY.*

SPLIT, MAN-- *RUN!* I AIN'T TACKLIN' *THAT* BROAD!

WHAT ABOUT THE *BOSS?* HE'LL *KILL* US FER SCREWIN' UP.

OH, DON'T WORRY ABOUT *THAT,* PUNK. THERE WON'T BE ENOUGH *LEFT* OF YOU FOR *HIM* TO GET HIS HANDS ON.

SHOOT! I DON'T *LIKE* THIS, LEROY... NOT ONE BIG, BAD *BIT!*

SHE'S GONNA LET US HANG LIKE DEAD MEAT IN AN *ICE BOX!*

SKRASHHH

NOT *DEAD,* MISTER-- BUT YOU MIGHT *WISH* YOU WERE.

TODAY WAS DEFINITELY THE *WRONG* DAY TO PULL OFF A JOB IN *MY* NEIGHBORHOOD!

SWOK.

I'M *MAD,* FELLAS... MADDER THAN I'VE EVER *BEEN...*

I WANT TO *SMASH* SOMETHING... AND I DON'T PARTICULARLY CARE *WHAT.*

NO, THAT'S NOT *TRUE!* I *DO* CARE...

... BLAST IT, I *HAVE* TO CARE.

I MAY NOT *LIKE* IT, BUT AS MUCH AS I *WANT* TO HATE YOU, I *CAN'T.*

THESE FEELINGS GO AGAINST EVERYTHING I WAS *TAUGHT.*

2

WONDER GIRL BREATHES IN DEEPLY, THEN EXPELS HER HATRED ALONG WITH HER BREATH. CALMLY, SHE PRESSES THE ALARM BELL AND JUST WAITS UNTIL...

HEY, MAN, GET US *AWAY* FROM THAT LOONY. SHE COULD'A TORE US *APART*.

LOUIE, I CAN'T THINK OF A GUY WHO'D DESERVE IT *MORE*.

WE'VE BEEN HUNTING FOR THIS GANG FOR *MONTHS*. YOU'VE SAVED US AN AWFUL LOT OF *WORK*.

JUST WANT TO SAY *THANKS*, WONDER GIRL.

IT'S *OKAY*, OFFICER, I WAS JUST DOING MY *JOB*!

NO, THAT'S A *LIE*. I WENT OUT LOOKING FOR SOMEONE TO *HURT*.

AND *WHY*--? BECAUSE HYPERION USED SOME SORT OF *SPELL* ON ME--MADE ME *LOVE* HIM.*

I FELT LIKE A *PAWN*, NOT IN CONTROL--

*AS SHOWN LAST ISSUE. --Len.

SO, WHAT DO I *DO*? I GO OUT OF MY WAY TO *LOSE* THAT CONTROL ON *MY OWN*.

BRIGHT, DONNA-- REAL BRIGHT.

TERRY! I ALMOST *FORGOT* YOU WERE WAITING. I'M *SORRY*.

DON'T MENTION IT, LOVE. IT WAS... WELL... *FASCINATING* WATCHING YOU IN ACTION.

MY STRENGTH DOESN'T *INTIMIDATE* YOU?

WELL, I'M NOT ABOUT TO CHALLENGE YOU TO AN *ARM-WRESTLING MATCH*, BUT, NAH-- IT DOESN'T *BOTHER* ME.

I HAVE THREE *OLDER SISTERS*. I GREW UP BEING BEATEN UP BY *GIRLS*.

BESIDES, GORGEOUS, WITH YOU IT'S *KINKY*.

HEY, LOWER THAT ARCHED *EYEBROW*, LOVE... I'M JUST *KIDDING*.

3

I'VE GOT A GOOD GRASP OF WHO *I* AM AND YOUR SPECIAL POWERS DON'T MAKE ME LESS *IMPORTANT*.

BUT THAT'S NOT WHAT'S *TROUBLING* YOU, IS IT? IT'S *HYPERION*, RIGHT?

YOU SEE RIGHT *THROUGH* ME, TERRY. YEAH, IT'S *HYPERION*.

LITTLE LADY THAT I *LOVE*, I'M A *HISTORY PROFESSOR*, REMEMBER?

I *KNOW* ALL *ABOUT* GODS ENTHRALLING BEAUTIFUL YOUNG MORTALS.

THAT DOESN'T MAKE IT *EASIER*, TERRY. I FEEL HELPLESS KNOWING I COULD BE *CONTROLLED* SO EASILY.

WELL, YOU CAN *DWELL* ON THAT, DONNA, EVEN THOUGH IT CAN'T CHANGE THE *FACTS*.

OR YOU CAN PUT IT *ASIDE*, KNOW YOU'RE A *GOOD PERSON* INSIDE, THAT YOU ARE *LOVED* AND CAN LOVE *BACK*.

YOU'VE GOT YOUR WHOLE *FUTURE* AHEAD OF YOU, DONNA...

DON'T LET THIS CRIPPLE YOUR *BELIEF* IN YOURSELF.

I'VE GOT A FUTURE, BUT FOR HOW *LONG*, REALLY? GARFIELD'S *YOUNGER* THAN I AM--

--AND HE'S ONLY *CLINGING* TO LIFE BY A FINE *THREAD*. *

*THE TERMINATOR SHOT GAR LOGAN, A.K.A. THE CHANGELING, IN TITANS #10. -- Len.

"WE RUSHED HIM TO *PARADISE ISLAND*, PLACED HIM UNDER THE *PURPLE RAY*... HOPING ITS LIFE-RESTORING RAYS COULD SAVE HIM."

"DIDN'T YOU SAY HE WAS *RECUPERATING*?"

HE'S NOT *DYING*, TERRY... BUT THAT'S FAR FROM BEING *HEALTHY*.

WHO KNOWS WHAT THIS WILL *DO* TO HIM... OR TO ANY OF US...

WE SUPER-HEROES AREN'T *USED* TO HAVING OUR FACES RUBBED IN OUR OWN *MORTALITY*.

READ ALL-STAR SQUADRON

TAXI

AND THAT'S WHY YOU'RE GOING BACK... TO *PARADISE ISLAND*, RIGHT?

I *HAVE* TO, TERRY... TO MAKE CERTAIN HE'S *ALL RIGHT*.

I'LL BE *WAITING* FOR YOU, DONNA.

GOD, TERRY, I *HOPE* SO. PLEASE... *KEEP WELL*.

ALWAYS *KEEP WELL*.

YOU'RE TOO GOOD A MAN TO EVER HAVE ANYONE *HURT* YOU.

4

THE FLAG DROPS, AND THE TOURNEY BEGINS...

THEY'RE BETTER TRAINED IN *RIDING* THESE BEASTS, BUT THAT WON'T *STOP* ME.

THE WARLORDS OF OKAARA TAUGHT ME HOW TO TAME *ANY* CREATURE.

THE FIRST HIT IS *MINE!*

THIS EXCITES ME LIKE THE TOURNAMENTS ON *TAMARAN...*

THOK!

I FEEL SO *FREE,* SO FILLED WITH *JOY!*

BUT...

WOK!

X'HAL! I DIDN'T SEE THAT *RIDER!*

HMMM, I FEEL WARM *BLOOD* ON MY CHEEK! I'VE BEEN *CUT.*

KORIAND'R IS *HURT...* PLEASE, STOP THE *GAMES.*

ONCE BEGUN THEY *CANNOT* BE STOPPED, RAVEN, BUT IF SHE *FALLS,* SHE'LL BE TAKEN FROM THE ARENA AND *TREATED.*

I WRENCHED MY *ARM,* BUT I'LL NOT FALL TO DEFEAT SO *EASILY...* AND CERTAINLY NOT SO *QUICKLY.*

AGHHH... I HAVE THE BEAST BY ITS *MANE...* IF I CAN HOLD ON BUT A MOMENT *MORE...*

...REPOSITION MYSELF IN THE *SADDLE...*

I'VE *DONE* IT!

AND THEY WERE NOT *READY* FOR ME TO MAKE MY *MOVE.*

STARFIRE LETS LOOSE WITH AN UNBRIDLED WHOOP OF VICTORY...

...AS THE CHEERING CROWD RISES TO ITS FEET, REJOICING IN HER MAGNIFICENT TRIUMPH!

6

SHE'S *GOOD*, HIPPOLYTA--BETTER TRAINED THAN I *REALIZED*.

INDEED, RAVEN-- I'D SAY SHE'D *RIVAL* MY DAUGHTER, *DIANA*, HERSELF.

BUT LET US SEE HOW SHE HANDLES THE *BATTLE STAFFS*.

YOU KNOW HOW TO *USE* THIS WEAPON, KORIAND'R?

I *DO*, TIBYA... I *GREW UP* WIELDING SUCH A STAFF.

THE WARLORDS TRAINED ME FOR THE BETTER PART OF A *YEAR* IN ITS *SUBTLETIES*.

THE WARLORDS OF OKAARA-- HOW *SCARED* OF THEM I WAS WHEN *TRAINING* ON THEIR WORLD.

YET, *WITHOUT* THEIR TRAINING, I DOUBT IF I COULD HAVE *SURVIVED* THE CITADEL'S *TORTURE*.

MEMORIES:

THE STAFF MUST BECOME *PART* OF YOU, KORIAND'R...

THINK OF YOURSELVES AS *ONE ENTITY*.

AND THINK OF YOUR ENEMIES AS MERELY COMPOSED OF *ATOMS*--

--ATOMS YOU CAN PENETRATE WITHOUT *HARM*, USING THE *KNOWLEDGE* WE GIVE YOU.

THINK FIRST BEFORE ENGAGING AN ENEMY IN *BATTLE*--

--FOR ONCE THAT COMMITMENT IS *MADE*, YOU CAN-NOT RETREAT UNTIL VICTORY IS *YOURS*.

BUT...

THOK

UNHH! *TOO MANY* OF THEM... HAVE TO *CONCENTRATE*...

7

YOU CAN FEEL YOUR *ENEMY* ABOUT YOU, YOUNG ONE...

...FEEL THE *RIPPLES* IN THE AIR AS THEY *MOVE.*

THEY WILL *ALERT* YOU TO THEIR PRESENCE EVEN BEFORE THEY ARE *SEEN.*

THREE OF THEM *SURROUNDING* ME.

THEY THINK I'VE BEEN *HURT* MORE THAN I AM.

GOOD, I WILL LURE THEM *CLOSER*--

FAK!

--THEN *STRIKE!*

REMEMBER, LITTLE ONE, YOU CAN *DEFEAT* YOUR ENEMY NO MATTER THEIR *SIZE,* NO MATTER THEIR *POWER.*

THAKK!

AHHH, I'VE *MISSED* THESE TESTS OF COURAGE... THESE *TRIALS BY COMBAT.*

FOCUS ALL YOUR *STRENGTH* INTO THE MOMENT OF ACTUAL *CONTACT* WITH YOUR ENEMY...

...AND THEY WILL NOT *SURVIVE.*

WHAK

FOR TOO LONG NOW I'VE *FORSAKEN* THE OKAARAN TRAINING RITUALS, BUT *NO LONGER.*

I WILL NEVER AGAIN ALLOW MYSELF TO GROW *WEAK!*

8

SHE RISES NOW, EXULTANT IN HER VICTORY. A PROUD, ALMOST VAIN SMILE CROSSES HER LIPS -- THEN QUICKLY VANISHES.

SHE REMEMBERS THE WARLORD'S WARNING...

THERE IS NO *JOY* TO BE HAD IN BATTLE. YOU FIGHT ONLY BECAUSE YOU *MUST*. IT IS *DUTY*.

"DO NOT *RELISH* VICTORY, FOR THAT *WEAKENS* YOU AND OPENS *YOU* TO A MOST HUMBLING *DEFEAT*."

YET, *KORIAND'R* CANNOT RESIST THE *SATISFACTION* SHE FEELS IN THIS TOURNAMENT VICTORY. SHE FEELS THE JOY SPREAD WARMLY THROUGHOUT HER BODY...

... AND THE *THUNDEROUS* OVATION IN HER HONOR ONLY SERVES THAT PLEASURE.

YOUR ISLAND IS SO MUCH LIKE *TAMARAN*... THE TRAINING FOR *COMBAT*, THE TOURNAMENTS OF *POWER*...

NO, KORIAND'R-- THE AMAZONS *DECRY* VIOLENCE, THEY EMBRACE *PEACE*.

INDEED, THIS ISLAND WAS *FOUNDED* AS A MEANS TO *AVOID* THE WARS OF MAN.

IT IS FAR MORE LIKE MY *TEMPLE AZARATH* THAN *YOUR* WARLIKE WORLD.

RAVEN, WE *DO* BELIEVE IN PEACE AND COMPASSION AND LOVE...

... BUT WE *ALSO* BELIEVE IN FIGHTING TO *KEEP* WHAT WE-- EH--?

THE GROUND IS *SHAKING!* SOMETHING'S *WRONG!*

BTOOM!!

GREAT *HERA!* PAULA'S LABORATORY ISLAND--IT'S *EXPLODING!*

THE *LABORATORY?* THAT IS WHERE *GARFIELD* IS!

WHAT'S *HAPPENED* TO HIM?

9

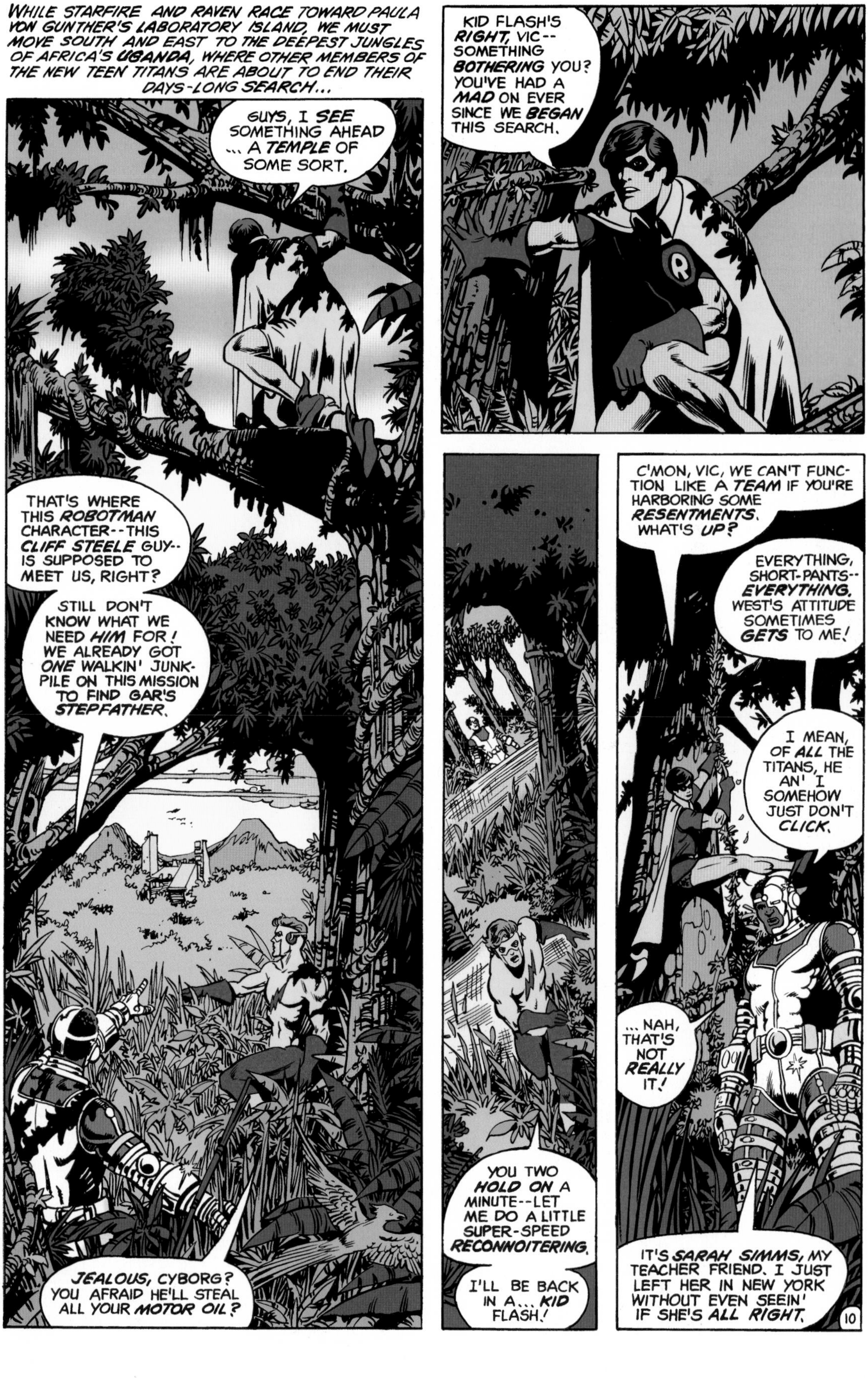
WHILE STARFIRE AND RAVEN RACE TOWARD PAULA VON GUNTHER'S LABORATORY ISLAND, WE MUST MOVE SOUTH AND EAST TO THE DEEPEST JUNGLES OF AFRICA'S UGANDA, WHERE OTHER MEMBERS OF THE NEW TEEN TITANS ARE ABOUT TO END THEIR DAYS-LONG SEARCH...
GUYS, I SEE SOMETHING AHEAD ... A TEMPLE OF SOME SORT.
THAT'S WHERE THIS ROBOTMAN CHARACTER--THIS CLIFF STEELE GUY--IS SUPPOSED TO MEET US, RIGHT?
STILL DON'T KNOW WHAT WE NEED HIM FOR! WE ALREADY GOT ONE WALKIN' JUNK-PILE ON THIS MISSION TO FIND GAR'S STEPFATHER.
JEALOUS, CYBORG? YOU AFRAID HE'LL STEAL ALL YOUR MOTOR OIL?
KID FLASH'S RIGHT, VIC--SOMETHING BOTHERING YOU? YOU'VE HAD A MAD ON EVER SINCE WE BEGAN THIS SEARCH.
YOU TWO HOLD ON A MINUTE--LET ME DO A LITTLE SUPER-SPEED RECONNOITERING.
I'LL BE BACK IN A... KID FLASH!
C'MON, VIC, WE CAN'T FUNCTION LIKE A TEAM IF YOU'RE HARBORING SOME RESENTMENTS. WHAT'S UP?
EVERYTHING, SHORT-PANTS--EVERYTHING. WEST'S ATTITUDE SOMETIMES GETS TO ME!
I MEAN, OF ALL THE TITANS, HE AN' I SOMEHOW JUST DON'T CLICK.
... NAH, THAT'S NOT REALLY IT!
IT'S SARAH SIMMS, MY TEACHER FRIEND. I JUST LEFT HER IN NEW YORK WITHOUT EVEN SEEIN' IF SHE'S ALL RIGHT.
10

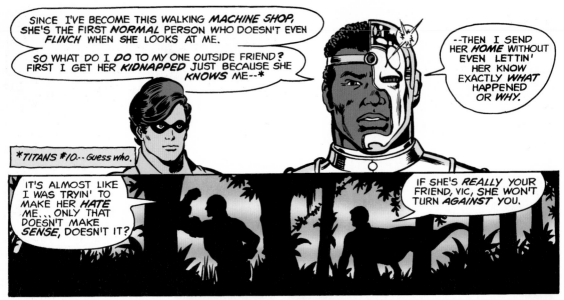

SINCE I'VE BECOME THIS WALKING *MACHINE SHOP*, SHE'S THE FIRST *NORMAL* PERSON WHO DOESN'T EVEN *FLINCH* WHEN SHE LOOKS AT ME.

SO WHAT DO I *DO* TO MY ONE OUTSIDE FRIEND? FIRST I GET HER *KIDNAPPED* JUST BECAUSE SHE *KNOWS* ME--*

--THEN I SEND HER *HOME* WITHOUT EVEN LETTIN' HER KNOW EXACTLY *WHAT* HAPPENED OR *WHY.*

*TITANS #10.--Guess who.

IT'S ALMOST LIKE I WAS TRYIN' TO MAKE HER *HATE* ME... ONLY THAT DOESN'T MAKE *SENSE*, DOESN'T IT?

IF SHE'S *REALLY* YOUR FRIEND, VIC, SHE WON'T TURN *AGAINST* YOU.

GUYS, SOMETHING'S WRONG... *DREADFULLY* WRONG.

YOU FIND *ROBOTMAN?*

JUST *HURRY,* PLEASE-- RIGHT *AHEAD.* IT'S *AWFUL...*

WONDER IF WEST'S *RIGHT*--THIS ROBOTMAN WAS GAR LOGAN'S *BUDDY* BACK IN HIS *DOOM PATROL* DAYS.

MEBBE I'M JUST SCARED I'LL *LOSE* ANOTHER FRIEND.

ROBOTMAN WAS SEARCHING FOR GAR'S STEPFATHER, *STEVE DAYTON*--AND DAYTON WAS SEARCHING FOR THE DOOM PATROL'S *KILLERS...*

DID HE *FIND* THEM? WHAT *HAPPENED* TO HIM?

MAN, SEEING *STEELE* THERE... IT MADE ME *SICK*...THAT COULD'VE BEEN *ME*... OR *ANY* OF US.

AND AFTER WHAT HAPPENED TO *GAR*... MY DOUBTS ABOUT BEING A FULL-TIME SUPER-HERO HAVE *RESURFACED* AGAIN-- IN SPADES!

11

THEY *STARE* AT THE TORN AND MANGLED FIGURE HOISTED BEFORE THEM, AND THEY ARE SUDDENLY VERY MUCH *FRIGHTENED.*

IT'S H-HIM... IT'S *ROBOTMAN!*

BUT--WHAT *HAPPENED* TO HIM?

WARNING TRESPASSERS WILL BE EXECUTED!

THE *LEGENDS* OF *ROBOTMAN* AND HIS FABLED *STRENGTH* ECHO THROUGH THEIR *HORRIFIED* MINDS.

WHAT COULD POSSIBLY HAVE *DONE* THIS TO HIM?

VIC, IS HE--?

MY EAR AMPLIFIERS ARE PICKIN' UP HIS *INTERNAL* GENERATORS...

HIS *BODY* MAY BE FIT FER A SCRAP PILE, BUT HE'S STILL *ALIVE* IN THERE...

...SOMEWHERE.

I'M GONNA MAKE SURE HE *STAYS* ALIVE.

DO YOU NEED HELP?

NO WAY, I'M HANDLING THIS *ALONE!*

MY *DAD* TAUGHT ME ALL ABOUT *CYBERNETICS* -- SO I COULD *REPAIR* MY *OWN* BODY PARTS.

'SIDES, *LOOKIN'* AT HIM MAKES ME THINK OF THAT OLD SAYIN' ABOUT THE *GRACE OF GOD.* THIS COULD'A BEEN *ME.*

IF THERE'S ANY WAY A' BRINGIN' 'IM BACK TO *LIFE,* I'LL *FIND* IT...

...'CAUSE, IF I *FAIL,* I'LL NEVER BE ABLE TO LOOK *LOGAN* IN THE FACE *AGAIN!*

12

SILENCE...

...AND THEY WAIT FOR WHAT SEEMS AT LEAST CENTURIES...

UNTIL...

UNHHHHH...

I'M DREAMIN'... I GOTTA BE DREAMIN'...

...OR MEBBE I'M JUST DEAD!

ROBIN... KID FLASH... YOU TWO I KNOW--

--BUT WHAT IN BLUE BLAZES ARE YOU?

I'M THE NEW 1981-STYLE SUPER-CYBORG.

IT'S A GOOD THING I'M DEAD--OTHERWISE I'D BARF!

STEELE, WHAT HAPPENED TO YOU? WHO DID THIS?

I... I DON'T REALLY REMEMBER, KID. I WAS LOOKIN' FOR DAYTON-- FOUND THIS UNDERGROUND FORTRESS...

...THEN, SUDDENLY, WHAMMO! I WAS BLOWN APART LIKE A USED KLEENEX.

NOW I'M AWAKE AGAIN! ONLY I CAN'T MOVE.

JUST HOLD YOUR CATHODE TUBES, OLD-TIMER... I'M RECONNECTIN' YOUR LEG JOINTS NOW.

BY THE WAY, MY NAME'S VIC STONE, AND I THINK WE GOT OURSELVES A MUTUAL FRIEND.

13

AND THAT BRINGS US RIGHT BACK TO *PARADISE ISLAND*, WHERE...

PAULA'S LABORATORY-- *DESTROYED*. BUT WHAT COULD HAVE *DONE* THAT?

WAS GARFIELD *HURT?* THAT'S ALL THAT *MATTERS.*

HESTIA, WHAT *HAPPENED* HERE?

THE *PURPLE RAY*... THERE WAS TOO MUCH *POWER*...

...FEEDBACK CAUSED THE *EXPLOSION*...

YOU *REST*, HESTIA...YOU'LL WAKE UP WITH NO *PAINS*...

...BUT, KORIAND'R-- WE'VE GOT TO FIND *GARFIELD*...

TOO LATE, WITCH-- I'VE FOUND *YOU!* I'M *ALIVE*...

...ALIVE AND READY TO *KILL!*

ATHENA-- WE NEED YOUR *WISDOM* NOW, GREAT GODDESS.

THE PURPLE RAY HAS DRIVEN THE MANLING *MAD!*

HE WAS GARFIELD LOGAN, THE CHANGELING, A SHAPE-SHIFTER... BUT NOW HE IS ONE HUNDRED TONS OF RAGING, THICK-SKINNED BEAST... A DEADLY BRACHIOSAURUS WHOSE ONLY CRAZED THOUGHTS ARE OF DEATH...

QUEEN HIPPOLYTA-- DO WE *KILL* THE BEAST?

I... I DO NOT *KNOW*... THAT IS A *MAN*...

... AND YET--

GRAWWLL!

BACK OFF, YOU FOOLS-- *TREMBLE*-- FOR THESE ARE YOUR LAST MOMENTS ALIVE!

I WANT TO KILL! I WANT TO *DESTROY!*

SISTERS, HE HAS GIVEN US NO *CHOICE*--

ATTACK!!

THE AMAZONS ARE *FEARFUL* AS THEY HURL THEIR SHARP-POINTED SPEARS, AND THEY HAVE EVERY REASON TO BE...

...FOR EACH STRONG SHAFT MERELY SNAPS IN *TWO* AS THEY GRAZE THE GREAT BEASTS' SCALY HIDE.

THAT RAY OF YOURS *DID MORE* THAN MERELY DRIVE HIM *INSANE*--

--HE COULD NEVER HAVE MADE SUCH A *TRANSFORMATION* BEFORE!

AGGHHHH!

COME TO ME, ALL OF YOU, LET ME *DESTROY* YOU ALL AT ONCE!

GRAWLL!

HERA HELP US! HE'S MORE A *BEAST* THAN A MAN...

I FEAR ONLY THE *GODS* CAN STOP HIM NOW.

NO, HIPPOLYTA, WE DO NOT *REQUIRE* A GOD...

...ONLY THE *EMPATH* NAMED *RAVEN!*

THE GREAT GREEN BEAST LIFTS HIS MASSIVE HEAD SKYWARD, HIS LONG TONGUE SWEEPS ACROSS HIS CRAGGY LIPS, THIS DARK ONE WILL PROVIDE A FEAST TONIGHT...

15

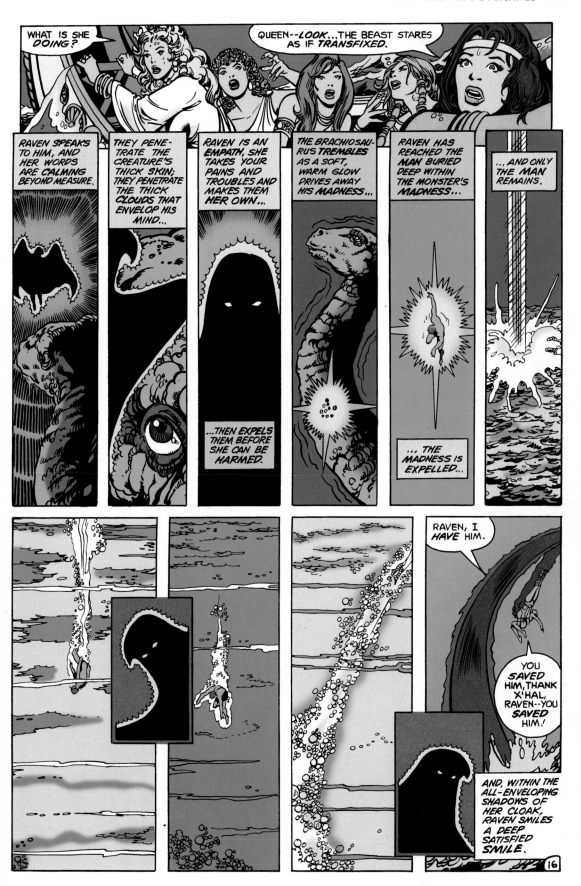

FOR LONG MOMENTS THERE IS ONLY DARKNESS...

LOGAN'S MIND SORTS OUT *THE REALITY* FROM THE *NIGHTMARE*...

THEN...

OH, WOW!

I *DIED!* I DIED AND I'M IN *HEAVEN.*

'CAUSE IF *THIS* ISN'T THE LAND OF ANGELS, I DON'T KNOW WHAT *IS!*

YOU'RE *ALIVE,* GARFIELD, THANK GOODNESS.

KORIAND'R? YOU'RE HERE, *TOO?* HEY, THEN I'M *NOT* DEAD, AM I?

I *KNOW!* I WOKE UP IN A CONVENTION FOR *CENTERFOLD GIRLS,* RIGHT?

SO IF I'M *ALIVE...* LEMME *AT* 'EM!

NO, MY FRIEND, YOU MAY NOT SET FOOT OFF THIS *TABLE.*

IF ANY MAN TOUCHES THE *GROUND* OF PARADISE ISLAND, WE AMAZONS WILL *LOSE* OUR FABLED POWERS.

HUH?

YOU MEAN I'M *STUCK* UP HERE?

WITH ALL THOSE GORGEOUS GALS JUST OUTTA *ARM'S REACH?*

ARGGHHH!

IT'S NOT *FAIR!* WHAT HAVE I DONE *WRONG* IN MY LIFE?

NOW I'M *SURE* I DIED... ONLY THIS ISN'T *HEAVEN*--

--IT'S *HELL!*

MY *OMNI-WAVE RECEIVER!*

AS AN IMAGE SHIMMERS INTO VIEW ON QUEEN HIPPOLYTA'S BRACELET...

DONNA... *DAUGHTER?* WHERE *ARE* YOU?

I'M HOVERING OVER THE *MAIN ISLAND,* MOTHER... WHERE *ARE* YOU?

COME, DAUGHTER... LAND ON PAULA'S ISLAND... WE'LL MEET YOU *THERE.*

BUT AS WONDER GIRL'S T-JET LANDS AMIDST THE JOYOUS THRONG, LET US ONCE MORE RETURN TO THE AFRICAN VELDT, WHERE...

...TOOK ME MORE'N *TWO WEEKS* TO STUMBLE ACROSS THIS SECRET ENTRANCEWAY ...AND THAT WAS WITH *KNOWIN'* IT WAS SOMEWHERE NEARBY.

THERE'S *NO WAY* YOU COULD FIND IT BY *ACCIDENT.*

AND THIS IS WHERE *MADAME ROUGE* AND *GENERAL ZAHL* ARE PLAYING HIDE-AND-SEEK?

OKAY, IT'S UP TO *ME* NOW. YOU GUYS STAY PUT WHILE I DO SOME SUPER-SPEED *SCOUTING.*

WATCH YOURSELF, HUH? IF THOSE TWO COULD TRUSS UP *ROBOTMAN...*

...EVEN YOU'RE NOT *IMMUNE!*

DON'T I *KNOW* IT... WHICH IS WHY I'VE *GOT* TO DO THIS.

GOT TO *PROVE* TO MYSELF THAT MY WAFFLING ABOUT BEING EITHER ORDINARY *WALLY WEST* OR SUPERHERO *KID FLASH--*

--IS A MATTER OF LOGICAL *CHOICE...*

... AND NOT BECAUSE I'M *AFRAID...* NOT BECAUSE I'M A *COWARD!*

18

BECAUSE, HEAVEN HELP ME, WHY ELSE AM I *AVOIDING* BEING WHAT I REALLY *AM?*

I'VE GOT MY SUPER-POWERS... I CAN'T AVOID *USING* THEM.

YET, SOMETHING KEEPS ME FROM SAYING-- YES, I'M KID FLASH, *SUPER-SPEEDSTER...*

I CAN'T BE A *NORMAL* KID ANY MORE... EVEN IF THAT'S WHAT I TRULY *WANT* TO BE.

YES, SOMEONE *SPECIAL* WITH SPECIAL *POWERS* AND SPECIAL *RESPONSIBILITES.*

I'VE GOT TO LEARN IF THAT SOME-THING IS THE FACT THAT I'M JUST PLAIN *SCARED,* OR--

UH-OH, *VOICES* --COMING FROM BEHIND THIS ROCK...

THERE MUST BE AN *ENTRANCEWAY* SOMEWHERE, BUT WHY BOTHER *LOOKING* FOR IT--

-- WHEN I CAN SIMPLY VIBRATE MY *ATOMS,...*

... AND ACTUALLY PASS THROUGH THE *WALL* ITSELF TO -- *HOLY HANNAH!*

A MAN-MADE CHAMBER ... WITH *GUARDS* OF SOME SORT.

THIS MUST BE THE WAY TO *MADAME ROUGE* AND COMPANY...

THAT IS, COMPANY SPELLED *TROUBLE* -- WITH A CAPITAL *"T"!*

19

OKAY, FIRST THINGS *FIRST*-- GET RID OF *THOSE* TWO, THEN CALL FOR THE OTHER *TITANS!*

AND A LITTLE SUPER-SPEED *WIND* BLAST SHOULD DO THE TRICK.

THEY DON'T *FEEL* THE WIND WHERE THEY STAND, BUT THEY HEAR THE SUDDEN, INEXPLICABLE HOWLING...

THEY GLANCE UPWARD IN AN ATTEMPT TO SEE WHAT IS *HAPPENING*...

BUT, IT IS A *VAIN* ATTEMPT AT BEST.

DUST STORM!

NO--THERE CAN *BE* NO DUST STORM DOWN HERE. WE ARE *UNDER ATTACK!*

SHOOT!

GREAT *ORDER* THERE, PAL. HOW DO YOU EXPECT TO *HIT* SOMETHING YOU CAN'T *SEE?*

NOT THAT I'M GOING TO GIVE YOU THE *CHANCE* ANYWAY.

KRAK!

SPLAK!

HMM, MUST BE *SLOWING DOWN*... IT TOOK MORE THAN TWO SECONDS TO *SUBDUE* THEM. OH, WELL ... *NEXT* TIME.

HEY, GUYS... ALL *CLEAR.* C'MON *DOWN.*

WE'LL BE RIGHT *THERE,* BUDDY.

FOLLOW ME. I KNOW THE *WAY.*

I CHECKED IT ALL OUT BEFORE THEY *WAYLAID* ME.

AND SHORTLY...

CRIPES! YOU SAID THEY WERE HEADQUARTERED DOWN HERE, BUT I NEVER EXPECTED *THIS!*

20

IT'S ALSO OBVIOUS WE CAN'T TAKE THEM *ALL* ON BY OURSELVES.

LET'S JUST FIND *STEVE DAYTON* AND GET *OUT* OF HERE.

THEN WE CONTACT THE *GIRLS* AND MAYBE EVEN THE JUSTICE LEAGUE.

HOLD IT, GUYS-- OVER *THERE*, ON THAT VIEW SCREEN...

ISN'T THAT *MADAME ROUGE?*

SOLDIERS! *ATTENTION!* SECURITY HAS BEEN *BREACHED!*

WE HAVE *INTRUDERS!* FIND THEM! *DESTROY THEM!*

IT'S *HER!* THAT BLASTED *KILLER!*

SHE AN' ZAHL MURDERED THE *DOOM PATROL!*

I WANNA BREAK HER STINKIN' LITTLE *NECK!*

HOLD ON, STEELE... C'MON, *CALM DOWN.*

LET ME *GO*, BLAST YOU! I'VE BEEN HUNTIN' DOWN THAT *WITCH* FER *YEARS!* LEMME *AT* HER!

STOP IT, CLIFF... WE'RE *HERE* TO FREE *DAYTON*, NOT TO GAIN *VENGEANCE*...AT LEAST NOT *YET*.

OKAY, KID--*OKAY!* I'LL DO WHAT YOU SAY... FER *NOW.*

BUT WHEN WE *COME BACK* HERE, I'M *TEARIN'* APART ROUGE AND ZAHL *MYSELF!*

AN' I'M WARNIN' YA *NOW*-- DON'T DARE GET IN *MY WAY!*

22

BUT WHERE DO WE BEGIN *LOOKIN'*? DAYTON COULD BE *ANYWHERE.*

WHICH IS WHY THIS RECON JOB'S BEST SUITED TO *ME.*

I'LL HAVE EVERY *CORRIDOR* HERE CHECKED IN *SECONDS.*

AND, JUST AS PREDICTED...

YA SURE THIS IS THE *RIGHT ONE,* FLASHER?

TRUST ME, STONE. WHEN HAVE I EVER *LIED* TO YOU?

DAYTON'S IN CORRIDOR C-6.

RIGHT *THERE!*

TROUBLE IS, THE CELL'S *LOCKED.* I CAN *VIBRATE* THROUGH, BUT YOU *CAN'T.*

LEMME *SMASH* IT DOWN, WHIZ KID.

NO, WE'VE GOT TO KEEP THIS *QUIET.*

BESIDES, WE DON'T NEED *MUSCLE* WHEN I'VE GOT A WELL-STOCKED *UTILITY BELT.*

STEELE, YOU HAVEN'T YET ASKED ABOUT *LOGAN.* HOWCUM?

HE'S NOT WITH *YOU* GUYS, RIGHT? I FIGGER SOMETHING MUST'A *HAPPENED.*

SO I'D RATHER NOT *KNOW* WHAT IT IS UNTIL I GET *ONE* REAL MAD OUT OF THE WAY.

OKAY, GUYS, IT'S *OPEN.*

WOW! YOU EVER THINK OF A CAREER IN *CRIME?*

NAH! I HATE *NIGHT WORK!*

WHIZ KID, I OWE YA AN *APOLOGY--* YOU WERE *RIGHT!*

THERE'S OUR BOY *NOW!*

23

AND, FROM DEEP WITHIN THE MISTY SHADOWS...

UHH, THAT *LIGHT* ...PLEASE, SHUT IT *OFF*... IT'S *BLINDING* ME.

WHO'S *THERE?* PLEASE -- TELL ME *WHO'S THERE.*

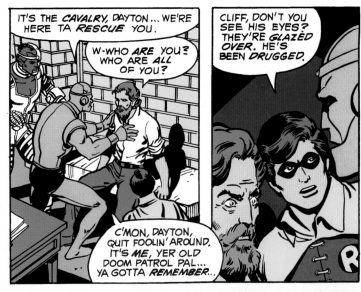

IT'S THE *CAVALRY*, DAYTON... WE'RE HERE TA *RESCUE* YOU.

W-WHO *ARE* YOU? WHO ARE *ALL* OF YOU?

C'MON, DAYTON, QUIT FOOLIN' AROUND. IT'S *ME*, YER OLD *DOOM PATROL* PAL... YA GOTTA *REMEMBER*...

CLIFF, DON'T YOU *SEE* HIS EYES? THEY'RE *GLAZED OVER.* HE'S BEEN *DRUGGED.*

HEY, GUYS... SORRY TO INTERRUPT YOUR *HELLOS*, BUT--

--WE'VE GOT *BAD COMPANY* COME A-CALLING!

THEY CAN'T *SEE* ME WHILE I'M MOVING AT *SUPER-SPEED*...

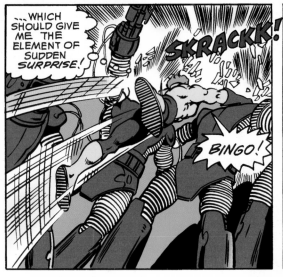

...WHICH SHOULD GIVE ME THE ELEMENT OF *SUDDEN SURPRISE!*

SKRACKK!

BINGO!

RED'S *GOT 'EM!* NOW LET'S MAKE SURE THEY *STAY DOWN!*

...MENTO... MENTO SUIT... I REMEMBER *MENTO* SUIT... KNOW WHERE IT'S BEEN *HIDDEN*...

24

JUST *WATCH OUT* FOR THEM, CYBORG.

THESE CREEPS ARE PRETTY *FAST!*

HE MOVES TOO *QUICKLY.*

I-I CANNOT *SHOOT HIM!*

BEHIND MY COLLAPSIBLE *SHIELD,* CYBORG... AND GET READY FOR THAT *MANEUVER* WE WORKED OUT LAST WEEK.

SHIELD? YOU GOT A *KITCHEN SINK* IN THAT BELT OF YOURS, TOO?

NAH, I DIDN'T HAVE *ROOM* AFTER I INSTALLED THE *BATHTUB.*

SPANG

KLANG

TROUBLE WITH *YOU,* SHORTY, IS I NEVER KNOW WHEN YOU'RE *JOKIN'* OR NOT.

PAL, I WAS CRACKING JOKES WHILE *YOU* WERE RUNNING HURDLES IN *HIGH SCHOOL.*

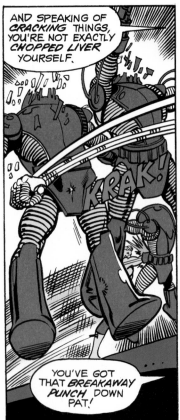

AND SPEAKING OF *CRACKING* THINGS, YOU'RE NOT EXACTLY *CHOPPED LIVER* YOURSELF.

KRAK!

YOU'VE GOT THAT *BREAKAWAY PUNCH* DOWN PAT!

YEAH, BUT IT WAS *YOUR* IDEA, ROBBIE.

Y'KNOW, YOU'RE NOT ALL THAT *BAD.* BUT MEBBE IF YA WORE *LONG PANTS* PEOPLE WOULD TAKE YA MORE *SERIOUSLY.*

SPROK!

OH, I'VE *THOUGHT* ABOUT CHANGING MY COSTUME...

SKRINK

STRAKK!

SEE?

...BUT IT'S SERVED ME PRETTY *WELL* TILL NOW.

25

"THAT'S *IT*? THEY SEND LESS THAN A DOZEN JERKS TO FIGHT US?"

"AN' I WAS JUST GETTIN' *WARMED UP*, TOO."

"SOMETHING'S *WRONG*... WE SAW *HUNDREDS* OF THEM OUT THERE."

"UNLESS THIS IS JUST A *TRAP*."

"WHICH MEANS WE'D BETTER *SPLIT*-- AND *FAST!*"

"HE HAD HIS SCIENTISTS DESIGN A *SUPER-SUIT*... IT FOCUSES HIS *BRAIN ENERGY*."

"LISSEN, IF HE KNOWS WHERE IT *IS*, WE CAN *USE* IT."

"*FORGET* IT, STEELE! WE DON'T HAVE THE TIME TO *WASTE*."

"TAKE IT *EASY*, VIC -- KID FLASH JUST *TOOK OFF* TO--"

"HE'S ALREADY *BACK*?"

"MENTO... MENTO SUIT ...MUST HAVE *MENTO SUIT*..."

"CAN'T YA *CLAM* HIM UP OR SOMETHIN'? WHAT'S THIS *MENTO SUIT* GARBAGE HE KEEPS MUMBLIN' ABOUT?"

"SORRY I TOOK SO *LONG*, BUDDY."

BUT THERE WERE A HALF DOZEN MEMBERS OF ROUGE'S GOON SQUAD *GUARDING* THIS BROOKS BROTHERS' REJECT.

"BUT, FRANKLY, WHAT *GOOD* IS THE SUIT GOING TO DO HIM IN THE *DAZED CONDITION* HE'S IN?"

"WE'LL WORRY ABOUT THAT *LATER*..."

"RIGHT NOW, CONCENTRATE ON GETTING OUT OF HERE *ALIVE!*"

26

THERE ARE NO GUARDS BLOCKING THEIR WAY TO FREEDOM, AND SO, JUST MINUTES LATER...

WE MADE IT.

YEAH, BUT I STILL DON'T *LIKE* IT. SOMETHING'S *WRONG*...

...AND I CAN'T SHAKE THIS QUEASY FEELING THAT ROUGE AND ZAHL HAD THIS *PLANNED* ALL ALONG.

YOU ARE *CORRECT,* MON PETITE AMI.

EVERYTHING HAS BEEN PLANNED AND EXECUTED JUST AS I *PREDICTED.*

DER WAR IS NOT YET *OVER,* ROUGE... DEY MAY YET *DEFEAT* YOU IN YOUR MOMENT OF *TRIUMPH!*

NEVER, ZAHL! *NEVER!*

FOR NOW WE HAVE AN *INSIDE MAN* AMONGST THEIR RANKS.

I SWEAR TO YOU, MON AMI, *THE TITANS WILL DIE!*

TAKE OFF IN TWO MINUTES, ROBIN... EVERYTHING'S *SET.*

GOOD, THE FASTER WE GET *AWAY* FROM HERE, THE BETTER I'LL *LIKE* IT.

AH, DON'T CREASE YER CAPE *WORRYIN',* KID. WE'RE *SAFE.*

NOTHIN' COULD HURT US *NOW!*

DAYTON SMILES AT ROBOTMAN'S *LAST* REMARK, AND HIS EYES *GLEAM* FOR A VERY BRIEF MOMENT. BUT THIS IS NOT THE TIME. HE WILL *WAIT.*

NEXT ISSUE: THE TITANS REUNITE AT LAST! PLUS MADAME ROUGE'S SCHEME REVEALED:

REVOLUTION!

PLUS A SURPRISE FROM THE PAST!

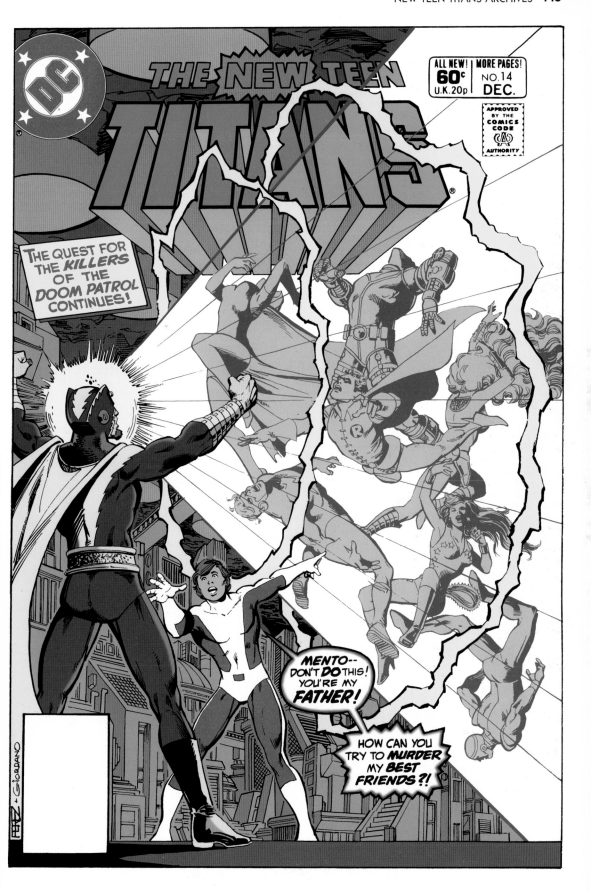

NO, THEY'RE WONDER GIRL, STARFIRE AND RAVEN -- OUR *OTHER* MEMBERS.

BUT BELIEVE ME, THEY ARE POWERFUL ENOUGH TO *HELP* US NOW.

I JUST WANNA SEE *LOGAN*... WANNA SEE IF THAT GREEN-HAIRED SQUIRT'S STILL UP TA CAUSIN' *TROUBLE!*

WONDER GIRL, YOU'RE CLEAR FOR *LANDING.*

GOT YOU, ROB -- CONVERTING TO *V.T.O.L.* NOW.*

*VERTICAL TAKE OFF AND LANDING--*Len.*

FORWARD MOMENTUM GIVES WAY TO POWERFUL VERTICAL THRUST FROM THE T-JET'S SLEEK BELLY--

--AND THE GREAT SHIP LOWERS ITSELF ONTO THE GRASSY KNOLL...

WE GOT YOUR MESSAGE ON *PARADISE ISLAND.* CONGRATULATIONS ON FINDING *DAYTON.*

TROUBLE IS, WONDER GIRL -- THAT WAS THE *EASY* PART.

HEY! YER *ALIVE!* YER *REALLY ALIVE!*

THAT'S WHAT I *LIKE* ABOUT YOU, GLITTER-BRAIN -- YOU'RE REALLY QUICK TO GRASP THE *OBVIOUS!*

Y'KNOW, I *MISSED YOU,* VIC -- *REALLY.*

SOMETHING *WRONG,* WONDER GIRL? SOMETHING *BAD* HAPPEN ON PARADISE ISLAND?

SOMETHING I'D RATHER NOT *TALK* ABOUT, ROBIN. IT WAS *PERSONAL.*

LISTEN, WE'VE BEEN *FRIENDS* PROBABLY LONGER THAN ANYONE *ELSE* HERE... AND I THINK WE'VE BEEN GOOD FRIENDS.

IF THERE'S ANYTHING *BOTHERING* YOU, OR ANYTHING YOU WANT TO TALK ABOUT -- I'M HERE, *REALLY,* ANYTIME.

TH-THANKS... I MAY TAKE YOU UP ON THAT... *SOMEDAY.*

WALLACE, CAN WE... TALK?

UHH, SURE, RAVEN... WHAT ABOUT?

US.

US? IS THERE AN US? I WASN'T SURE.

I CARE FOR YOU, WALLACE, I TRULY DO -- AND WHAT I DID TO YOU --

-- EMPATHICALLY FORCING YOU TO LOVE ME -- I KNOW IT WAS TERRIBLY WRONG.

RAVEN, I --

NO, PLEASE -- LET ME FINISH. I HAVE JUST FREED MYSELF FROM AZARATH'S CONTROL --

-- AND I MUST LEARN MORE ABOUT MYSELF BEFORE I CAN PLEDGE MYSELF TO ANYONE ELSE ... INCLUDING YOU.

DO YOU UNDERSTAND?

I -- THINK SO.

OH WALLACE, I TRULY HOPE SO.

IT WAS INCREDIBLE -- ALL THESE GORGEOUS WOMEN ON PARADISE ISLAND, ALL WAITING JUST FOR ME.

I TELL YA, I SWEPT 'EM ALL OFF THEIR DAINTY LITTLE COMBAT SANDALS!

SURE, SALAD-HEAD... A REAL LOVER BOY, THAT'S YOU.

HUH? I... UHH...

BRONZE THIS MOMENT, GUYS -- LOGAN'S CAUGHT WITHOUT SOMETHIN' STUPID TO SAY.

MY GOD, CLIFF. THEY DIDN'T TELL ME.

AND YOU'VE GOT DAYTON? WOW! MAN, AM I GLAD TO SEE YOU!

THEY'VE GOT TWO FOOTBALL STADIUMS FILLED WITH PAPERWORK BACK IN --

HEY -- WHAT'S WRONG WITH HIM? HE'S JUST STARING OFF INTO SPACE?

YEAH, HE DOESN'T SEEM TO REMEMBER ANYTHING, OR KNOW ANYTHING.

HE'S BEEN LIKE THIS EVER SINCE WE FOUND HIM, KID.

C'MON, DAYTON, YOU CAN'T *DO* THIS TO ME ... VIC--CAN'T WE DO *ANYTHING* FOR HIM?

WE GOTTA DO *SOMETHING!*

YOU KNOW, THIS LAND IS SO LUSH AND BEAUTIFUL -- WE REALLY SHOULD CONSIDER MOVING *TITANS' TOWER* HERE.

NEW YORK IS MAJESTIC, BUT THIS IS JUST SO *LOVELY*.

AHH, VIC, WALLY... HOW HAVE YOU TWO *BEEN?*

BELIEVE ME, PAL-- WE'VE BEEN *TRYIN'.*

AND *YOU*, DICK... I'VE *MISSED* YOU. I REALLY *DID*, YOU KNOW.

STARFIRE, PLEASE... WE'VE *GOT WORK TO DO*.

SO--?

SHE'S ONE OF THE NEW TITANS? *NO WONDER* YOU'RE A MEMBER. HOW DO I JOIN?

FORGET IT, RUSTPOT-- WE *DON'T TRUST ROBOTS* OVER TWENTY!

BESIDES, I DON'T NEED ANY MORE COMPETITION.

UNHH... COSTUME... *MENTO* ... MUST HAVE MENTO...

WHERE IS IT? WHERE IS *COSTUME*...?

DAYTON'S *FLIPPING OUT?* I THOUGHT YOU SAID HE WAS *WIPED OUT?*

MENTO... MUST HAVE *MENTO*...

HE'S *GIBBERING* ABOUT THAT OLD STUPID *SUPER-HERO* HE ONCE PRETENDED TO BE.

MAN, HE REALLY *HAS* FLIPPED OUT! MENTO WAS A NOWHERE *JERK!*

STEVE DAYTON.... THERE IS NO NEED TO *RUN*... WE CAN *HELP* YOU.

COSTUME .... MENTO COSTUME ... MUST *HAVE* IT...

HMMM, YES, I CAN *SENSE* SOMETHING... AN EMOTIONAL *DISTURBANCE*-- AND --

--THERE IS SOME *MENTAL BLOCKAGE* IN HIS SUBCON- SCIOUS ... SOMETHING THAT FORCES HIM TO ASK FOR THIS *COSTUME*, WHATEVER IT IS.

④

I AM TRYING TO CALM HIM DOWN, BUT I *CANNOT*... THE ROOT OF HIS DISTURBANCE IS *POWERFUL*...TOO POWERFUL FOR *ME*.

JUST *GREAT!* AND I WAS NEVER TOO WILD ABOUT DAYTON *BEFORE* THIS!

I MEAN, IF IT WAS UP TO *HIM*, HE'D'A LEFT ME STANDING IN THE COLD. HE NEVER *WANTED* TO ADOPT ME.

DON'T *BELIEVE* IT, SHORT-STUFF. DAYTON ACTUALLY *LIKED* YA IN HIS OWN SCREWY WAY.

LIKE HECK HE DID.

RAVEN--

--THIS IS HIS *MENTO* COSTUME... I FOUND IT IN ROUGE'S UNDER-GROUND CITY.

DO YOU THINK MAYBE IF HE TRIED IT *ON*--?

HE *WANTS* THE COSTUME ...PERHAPS HE *NEEDS* IT.

ROBIN, TELL ME IF I AM *WRONG*--BUT ISN'T THAT UNIFORM ...RATHER *LUDICROUS?*

AND THAT'S AN *IMPROVEMENT* OVER HIS *OLD* FIGHTING TOGS.

DAYTON *BECAME* A SUPER-HERO ONLY TO WIN OVER *RITA FARR* OF THE *DOOM PATROL*-- TO MAKE HER HIS *WIFE*.

I DON'T THINK *STYLE* WAS ON HIS MIND.

HE STILL SEEMS TO BE SOMEWHERE ON *CLOUD NINE*.

C'MON, DAYTON--DON'T YOU REMEMBER *ANYTHING?*

C'MON, BLAST IT--*TRY!*

THERE IS NO REPLY...

...ALTHOUGH DAYTON'S EXPRESSIONLESS FACE SUDDENLY TAKES ON A DECIDEDLY *ANGRY* CAST...

...AS ROBIN'S MIND CLICKS OVER -- *BATTLE WARY* AFTER SO MANY YEARS OF WORKING ALONGSIDE THE *BATMAN*...

5

RUN! SOMETHING'S WRON--

BUT, THE TEEN WONDER'S WARNING COMES A TAD *TOO LATE*, AS STEVE DAYTON'S EYES SUDDENLY *BURN* WITH A HELLISH GLOW...

...AND *CHAOS* ENSUES...

INDEED, ONLY *ONE TITAN* WAS ABLE TO *ACT* ON ROBIN'S CRY.

ONLY ONE TITAN WHOSE INNER *VIBRATIONS* ALLOWED MENTO'S TELEKINETIC BLAST TO HARMLESSLY PASS THROUGH HIS VERY ATOMS.

ONE TITAN WHO NOT ONLY *RECOGNIZED* THE DANGER, BUT HAS BEEN ABLE TO *RESPOND* TO IT:

KID FLASH!

CAN'T BELIEVE DAYTON WAS PLAYING *POSSUM*. DEEP DOWN HE'S A *GOOD GUY--* ONE OF *US*!

SO MAYBE THAT EXPLAINS WHY ROUGE AND ZAHL SENT SO *FEW* OF THEIR WARRIORS AFTER US WHEN WE ESCAPED HER CITY.

SHE *WANTED* US TO TAKE DAYTON TO FREEDOM--BECAUSE SOMEHOW SHE *CONTROLLED* HIM!

TROUBLE IS, HOW DO WE TAKE ON DAYTON WITHOUT *HARMING* HIM?

IF I REMEMBER, HIS TELEKINETIC POWERS CAN BE *DEADLY!*

6

SOMETHING'S GOTTA BE *WRONG* WITH DAYTON. HE'D NEVER ACT LIKE THIS *OTHERWISE.*

THAT'S A *RELIEF*, PAL. SO WHEN HE MANAGES TO *KILL* ME, I'LL KNOW IT WAS ONLY A *MISTAKE!*

SHEESH!

CYBORG'S WHITE-SOUND BLASTERS *SHATTER* THE FALLING TREES INTO A MILLION USELESS *SPLINTERS...*

...*WHILE WONDER GIRL ATTACKS THE PROBLEM IN HER OWN INIMITABLE FASHION.*

CAN'T YOU GET *CLOSER* TO HIM, RAVEN... DIG *DEEPER* INTO HIS *MIND?*

I HAVE *TRIED...* BUT I AM *BLOCKED* IN EVERY *ATTEMPT!*

I CAN SENSE THE *HORROR* HE FEELS AT HIS OWN DEEDS, BUT NOT THE *REASON* BEHIND HIS ATTACK.

I TELL YOU, DONNA--STEVEN DAYTON IS BEING *CONTROLLED* BY FORCES BEYOND HIS *WILL*--

--AND IF WE CANNOT *SAVE* HIM, THOSE VERY FORCES WILL TEAR HIS MIND *ASUNDER!*

NO MAN CAN WITHSTAND THAT *MENTAL PRESSURE* ON HIM FOR LONG.

IF THAT'S *TRUE*, RAVEN --IF HE *IS* BEING CON-TROLLED, THEN I CAN'T USE ALL THE POWER OF MY *STARBOLTS* ON HIM.

BUT I *CAN* CONTROL THE *INTENSITY* OF MY BLAST...

...TRY TO *STUN* HIM UNTIL YOU CAN MOVE *CLOSER*--

SKRE

X'HAL!! IT'S NO *USE!*

HE CAN *REPEL* MY STARBOLTS-- SEND THEM *BACK* AT ME!

UNLESS I USE MY FULL POWER AND *KILL* HIM-- I'LL NEVER GET THROUGH HIS *DEFENSES!*

C'MON, STEVE--QUIT *STARING* AT ME THAT WAY, HUH?

OKAY, SO MAYBE WE WERE NEVER THE WAY A KID AND HIS DAD *SHOULD* BE, BUT THAT DOESN'T MEAN...

NO--I'M NOT GETTING *THROUGH* TO HIM--! HE'S *GLARING* AT ME-- OUT FOR *BLOOD*--

7

RAVEN, BORN IN THE OTHERDIMENSIONAL TEMPLE OF AZARATH, IS AN EMPATH...A HEALER OF SOULS...

SHE CAN DIG INTO YOUR DEEPEST SUBCONSCIOUS, SHE CAN TAKE YOUR MOST TERRIBLE PAINS...

...AND MAKE THEM HER OWN.

SHE CAN REACH INTO YOUR MIND AND IMPERCEPTIBLY ALTER IT.

STEVE! PLEASE... YOU'RE *HURTING* ME. STEVE, DON'T YOU SEE WHO I *AM?*

...AND--

MY GOD, STEVE, I'M *RITA*-- I'M YOUR *WIFE.*

SHE CAN SENSE YOUR DEEPEST FEARS, AND *EXPLOIT* THEM, SHE CAN LEARN OF YOUR TRUEST *LOVE*...

WHY ARE YOU *HURTING* ME THIS WAY, STEVE? DON'T YOU KNOW YOU'RE *KILLING* ME?

PLEASE... DON'T *DO* THIS... PLEASE...

...DON'T HURT ME...DON'T *HURT*...SO MUCH *PAIN*--

--SO TERRIBLE...SO VERY *TERRIBLE*...

RI... RIT...

OH, LORD... LORD... I'M *BURNING UP*, STEVE... I CAN'T LAST MUCH LONGER...

RITA--?

RITA! NOOOO!

YOU *DID* IT, RAVEN -- HE *STOPPED.*

JUST NEXT TIME, GAL, DON'T *WAIT* SO LONG, EH?

9

YOU WERE *INCREDIBLE,* RAVEN-- YOU REALLY *WERE.*

I JUST DID MY *JOB,* WALLACE.

WHO'S SHE *KIDDING?* SHE'S IN *PAIN.*

USING HER POWERS LIKE THAT *HURT* HER AS MUCH AS IT HELPED ROBOTMAN.

ONLY SHE *HIDES* THE PAIN ... PRETENDS SHE'S *COLD.* LORD, WHY DO I FEEL THAT ONE DAY SHE'S GOING TO *BREAK?*

BLAST!

I HADN'T *PREDICTED* THIS-- THEY FREED THAT LUDICROUS FOOL FROM THE *MIND-CONTROL* I PLACED HIM UNDER.

ZAHL, THIS COULD *DELAY* EVERYTHING I HAVE WORKED SO HARD FOR.

IT VILL DELAY *NOTHING,* MADAME ROUGE. I *SWEAR* IT!

MY ARMIES HAVE TRAINED *WELL* FOR THIS COUP!

ZANDIA WILL BE OURS BY *DAWN!*

IT HAD *BETTER* BE, ZAHL. I DO NOT LIKE HAVING TO PLACE MY HOPES IN THE HANDS OF *OTHERS.* I PREFER CONTROLLING ALL THE EVENTS *MYSELF.*

WE *ALL* DO, MADAME, BUT THERE ARE TIMES WHEN ONE *MUST* WORK WITH OTHERS FOR *MUTUAL* GOALS, EH?

BE CERTAIN WE WORK *TOGETHER,* ZAHL. I HAVE NOT FORGOTTEN THAT YOU *DISOBEYED* ME AND DESTROYED THE *DOOM* PATROL.

YOU MURDERED THEIR *LEADER*-- THE MAN I HAD ONCE *LOVED.*

DISOBEY ME *AGAIN,* AND THIS TIME IT SHALL BE *YOU* WHO SUFFERS THE BLOODY *CONSEQUENCES.*

10

BUT WE HAVE WORKED TOGETHER FOR *YEARS*. WHY DO YOU QUESTION ME *NOW*?

I QUESTION *YOU*, I QUESTION *MYSELF*. WE ARE TOO CLOSE TO SUCCESS *NOT* TO QUESTION OURSELVES.

THE MAN I LOVE IS *DEAD* ... THE WORLD HAS TURNED AGAINST ME FOR *PARTICIPATING* IN HIS DEATH.

I HAVE *NOTHING ELSE* TO LIVE FOR BUT THE SUCCESS OF MY PLAN.

ZANDIA WILL BE *OURS* -- I WILL BE *ZANDIA*. I WILL BE THE *STATE* -- AS MY OWN *COUNTRYMAN* ONCE SAID.

ZANDIA: A SEEMINGLY CONTENTED RURAL COUNTRY. ITS PEOPLE APPEAR HAPPY, THOUGH SUCH IS NOT THE CASE.

YET, THAT IS A MATTER FOR *ANOTHER* DAY. NOW, HOWEVER, WE FOCUS ONLY ON A SMALL FLAT OVERLOOKING THE *PLAZA DEGRAN*...

OUI, MADAME, ALL IS *READY*.

THE GENERALS WILL LEAD THEIR SOLDIERS AGAINST THE *CURRENT REGIME* WHEN YOU ORDER THEM TO.

NO, *NO*, MADAME! I PROMISE YOU, THE COUP WILL NOT *FAIL*.

NOW I MUST--

AH, MONSIEUR, IT HAS TAKEN ME QUITE A WHILE TO *TRACK YOU DOWN*.

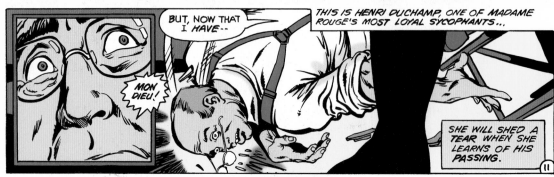

BUT, NOW THAT I *HAVE*--

MON DIEU!

THIS IS HENRI DUCHAMP, ONE OF MADAME ROUGE'S MOST LOYAL SYCOPHANTS...

SHE WILL SHED A *TEAR* WHEN SHE LEARNS OF HIS *PASSING*.

11

WHILE *BIZARRE* EVENTS BREW ON THE *BALTIC SEA* ISLAND OF *ZANDIA*, WE RETURN TO *AFRICA*, WHERE...

.... IT'S LIKE WAKING UP FROM A *NIGHTMARE!*

I--I DON'T THINK I CAN THANK YOU *ENOUGH.*

AND I CAN'T POSSIBLY BELIEVE IT'S BEEN A *YEAR* SINCE I VANISHED I CAN'T *REMEMBER* A THING THAT HAPPENED.

YOU'RE SURE OF THAT, SIR? NOTHING THAT COULD *HELP* US?

HE *SAID* HE CAN'T REMEMBER, SHORT-PANTS. ISN'T THAT *ENOUGH?*

CALM *DOWN,* GAR-- ROBIN'S ONLY DOING HIS *JOB.*

I KNOW THIS IS *DIFFICULT,* SIR, BUT PLEASE *TRY* TO REMEMBER.

FUNNY, I REMEMBER *YEARS* AGO --WHEN IT ACTUALLY *BEGAN...* BUT *YESTERDAY,* I DON'T REMEMBER A *THING!*

IT BEGAN, I GUESS, WITH THE FORMATION OF THE *DOOM PATROL.*

NOW, I WASN'T *THERE*--THAT DAY BELONGED TO SOMEONE *ELSE...* A CRIPPLE NAMED *NILES CAULDER!* ONLY HE CALLED HIMSELF-- *THE CHIEF!*

I SUMMONED YOU THREE HERE BECAUSE, IN ONE FASHION OR ANOTHER, THE OUTSIDE WORLD CONSIDERS YOU *FREAKS!*

YOU'RE SHUNNED AS SOMETHING *DIFFERENT,* SOMETHING NOT TO BE DESIRED -- BUT I--

-- I CAN OFFER YOU A *WORLD!*

12

"HE BROUGHT THESE THREE TOGETHER.

FIRST, LARRY TRAINOR, A TEST PILOT.

"CLIFF STEELE WAS THE BEST RACECAR DRIVER ON THE CIRCUIT--

"AND RITA... MY GOD, RITA FARR-- THE MOST BEAUTIFUL ACTRESS WHO EVER LIVED.

"TRAINOR WAS FLYING AN EXPERIMENTAL PLANE THROUGH A RADIOACTIVE BELT IN THE UPPER IONOSPHERE.

"THE RADIOACTIVITY CHANGED HIM -- HE BECAME -- NEGATIVE MAN!

"--UNTIL HIS CAR SMASHED INTO A WALL, DESTROYING STEELE'S BODY IN THE PROCESS.

"ONLY THE CHIEF'S SURGICAL SKILL SAVED HIM... BY TRANSFERRING STEELE'S STILL-LIVING BRAIN INTO THE METAL BODY OF--ROBOTMAN!

"SHE FELL INTO A RIVER POLLUTED BY STRANGE, UNKNOWN CHEMICALS.

"AND THEY CHANGED HER... ALTERED HER BODY CHEMISTRY UNTIL SHE BECAME-- ELASTI-GIRL!

"NEGATIVE MAN! ROBOTMAN! ELASTI-GIRL! THEY THOUGHT OF THEMSELVES AS FREAKS, BUT THEY WERE REALLY HEROES IN THE TRUEST SENSE OF THE WORD.

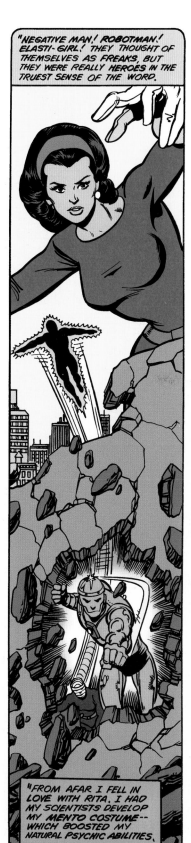

"FROM AFAR I FELL IN LOVE WITH RITA. I HAD MY SCIENTISTS DEVELOP MY *MENTO* COSTUME-- WHICH *BOOSTED* MY NATURAL *PSYCHIC ABILITIES*.

"AND I SET OUT TO MAKE HER FALL IN LOVE WITH *ME*. SHE DID, YOU KNOW -- DESPITE MY POWERS AND DESPITE THE FACT THAT, AS STEVE DAYTON, I WAS THE FIFTH RICHEST MAN IN THE WORLD.

"--BUT, BLAST IT ALL, THAT LIFE WERE CUT SHORT!"

"SHE AND THE REST OF THE PATROL WERE KILLED BY THEN-CAPTAIN ZAHL, WHO FORCED THE PATROL TO SACRIFICE THEMSELVES TO SAVE THE LIVES OF 14 INNOCENT PEOPLE IN THE FISHING VILLAGE OF CODSVILLE, MAINE.

"WE WERE MARRIED AND WE LOOKED FORWARD TO A LONG, HAPPY *LIFE* TOGETHER --

ALL OF THEM -- THE CHIEF, CLIFF, LARRY, AND MY DARLING RITA.... ALL *DEAD*.

NOT *ALL* DEAD, BUT YOU DIDN'T KNOW I'D *SURVIVED*, THOUGH I WAS PROBABLY MORE READY FER THE *JUNK HEAP* THAN I WAS FER *SUPER-HEROING*.

I WAS *REBUILT*, BUT I DIDN'T LIKE THAT NEW ROBOT-SHAPE I WAS GIVEN, SO I CONVINCED DAYTON'S LAB BOYS TO REBUILD MY *ORIGINAL* TIN-CAN BODY. I'M AS GOOD AS *OLD* AGAIN!

14

THEN YOU'RE *NOT* LIKE ME? YOU'RE TOTALLY A *MACHINE*.

AND I COME WITH A *FIVE-YEAR WARRANTY*, TOO!

LORD, AND I USED TO FEEL *SORRY* FOR MYSELF! AT LEAST I'M STILL *HALF-HUMAN*!

OKAY, *OKAY*, DO WE HAVE TO LIVE 'THROUGH THOSE DAYS AGAIN?

WE ALL KNOW THE GORY PARTS AND I DON'T WANNA *HEAR* 'EM ANYMORE.

BUT THE *QUESTION* IS-- DID ALL THAT HELP YOU *REMEMBER* ANYTHIN'?

I-I REMEMBER THE *GRIEF* I FELT AT RITA'S DEATH, AND THE UNENDING *ANGER*.

"I HAD MY *SCIENTISTS* BOOST MY *SUPER-SUIT* FOR ME--

"--AND I REMEMBER *BEGINNING THE HUNT*, SEARCHING FOR THOSE *KILLERS* IN COUNTRY AFTER BACKWATER COUNTRY.

"I CAN'T TELL YOU HOW MANY *MONTHS* IT TOOK BEFORE I GOT A CLUE THAT LED ME TO *AFRICA*.

"AND THAT -- THAT WAS WHEN I SAW--

--*RITA!*

WELL, IT'S CERTAINLY *TAKEN* A WHILE, *DARLING*, I WAS WONDERING WHEN YOU'D *SHOW UP*.

RITA? BUT, IT'S IMPOS- SIBLE--?!?

OH, YOU *REALLY* THOUGHT I WAS *DEAD*, DID YOU? *GOOD*.

THAT'S WHAT I *WANTED* EVERY- ONE TO BELIEVE WHILE I HUNTED DOWN *MADAME ROUGE* AND *CAPTAIN ZAHL*.

WH-WHAT ABOUT THE *OTHERS*? THE CHIEF... *NEGATIVE MAN*-- WHAT ABOUT *CLIFF*?

THEY ALL *DIED*-- BUT SOMEHOW I WAS BLOWN *FREE*.

BUT WHY ARE WE *TALKING*? WE'VE FOUND EACH OTHER AT LAST.

"SOMETHING WAS TERRIBLY *WRONG*. RITA'S LIPS WERE LIKE *ICE*.

(15)

"I KNEW THIS WASN'T MY WIFE... IT COULDN'T BE.

"I TRIED TO SQUIRM FREE, BUT IT WAS ALREADY TOO LATE."

YOU MORONIC SIMPLETON! HOW EASY IT WAS TO FOOL YOU BY SIMPLY ALTERING MY BODY SHAPE.

"I HAD TOTALLY FORGOTTEN HER CURSED POWER. I FELT LIKE A STUPID FOOL!"

SHE DIDN'T KILL ME... SHE SIMPLY BROUGHT ME TO HER UNDERGROUND CITY...

AND, I GUESS, FOR A YEAR SHE FED ME DRUGS... NUMBED MY WILL... UNTIL YOU FREED ME.

BUT NOW YOUR SOUL IS YOUR OWN YOU ARE A FREE MAN.

SO, WHAT NOW?

WE COULD GO BACK TO THAT JOINT AND SMASH ZAHL AND ROUGE.

YEAH, GUESS WE COULD. BUT YOU THINK WE GOT THE POWER?

I MEAN THOSE DUDES ARE PRETTY TOUGH.

MEBBE WE OUGHTTA--

SHUT UP! ALL OF YOU -- SHUT THE HECK UP!

YOU'RE GABBING AWAY LIKE THIS WAS JUST SOME SUPER-HERO GET-TOGETHER.

THOSE TWO ARE KILLERS, AND I WANT THEM TO PAY!

PAY FOR WHAT THEY DID TO ME... WHAT THEY DID TO THE PATROL!

GARFIELD, PLEASE -- BE CALM --

GET AWAY FROM ME, RAVEN... DON'T USE YOUR BLASTED CALMING POWERS ON ME.

I WANT TO STAY ANGRY... I WANT TO BE MAD!

I DESERVE THE RIGHT TO BE MAD FOR A CHANGE!

16

WE CAN ALL *FEEL* FOR THE DOOM PATROL, WHAT HAPPENED TO *THEM*, GAR, COULD HAPPEN TO *ANY* OF US... OR *ALL* OF US.

WE'RE *ALL* ANGRY WHEN SOMETHING LIKE THIS GOES ON. BELIEVE ME--THE *RAGE* YOU'RE FEELING ISN'T FELT BY YOU *ALONE*.

WE ALL WANT TO SEE THOSE KILLERS *CAUGHT*.

WE WILL *STOP* THEM, GAR -- YOU CAN *BELIEVE* ME!

I WILL NOT LET THEM SQUIRM THROUGH MY GRASP -- NO MATTER *WHAT* I MUST DO.

YOU THINK YOU *UNDERSTAND* THIS, BUT YOU REALLY *DON'T*.

FOR YEARS I'VE BEEN SUFFERING BECAUSE I'VE VIRTUALLY SEEN *TWO* SETS OF PARENTS *KILLED*.

OH, I'VE *GONE ON*, HAVEN'T I? LAUGHING LIKE A LUNATIC -- SPOUTING STUPID *JOKES* --

-- HOPING THEY'D EASE THE *PAIN*. BUT YOU KNOW, EVERY JOKE ONLY MADE THE PAIN HURT *MORE*.

NOW YOU WANT TO GUIDE ME ALONG AND SOLVE MY PROBLEMS FOR ME LIKE SOME *SURROGATE* PARENTS ...

... BUT, BLAST IT--I HAVE TO DO THIS BY *MYSELF* OR I'LL NEVER FEEL LIKE I'VE AMOUNTED TO MUCH OF *ANYTHING*!

HE'S *CRAZY*! HE DOESN'T KNOW WHAT HE'S GETTING INTO.

I'LL *STOP* HIM--

NO, *DON'T*. LET HIM GO. MAYBE HE'S *RIGHT*.

EVERYONE HAS THE RIGHT TO *PROVE* HIMSELF SOMETIME.

DOES THAT MEAN WE GOTTA SIT BACK AN' WATCH THAT LITTLE WITCH AN' HER GOOSE-STEPPIN' PAL *SKRAG* LOGAN FER KICKS?

LISSEN--THAT KID'S CONFUSED AND LOST--HE'S TRYIN' TA *PROVE* HIMSELF BECAUSE NONE OF US TAKES HIM *SERIOUSLY*.

WE LISSEN TO HIS CORNY *JOKES* AN' THINK HE'S A FLAKE AN' ORDER 'IM AROUND WITH A "DO THIS," OR "DO THAT"!

BUT HE'S A KID WHO'S DEEP-DOWN *GOOD*... AN' HE'S REAL TROUBLED... AND WHY THE HECK AM I STANDIN' HERE *GABBIN'* WHEN I SHOULD BE *TRAILIN'* HIM?

17

I DON'T HAVE TO BE A BRAIN LIKE ROBIN TO GUESS *MADAME ROUGE* IS BEHIND THIS FLYING CITY!

SO THAT MAKES IT REAL *EASY* ON LITTLE GAR LOGAN!

WHEREVER THIS REFUGEE FROM A FLASH GORDON MOVIE GOES, I GO *WITH IT!*

PROVIDING I *LIVE* LONG ENOUGH!

THE WINDS UP HERE ARE *TERRIBLE* ...THEY'RE CUTTING RIGHT THROUGH ME LIKE A SURGEON'S *SCALPEL!*

GOTTA KEEP MY EYES *CLOSED*...SO I CAN BARELY *SEE*...

...WHICH MAY BE THE ONLY *GOOD* THING ABOUT THIS CATASTROPHE!

IF I *SAW* WHAT I WAS DOING, I'D BE *SICK* OVER HALF OF AFRICA!

GAR LOGAN HOLDS FIRM... NOTHING ON EARTH WILL MAKE HIM RELEASE HIS IRON-TIGHT GRIP. MEANWHILE...

ALL RIGHT, I'VE RE-LEARNED *LESSON ONE*-- NEVER *UNDERESTIMATE* YOUR ENEMY!

I NEVER SUSPECTED ROUGE'S FORTRESS WAS *MOVABLE!*

MOVABLE AND MOVING *FAST*...LOOK AT THEIR SPEED ON THE *RADAR.*

AT THE RATE THEY'RE TRAVELING, THEY'LL BE OUT OF AFRICA IN MINUTES.

YOU GOT A BEAM ON WHERE SHE'S *HEADING?*

YOU CAN ACTUALLY GUESS THEIR *PATH*, VICTOR?

SURE *CAN*, GOLDIE... A LITTLE TRIANGULATION, AND *WHAMMO!*

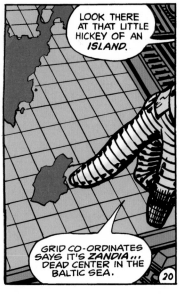

LOOK THERE AT THAT LITTLE HICKEY OF AN *ISLAND.*

GRID CO-ORDINATES SAYS IT'S *ZANDIA*... DEAD CENTER IN THE BALTIC SEA.

20

ZANDIA: POPULATION APPROX, --3,769, NO MAJOR INDUSTRY, NO IMPORTS, AND NO EXPORTS.

THOUGH THE SECRET OF HOW ZANDIA SURVIVES WILL NOT BE TOLD THIS DAY...

...TRUST US WHEN WE SAY ZANDIA DOES *INDEED* SURVIVE, AND QUITE WELL UNDER THE RULE OF *THIS* MAN...

...PRESIDENT FREDERICK GRAVES...

A NAME QUITE APROPOS CONSIDERING A GRAVE IS ALL HE WILL BE FIT FOR IN EXACTLY 3.7 SEC--

ZWITT!

MY, HOW TIME FLIES!

LORD, LOOK UP THERE!

WE'RE UNDER ATTACK!

YAGGHH!

ZANDIA'S EXPATRIATE CITIZENS FALL LIKE WHEAT BEFORE A VERY DEADLY *SCYTHE...*

...WIELDED BY CRUEL AND VICIOUS FLYING FORCES UNDER THE ORDERS OF A VERY SINISTER *GENERAL ZAHL.*

LIKE LOCUSTS, THEY SWEEP PAST ZANDIA'S CENTRAL *MICROFILM COMPLEX,* DESTROYING INVALUABLE *RECORDS* WITH INSIDIOUS *EASE.*

THEN THEY SOAR ON, LEAVING IN THEIR JET-STREAM WAKE THE MINGLED *TEARS* AND RUNNING *BLOOD* OF USELESS *DESTRUCTION...*

21

I FIND THIS BUTCHERY IMPOSSIBLE TO *BELIEVE.* THESE PEOPLE ARE *INNOCENTS,* BUT ZAHL IS HAVING THEM *SLAIN!*

SOLDIER 4-X... ENEMY TO YOUR *RIGHT!*

THEY'RE TURNING TOWARD *ME--?*

BUT IT WON'T DO THEM ANY *GOOD!*

SP-UNKKK!

I WASN'T ABOUT TO MISS OUT ON *THIS* FIGHT!

I CAN SET UP A SUPER-SPEED *UPDRAFT* TO LOWER ME TO THE GROUND AND TAKE OUT SOME OF ZAHL'S *GOON SQUAD* AT THE SAME TIME!

YOU SURE YOU DON'T SEE *GAR* DOWN THERE?

NOT A *SIGN,* CLIFF. YOU THINK HE DIDN'T *FOLLOW* ROUGE?

IF HE *DIDN'T,* BAT-BOY, THEN HE'S NOT THE GAR LOGAN I *KNOW!*

C'MON, *LAND* THIS HEAP -- HE'S GOTTA BE DOWN THERE *SOMEWHERE.*

AT LAST I'M *FREE* -- IN MY *ELEMENT!*

SKREEE

SKREEE

I MAY HAVE BEEN FORCED TO *REIN IN* MY FULL POWER IN THE PAST--

--BUT NOW I STRIKE OUT *UNFETTERED!*

23

BUT HOW MANY OF THEM *ARE* THERE?

FOR EACH *ONE* I BLAST, *FIVE* MORE APPEAR!

MY POWER ISN'T *INFINITE!*

THERE'S NO WAY I CAN *CONTINUE* TO--

GREAT *HERA!* THEY'VE GOT *KORIAND'R!*

THEN THEY WERE *READY* FOR US... THEY *KNEW* WE WERE *COMING!*

BAM

BLAM

BANG

DOES THAT MEAN THIS WAS A *TRAP* TO--

KREEE

NO! THAT *WALL*--

SK RASHH!

BOTH MY FRIENDS ARE *DOWNED*--THE OTHERS HAVEN'T *LANDED* YET-- I'M *ALONE*--

-- I HAVE NO *CHOICE* NOW. I CANNOT *HOLD BACK*, OR--

24

BUT RAVEN'S NEXT WORDS ARE SUDDENLY STOPPED SHORT, FOR, AS HER ASTRAL SOUL-SELF LOWERS TOWARD THE SOLITARY SOLDIER --

-- A MIND-NUMBING BEAM OF PLASMIC LIGHT STRIKES HER FROM BEHIND.

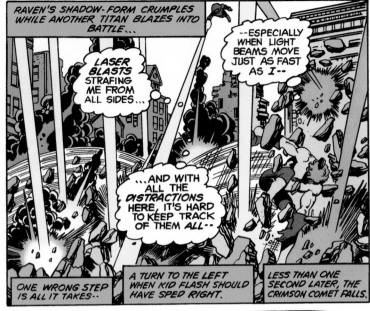

RAVEN'S SHADOW-FORM CRUMPLES WHILE ANOTHER TITAN BLAZES INTO BATTLE...

LASER BLASTS STRAFING ME FROM ALL SIDES...

--ESPECIALLY WHEN LIGHT BEAMS MOVE JUST AS FAST AS I--

...AND WITH ALL THE DISTRACTIONS HERE, IT'S HARD TO KEEP TRACK OF THEM ALL--

ONE WRONG STEP IS ALL IT TAKES--

A TURN TO THE LEFT WHEN KID FLASH SHOULD HAVE SPED RIGHT.

LESS THAN ONE SECOND LATER, THE CRIMSON COMET FALLS.

IT'S NO USE... WE'LL NEVER FIND LOGAN FROM UP HERE.

LET ME OUT NOW!

THERE ISN'T TIME FOR THAT, VIC-- JUST DO YOUR BEST UNTIL I CAN FIND A PLACE TO LAND THE T-JET!

I'M TRYIN' BAT-BOY--

I GOT ONE MILLION DECIBELS OF PURE SOUND BLASTIN' DOWN THERE--

-- BUT THEY MUST HAVE SOME KINDA SHIELD PROTECTIN' 'EM-- MY BLASTS AIN'T GETTIN' THROUGH!

HOLD IT, STONE--STOP! LOOK, OVER THERE, ON THE RIGHT TIP OF ROUGE'S FLYING CITY --

YOU SEE HIM?

HUH? WHERE'D HE POP UP FROM? HE WASN'T THERE A SECOND AGO, I'M SURE OF THAT!

THANK GOODNESS --YOU FOUND ME, GUYS--DROP LOWER ...LET ME REACH YOU.

25

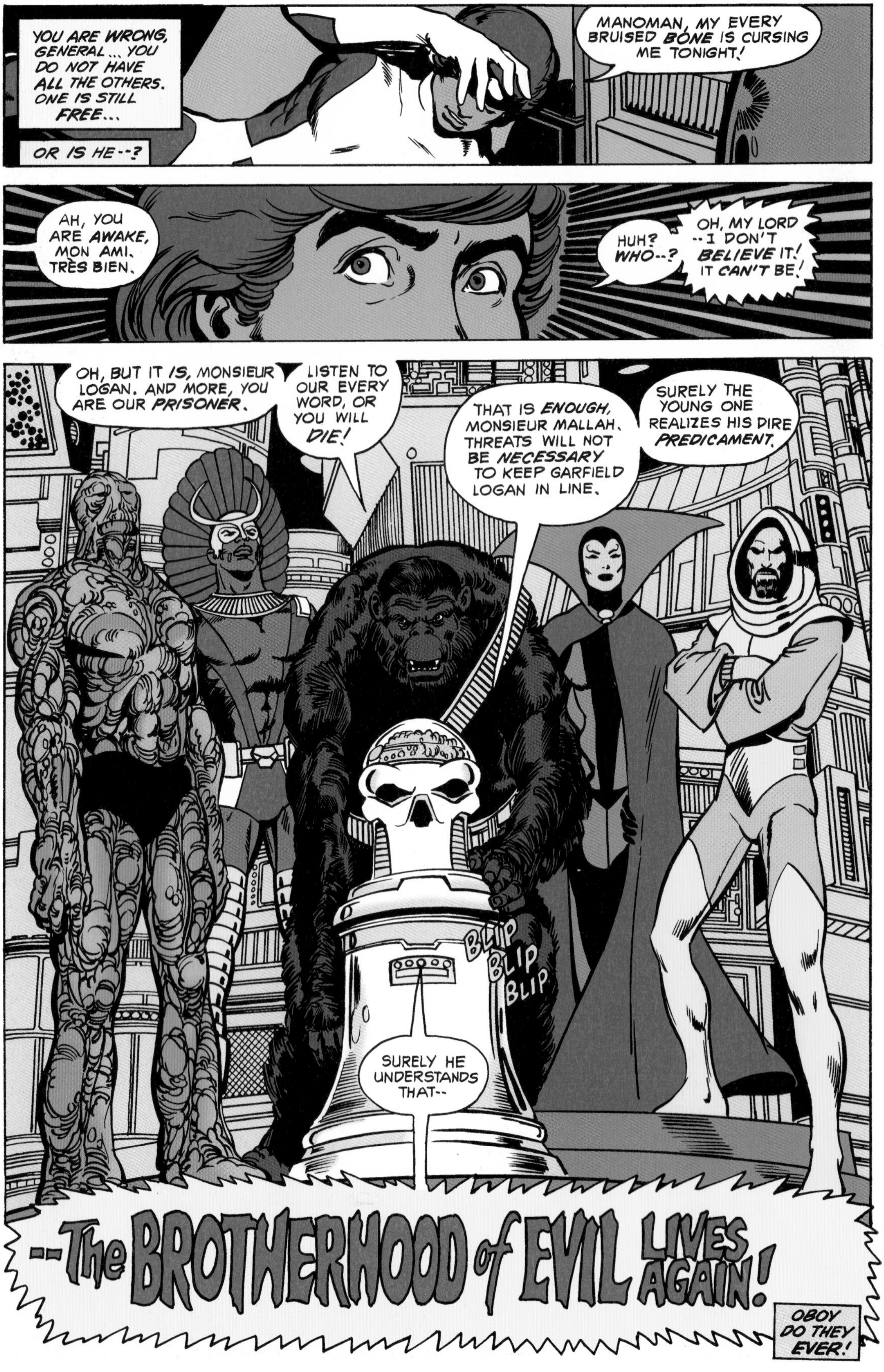

YOU ARE WRONG, GENERAL... YOU DO NOT HAVE ALL THE OTHERS. ONE IS STILL FREE...
OR IS HE--?
MANOMAN, MY EVERY BRUISED BONE IS CURSING ME TONIGHT!
AH, YOU ARE AWAKE, MON AMI. TRÈS BIEN.
HUH? WHO--?
OH, MY LORD --I DON'T BELIEVE IT! IT CAN'T BE!
OH, BUT IT IS, MONSIEUR LOGAN. AND MORE, YOU ARE OUR PRISONER.
LISTEN TO OUR EVERY WORD, OR YOU WILL DIE!
THAT IS ENOUGH, MONSIEUR MALLAH. THREATS WILL NOT BE NECESSARY TO KEEP GARFIELD LOGAN IN LINE.
SURELY THE YOUNG ONE REALIZES HIS DIRE PREDICAMENT.
BLIP BLIP BLIP
SURELY HE UNDERSTANDS THAT--
--The BROTHERHOOD of EVIL LIVES AGAIN!
OBOY DO THEY EVER!

JA, YOU PREFER THE MERE *CONQUERING* OF THE RABBLE WHILE I ENJOY WATCHING THEM *SUFFER!*

MMM? THIS *ROBOTMAN*... HE IS NOT *DEVOLVING.*

OF COURSE-- OUR PIT WOULD NOT AFFECT HIS *METAL BODY.* BUT THIS IS NOT TO *WORRY, NEIN?*

HIS FRIENDS ARE QUICKLY SINKING THROUGH THE *EVOLUTIONARY CHAIN*--

--VERY SOON THEIR NEANDERTHAL MADNESS WILL *OVERWHELM* THEM-- AND THEY WILL *CRUSH* THE METAL ONE FOR US.

ZAHL'S EVIL FRIGHTENS EVEN *ME* SOMETIMES. THERE IS NO *SOUL* IN THAT MADMAN.

BUT I WILL *PERMIT* HIM HIS PETTY PLEASURES, AT LEAST FOR *NOW.*

BUT, WHEN ZANDIA IS TOTALLY *MINE*... WELL, *C'EST LA GUERRE!* THAT IS *WAR,* NON?

FOR EVERYONE IS THE ARCHITECT OF HIS *OWN FORTUNE!*

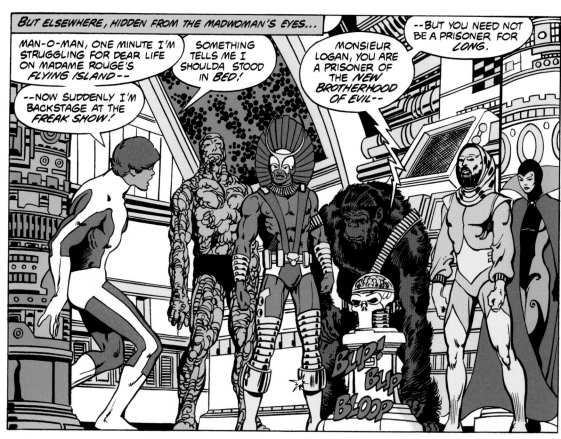

HE WILL MERELY *SHIFT* YOU TO WHERE YOU CAN DO NO *HARM*.

HOLY COW! I *LEAP* AT HIM-- AND SUDDENLY I'M ON THE OTHER SIDE OF THE *ROOM!*

I GOT A HUNCH I COULD BE IN *TROUBLE* HERE!

BE *PLEASED,* MY LITTLE ONE-- *WARP COULD* HAVE SENT YOU PLUNGING INTO AN ACTIVE *VOLCANO!*

AH, NOW THINGS ARE LOOKING *BRIGHTER.* HEY, GORGEOUS, WHY DON'T WE *BLOW* THIS JOINT-- AND *MAKE OUT* OR SOMETHING?

I THINK I'M IN *LOVE!*

LOVE? *PHOBIA* KNOWS NOTHING OF *LOVE.*

PHOBIA KNOWS ONLY *FEAR!!*

YOU WHO PROFESS TO LOVE WOMEN WILL NOW ONLY *FEAR* THEM!

GYNOPHOBIA GRIPS YOU IN TIGHT TALONS OF TERROR!

PLEASE-- *STOP* HER... SHE'S GONNA *HURT* ME...

I *BEG* YOU-- PLEASE TAKE HER *AWAY* FROM ME.

ENOUGH, PHOBIA! LET *HOUNGAN* HAVE HIS TURN!

I HAVE TAKEN MY COUNTRY'S *ANCIENT RITUALS* AND NOW USE THEM *SCIENTIFICALLY!*

THIS *COMPUTER FETISH* HOLDS A LOCK OF YOUR *EMERALD HAIR.*

IT HAS CYBERNETICALLY SORTED OUT YOUR BODY'S *CELLULAR STRUCTURE!*

A STRUCTURE I CAN AFFECT BY USING THIS *ELECTRONIC NEEDLE!*

BEHOLD! I MERELY GRAZE THE DOLL'S *APPENDAGE,* AND--

OH, WOW! *STOP IT!* WHAT ARE YOU DOING TO MY *LEG?*

YOU'RE *KILLING* IT-- *STOP!*

5

HAVE YOU SEEN *ENOUGH,* LOGAN?

UHH, LET'S JUST SAY I'M *CONVINCED,* OKAY?

SO, BRAIN, *TELL ME*-- WHAT HAVE YOU BEEN *UP TO* LATELY?

I MEAN, YOU AND YOUR BIG APE PAL, *MALLAH,* VANISHED THE SAME TIME THE *PATROL* WAS KILLED.

FACT IS, I THOUGHT *YOU* DIED, TOO.

THAT IS WHAT WE *WISHED* EVERYONE TO BELIEVE.

BLIP BLIP BLIP

"INDEED, MERE MOMENTS BEFORE MADAME ROUGE AND CAPTAIN ZAHL ATTACKED THE BROTHERHOOD'S HEADQUARTERS.."

MADAME ROUGE KNOWS THAT *I* CREATED THE FURNACE OF EVIL THAT BURNS WITHIN HER. SHE WILL DO ANYTHING TO DES--

WAIT! MALLAH, MY COMPUTER SENSORS REVEAL SHE IS *NEAR US*--READY TO *ATTACK.*

BLIP

ACTIVATE *DECOY* PROCEDURE NOW!

OUI, MONSIEUR BRAIN!

"IT WAS THIS SIMPLE, LOGAN-- OUR FLOOR REVOLVED...

...WE WERE SAFE IN OUR *UNDERGROUND CHAMBER*--

-- AND WHAT ROUGE AND ZAHL *THOUGHT* THEY HAD DESTROYED...

...WAS MERELY TWO *LIFELIKE REPLICAS!*

MONSIEUR MALLAH AND I REMAINED IN HIDING, SEARCHING TO FORM A *NEW BROTHERHOOD OF EVIL!*

A BROTHERHOOD YOU HAVE JUST NOW *MET!*

OUI, MONSIEUR BRAIN. I AM CALLED *WARP*-- WITH ZEE PROPER COORDINATES I CAN CREATE ZEE WARP-- BETWEEN ANY TWO LOCATIONS.

YOU HAVE *TASTED* THE FEAR-CREATING POWERS OF *PHOBIA*--PRAY I DO NOT DECIDE TO LET YOU *FEAST* ON THEM!

AND I, *HOUNGAN,* HAVE SHOWN YOU HOW SUPERSTITION AND SCIENCE CAN BE *MERGED*-- WITH VERY DEADLY RESULTS!

SCIENCE-- *BAH!* DIS SCIENCE CREATED *PLASMUS...* GENERAL ZAHL USED ME AS HIS GUINEA PIG AND IT ALMOST COST ME MY *LIFE!*

ZAHL AND HIS WITCH COMPANION MUST *PAY* FOR WHAT THEY DID TO ME!

6

WE *ALL* HAVE REASONS, MONSIEUR LOGAN, TO SEEK *VENGEANCE* ON ZAHL AND ROUGE.

JOIN WITH US AND PERHAPS WE SHALL ALL *SUCCEED*, NO?

YOU PEOPLE ARE *SCUM...* YOU, BRAIN, WERE ONE OF THE DOOM PATROL'S GREATEST *ENEMIES...* WHICH MAKES YOU *MY* ENEMY AS WELL.

BUT ZAHL AND ROUGE *DESTROYED* THE DOOM PATROL! THEY *KILLED* MY ADOPTIVE MOTHER... RITA FARR-- *ELASTI-GIRL!*

SO, FOR *NOW* I'LL PUT ASIDE THE CONTEMPTUOUS *HATRED* I FEEL FOR YOU, BRAIN, AND I'LL FIGHT *ALONGSIDE* YOU.

BUT WHEN ALL THIS IS *OVER...* AFTER WE'VE GONE OUR SEPARATE WAYS --THE *TRUCE* WILL BE OVER--

--AND I'LL FIND A WAY TO HUNT *YOU* DOWN FOR ALL YOUR FILTHY CRIMES!

MEANWHILE...

ZANDIA HAS JUST *FALLEN.* IT IS NOW *MINE!*

THERE WILL BE NO STOPPING ME *NOW!*

STOPPING *US,* MY DEAR-- *US!*

OF COURSE, ZAHL... OF *COURSE!*

ZANDIA FALLS, AND OUR ENEMIES HAVE REVERTED TO A PRIMITIVE STATE.

I FEAR THEY WILL PROBABLY RIP *EACH OTHER* APART *LONG* BEFORE THEY DEVOLVE INTO *ONE-CELLED AMOEBAS!*

IT SHOULD BE QUITE *ENJOYABLE* TO WATCH, NEIN, MADAME?

AHH, THE *FÜHRER* WOULD HAVE BEEN SO *PROUD.*

7

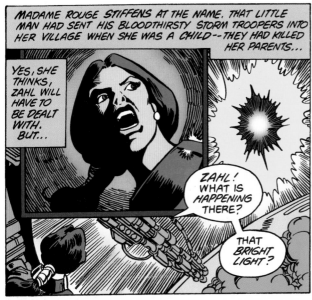

MADAME ROUGE *STIFFENS* AT THE NAME. THAT LITTLE MAN HAD SENT HIS BLOODTHIRSTY *STORM TROOPERS* INTO HER VILLAGE WHEN SHE WAS A *CHILD*--THEY HAD KILLED HER PARENTS...

YES, SHE THINKS, ZAHL WILL HAVE TO BE DEALT WITH. BUT...

ZAHL! WHAT IS HAPPENING THERE?

THAT *BRIGHT LIGHT?*

WELL, WELL, WARP-- RIGHT ON *TARGET* WITH THE *FIRST TRY!*

AND LOOK WHO'S *HERE*--TALL, DARK AND SLIMY-- JUST WAITING FOR US TO *MOW HIM DOWN!*

LOGAN? DO NOT TAKE ONE STEP *CLOSER,* MON AMI--

--LEST I PRESS THIS *DETONATOR* WHICH SHALL *DESTROY* YOUR NEANDERTHAL FRIENDS.

LORD, WHAT'S SHE *DONE* TO THEM? WHAT DO I *DO?* TRY TO *JUMP* HER?

MAN, IF I WERE *ROBIN,* I WOULDN'T HESITATE, I'D--

BUT WHILE THE SHAPE-CHANGER *MULLS* OVER THE ALTERNATIVES...

YOU HESITATE. GOOD, LOGAN-- PERHAPS YOU ARE NOT QUITE SO *STUPID* AFTER ALL.

NOW, MY LITTLE ONE-- DO AS I *SAY,* OR--

--OR *NOTHING,* KILLER!

YOU NO *LONGER* HOLD THE CARDS!

SKRASH!

BLAM

INDEED, THE GAME PLAY IS *MINE!*

MON DIEU! MONSIEUR MALLAH! Y-YOU ARE ALIVE...

THEN-- ALL OF YOU HERE--

CORRECT, MADAME, WE WORK FOR *ZEE BRAIN*... AND WE WORK TOGETHER TO *DEFEAT* YOU!

8

ZEE BROTHERHOOD OF EVIL SHALL BE TRIUMPHA--

ACHHH!

YOU SHALL *DIE*, SWINE-- AS YOU SHOULD HAVE DIED *YEARS* AGO!

THE BROTHERHOOD SHALL PERISH EVEN AS IT IS *BORN* ANEW!

ZAHL'S ARMIES, AUGMENTED BY VIRTUALLY INDESTRUCTIBLE BIO-SUITS, SURGE FORWARD GLEEFUL AT THIS CHANCE TO WREAK *DEVASTATION*...

BUT...

ZAHL, I OWE *YOU* FOR WHAT YOU HAF DONE TO ME!

MY PROTOPLASMIC BODY, THIS *HORROR* I HAF BECOME--

--IT SHALL BE DER *WEAPON OF YOUR DESTRUCTION!*

SSS

HOLY HANNAH! P-PLASMUS-- WHAT DID YOU *DO* TO HIM?

GOD!

DER FOOL HAS BEEN REDUCED TO A PROTOPLASMIC *BLOB!* HE DESERVED NOTHING MORE!

AHH, *THREE* OF THEM ATTACK AT *ONCE*. THEN THIS SHALL BE A *TEST* OF PHOBIA'S POWERS!

A MOMENT TO CONCENTRATE--

9

--AND THE *SAME* FEAR SHALL GNAW AT YOU *ALL!*

OPHIDIOPHOBIA! THE FEAR OF *REPTILES*--

YOU SEE *EACH OTHER* AS THE SLITHERING SNAKES YOU *ARE!*

SKREEEE

SO *EASY...* ...AND RATHER QUITE *AMUSING,* DO YOU NOT THINK?

OUI, MADAME, A *LAUGH!*

BUT A *SICK* ONE, NO?

SHE IS *WITHOUT HUMOR*-- SHE *FRIGHTENS* ME.

AHHH, A *WARP* FOR MY *FRIENDS* HERE--

THE *FURTHER* I SEND MY *ENEMIES,* THE MORE *STRAIN* I FEEL--

--BUT THIS WARP IS SURELY *WORTH* IT, NO?

"OH, ONE WORD OF *CAUTION*--

"*IN SPACE IT IS VERY DIFFICULT TO BREATHE!*"

10

ZAHL IS A *FOOL!* HE STANDS *BEHIND* AND FIGHTS! BUT *I* SHALL NOT BE SO *STUPID!*

IF MONSIEUR MALLAH AND THE OTHERS ACTUALLY *DEFEAT* OUR SOLDIERS, I WISH TO BE *SAFE--*

--TO PLAN STILL *GREATER PLANS!*

THOUGH THIS CONSTANT BATTLING BEGINS TO *GNAW* AT ME, THERE IS *NO TURNING BACK* NOW.

CURSE THE BRAIN FOR TAKING AN ORDINARY FRENCH SCHOOL TEACHER--

--AND TWISTING HER INTO THE INFAMOUS *MADAME ROUGE!*

HOW *DIFFER-ENT* MY LIFE MIGHT HAVE BEEN IF--

AND WHERE DO YOU THINK *YOU'RE* GOING, LITTLE *LETHAL* LADY?

LOGAN? IS THAT *YOU?*

RIGHT ON THE FIRST GUESS, GRUE-SOME...

...A *LIGHTNING BUG* TO LIGHT UP YOUR LIFE...

AND NOW THAT I HAVE YOUR CRUMMY ATTENTION-- *WHAMMO!*

MY, MY, WHAT GREAT BIG *TEETH* I HAVE, GRANNY--

--THE BETTER TO PLAY "*JAWS*" ON YOU, EH?

MON DIEU! IT IS *IMPOSSIBLE!*

MEANWHILE... IT'S *NO GOOD!* THEIR *MINDS* HAVE REGRESSED LIKE THEIR *BODIES!*

THEY'VE BECOME *PRIMITIVE SAVAGES--* READY TO FEAST ON A *STEEL-SKIN* SUPPER!

TROUBLE IS, THEY MAY *SUCCEED--* EVEN IN *THIS* STATE THEY STILL HAVE THEIR *POWERS.*

CAN'T *FIGHT* THEM OFF, SO USE THE *ONLY* THING YOU'VE GOT *WORKING* FOR YOU, STEELE--

NEXT TO *THEM*, THE LITTLE SUPER-STRENGTH I'VE GOT IS--

ARGHH!

--YOUR BRAIN, MAN-- USE YOUR BRAIN!!

11

ELSEWHERE...

WARRIOR! YOU HAVE FIRED YOUR LAST WEAPON!

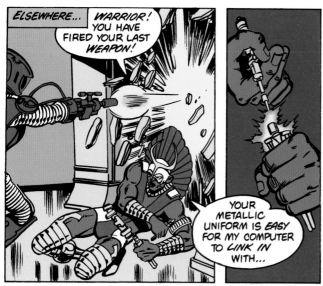

YOUR METALLIC UNIFORM IS *EASY* FOR MY COMPUTER TO *LINK IN* WITH...

...EASY FOR ME TO *TAMPER* WITH...

...EASY FOR MY COMPUTER FETISH TO *DESTROY!*

SPTRAKK

THE POWERS OF HOUNGAN ARE *NOT* TO BE *TOYED* WITH!

THIS *BETTER* WORK, OR ALL MY BRAIN IS GONNA BE *GOOD* FOR--

--IS TO MAKE ME THE *SMARTEST CORPSE* IN THE JUNKYARD!

IT'S *CYBORG* I WANT, MY METALLIC COMRADE-IN-CYBERNETIC-ARMS!

I'VE SEEN STONE *USE* HIS WEAPONS, KNOW WHAT HE CAN *DO*--

HEY! QUIT STRUGGLING, GUY-- I'M DOING THIS FOR *ALL* OF US!

THERE. I'VE GOT HIS *WHITE SOUND BLASTER* ATTACHED...

...SET IT FOR *FIFTY THOUSAND* DECIBELS--

12

-- MY VERY LIFE IS TO *HEAL!*

TO TAKE AWAY THE *PAIN* OF THE HELPLESS...

AZAR HELP ME! EACH TIME I EMPATHICALLY HEAL *ANOTHER...*

...*MY PAINS* GROW MORE *TERRIBLE!*

I HURT, GREAT *AZAR*-- I HURT... YET I *CANNOT STOP!*

T-TO BE AN EMPATH *MEANS* TO HEAL *OTHERS* AT THE *EXPENSE* OF *YOURSELF.*

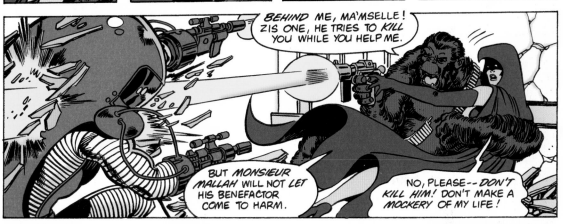

BEHIND ME, MA'MSELLE! ZIS ONE, HE TRIES TO *KILL* YOU WHILE YOU HELP ME.

BUT *MONSIEUR MALLAH* WILL NOT *LET* HIS BENEFACTOR COME TO HARM.

NO, PLEASE-- *DON'T KILL HIM!* DON'T MAKE A *MOCKERY* OF MY *LIFE!*

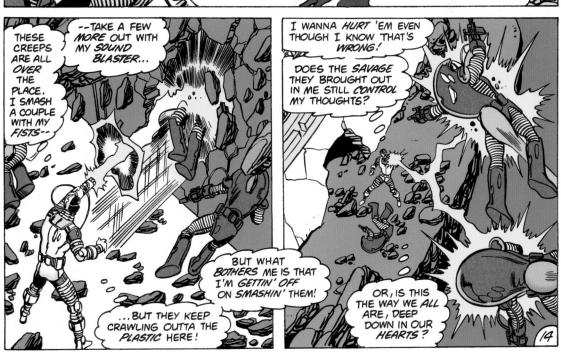

THESE CREEPS ARE ALL OVER THE PLACE. I SMASH A COUPLE WITH MY *FISTS*--

--TAKE A FEW *MORE* OUT WITH MY *SOUND BLASTER...*

...BUT THEY KEEP CRAWLING OUTTA THE *PLASTIC* HERE!

I WANNA *HURT* 'EM EVEN THOUGH I KNOW THAT'S *WRONG!*

DOES THE *SAVAGE* THEY BROUGHT OUT IN ME STILL *CONTROL* MY THOUGHTS?

BUT WHAT *BOTHERS* ME IS THAT I'M *GETTIN'* OFF ON *SMASHIN'* THEM!

OR, IS THIS THE WAY WE *ALL* ARE, DEEP DOWN IN OUR *HEARTS?*

14

THERE IS A SHARP CONTRAST IN STYLES HERE. THE BROTHERHOOD OF EVIL KILL THEIR FOES! THE TITANS SEEK MERELY TO STOP THEM, TO RENDER THEM INOPERATIVE.

A DIFFERENCE THAT RAVEN NOTES WITH APPRECIATION.

EVEN IN BATTLE, EVEN IN THE MIDST OF WAR, THERE IS A DIFFERENCE BETWEEN GOOD AND EVIL.

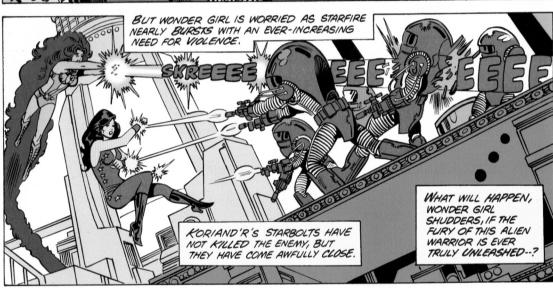

BUT WONDER GIRL IS WORRIED AS STARFIRE NEARLY BURSTS WITH AN EVER-INCREASING NEED FOR VIOLENCE.

SKREEEE SKREEEE SKREEEE

KORIAND'R'S STARBOLTS HAVE NOT KILLED THE ENEMY, BUT THEY HAVE COME AWFULLY CLOSE.

WHAT WILL HAPPEN, WONDER GIRL SHUDDERS, IF THE FURY OF THIS ALIEN WARRIOR IS EVER TRULY UNLEASHED--?

FAR BELOW HIM, GENERAL ZAHL SEES THE CASUALTIES MOUNT WITH HORRIFYING SPEED.

HE SEES HIS SOLDIERS CUT DOWN WITH TERRIFYING EASE.

AND THIS SOLDIER DECIDES THE TIME HAS COME TO FLEE, TO RUN AS HE RAN FROM ANOTHER LOSING BATTLE SO MANY YEARS BEFORE...

17

BUT TO GARFIELD LOGAN, THAT DOOR MIGHT WELL HAVE BEEN MADE FROM PAPIER-MÂCHÉ...

YOU KILLED THE *CHIEF*, YOU KILLED *LARRY...* AND, BLAST YOU, ROUGE -- YOU KILLED MY *MOTHER!*

SKRASH!

AND HE WILL KILL *ME*. NOTHING WILL *STOP* HIM.

NOTHING, UNLESS--

GUESS *WHAT*, GOOSE-STEPPER, A *DEAD END!*

SORTA *APPROPRIATE*, CONSIDERING!

LET ME *OUT!* DERE *MUST* BE A WAY OUT!

ONLY *ONE* WAY, ZAHL.

BAH! YOU VILL NOT *KILL* ME. YOU ARE *WEAK!*

YOU *COULD NOT* KILL.

ZAHL...

YEAH, MEBBE YOU'RE *RIGHT*, ZAHL!

BUT I CAN SURE MAKE *LIVING* ONE HELLUVA *NIGHTMARE!*

NEIN! NEIN! YOU VILL NOT *TOUCH* ME, YOU STEEL SWINE!

I HAVE NOT LIVED SO LONG TO BE IMPRISONED LIKE SOME PETTY *THUG!*

YOU VILL *DIE* BEFORE I--

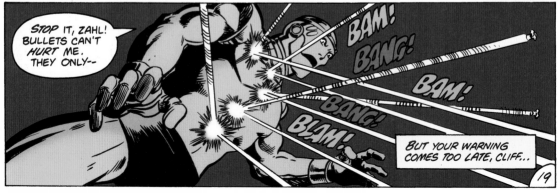

STOP IT, ZAHL! BULLETS CAN'T *HURT* ME. THEY ONLY--

BAM! BANG! BAM! BANG! BLAM!

BUT YOUR WARNING COMES TOO LATE, CLIFF...

19

THE DEED IS DONE...

ZAHL'S OWN HAND HAS BROUGHT DOWN RETRIBUTION.

I *TOLD* YOU, ROBOTMAN, YOU VOULD *NOT* TAKE ME.

I *DIE*, BUT DAT IS ALL *RIGHT*.

I HAF THE *LAST LAUGH*, ROBOTMAN!

DER FÜHRER WOULD HAF *WANTED* IT THIS WAY... THE LAST LAUGH...

H-HEI--

HEIL HITL--

THE LAST LAUGH, ZAHL?

UNHHH...

NOBODY GETS THE LAST LAUGH, ZAHL.

YOU DON'T GET IT. THE THOUSANDS YOU'VE *KILLED* DON'T GET IT... THE CHIEF, LARRY, RITA-- *THEY* DON'T GET IT. *I* DON'T GET IT.

NOT EVEN *GOD* ALLOWS HIMSELF THE LAST LAUGH, ZAHL.

HE ONLY *WEEPS* FOR HIS CHILDREN GONE ASTRAY!

C'MON, ROUGE, THERE'S NO *ESCAPE* FROM ME.

THIS HAS BEEN BUILDING IN ME FOR *TOO LONG!*

THIS HAS BEEN *DESTROYING* ME FOR TOO MANY YEARS TO LET YOU *GET AWAY!*

HE'S *INSANE!* HE'S EVEN METAMORPHOSING INTO CREATURES THAT DO NOT *EXIST!* CREATURES OF HIS OWN IRRATIONAL *MIND!*

AND THE NET TIGHTENS IRREVERSIBLY...

20

HE WON'T LET ME GET *AWAY.* THERE'S *NOTHING* I CAN TURN MYSELF INTO THAT WOULD *SAVE* ME.

IF I *HAVE* TO DIE, THEN I WILL TAKE THEM ALL WITH ME!

WHAT ARE YOU *DOING,* ROUGE? GET *AWAY* FROM THERE!

FORGET IT, MON PETITE-- WE WILL ALL GO TO A MORE GLORIOUS FOREVER *TOGETHER!*

NO! I SAID GET AWAY!

SWAK!

GAR LOGAN LASHES OUT WITH FEROCITY, AND ROUGE'S BODY IS LIMP AS IT SPILLS ACROSS THIS ELECTRONIC TOWER OF BABEL...

FOR A MOMENT, HER EYES BETRAY HER DEEPEST FEAR AS SHE REALIZES AT LAST THE END HAS COME.

MY GOD!

SKRAWKK!

IT IS *HARD* FOR THE CHANGELING TO ALTER HIS FORM BACK TO HUMAN. IT IS ALMOST AS IF HE *PREFERS* DISPLAYING THIS BEAST FROM WITHIN. BUT THEN, FINALLY...

ROUGE--? MADAME ROUGE?

D-DID I *KILL* HER?

I DIDN'T *MEAN* TO.

NO. THAT'S NOT TRUE, I *DID* MEAN TO...BUT I *WOULDN'T* HAVE...

...L-LOGAN...

Y-YOU'RE ALIVE?

THANK GOD, I DIDN'T *KILL* YOU... THANK *HEAVEN*...

:COUGH: WE'RE ALL *DEAD,* LOGAN ...ALL OF US...

21

...I--I DIED *LONG AGO*--WHEN THE BRAIN ALTERED MY MIND AND TURNED ME *EVIL*...

I AM GLAD THE *REST* OF ME DIES NOW...

THE SHOCK, LOGAN--IT SEEMED TO CLEAR MY MIND... PLEASE, ALL OF YOU *RUN*-- THIS ISLAND *COUGH* WILL BE THE *DEATH* OF YOU ALL...

...LOGAN... TH-THANK YOU FOR *FREEING* ME, LOGAN--THANK YOU...

OH, GOD, NILES... I *COME* TO YOU... I... COME... TO... YOU...

NO! NO! I--I *KILLED* HER... *I KILLED HER!!* HER DEATH'S NOW ON MY CONSCIENCE, TOO.

I--I *HATED* HER, I WANTED HER *DEAD*, I WANTED TO *DESTROY* HER, AND I DID... I *DID!*

I *HIT* HER... INTO THAT MACHINE... I CAUSED HER DEATH AS IF I HAD PULLED A *TRIGGER*...

BUT... I WON'T LET ANYONE *ELSE* DIE BECAUSE OF ME.

IF THIS BLASTED ISLAND IS GOING UP IN FLAMES, NO ONE *ELSE* IS GOING TO SUFFER.

HE RUNS BECAUSE HE HAS EXHAUSTED HIMSELF... THE LARGER THE MASS OF THE CREATURE HE BECOMES, THE MORE IT TAKES OUT OF HIM...

HE RUNS, BECAUSE, FOR NOW AT LEAST, GARFIELD LOGAN IS *INCAPABLE* OF SHIFTING SHAPES...

HE RUNS FOR HIS FRIENDS STILL IN THE MIDST OF *BATTLE*, AND AS HE RUNS, SO MANY THOUGHTS ENTER HIS TORTURED YOUNG MIND...

22

PERHAPS RAVEN SENSES THE CONFLICTING EMOTIONS THAT ASSAIL GAR LOGAN. PERHAPS THAT IS WHY SUDDENLY SHE CRIES OUT...

STOP! PLEASE LET THE FIGHTING END!

THE BATTLE IS OVER... THOSE WE CAME TO DEFEAT... ARE LOST.

ROUGE AND ZAHL DEAD?

I AM DISAPPOINTED. I WISHED TO BE THE INSTRUMENT OF THEIR DESTRUCTION.

WHAT GOOD DOES IT DO, HAVING ROUGE DIE? MY MOM IS STILL DEAD. AND THE REST OF THE PATROL WITH HER.

ALL THESE YEARS THE VENGEANCE I WAS HOPING FOR-- IT MEANS NOTHING TO ME NOW THAT IT'S BEEN HAD!

I--I DON'T EVER WANT TO HURT ANYONE AGAIN... ALL I WANT IS TO HELP--

LOGAN!

THE BRAIN? WHAT ARE YOU DOING HERE?

SHIFTING THIS FLOATING ISLAND, LOGAN-- I WANT ZANDIA SAFE-- FOR REASONS OF MY OWN!

AND YOU, LITTLE ONE, YOU HAVE DONE TRES BIEN... I LAUGHED AS I HEARD ROUGE BREATHE HER LAST!

BUT WE MUST SAVE OUR ALLIES, NON? ALERT THEM NOW!

AND... EVERYONE, THIS JOINT'S GONNA MAKE A BOOM! THAT MOUNT ST. HELENS WOULD ENVY. GET OUT OF HERE--FAST!

BUT HOW DO WE TAKE EVERYONE WITH US?

FOLLOW ME, MES AMIS--

YOU? HOW CAN WE TRUST YOU?

IT VOULD BE WISE, STEEL MAN. HERR WARP IS YOUR ONLY SALVATION!

HURRY! I SHALL BRING US ALL TO SAFETY THROUGH MY SPATIAL WARP.

ZE WARP STILL MAKES MALLAH NERVOUS.

YOU WANT TO BE NERVOUS --OR DEAD, MONSIEUR?

23

WOTTA YA *WAITING* FOR? LET'S *BLOW* THIS SECOND-RATE HINDEN-BURG!

LOGAN, YOU HAVE BROUGHT THE *MASTER* TO ME. GOOD! HAND HIM OVER *NOW*, OR ELSE.

I HAVE TOLD YOU, MONSIEUR, LOGAN IS A *COMRADE* ...THERE IS NO *NEED* TO MAKE THREATS.

HE IS RESPONSIBLE FOR ROUGE'S GLORIOUS *DEATH.*

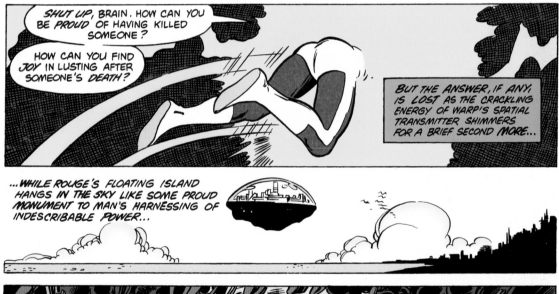

SHUT UP, BRAIN. HOW CAN YOU BE *PROUD* OF HAVING KILLED SOMEONE?

HOW CAN YOU FIND *JOY* IN LUSTING AFTER SOMEONE'S *DEATH?*

BUT THE *ANSWER,* IF ANY, IS *LOST* AS THE CRACKLING ENERGY OF WARP'S SPATIAL TRANSMITTER SHIMMERS FOR A BRIEF SECOND *MORE...*

...WHILE ROUGE'S FLOATING ISLAND HANGS IN THE SKY LIKE SOME PROUD MONUMENT TO MAN'S HARNESSING OF INDESCRIBABLE POWER...

BUT THE POWER HERE WAS FORGED FROM THE DREAMS OF A MADMAN...

AND LIKE THOSE DREAMS, IT, TOO, MUST COME TO AN END.

SWALLOWED WHOLE BY ITS OWN *EVIL...*

DESTROYED BY ITS OWN BANEFUL LUSTS...

24

GONE... ALONG WITH THEIR INSANE PLANS OF CONQUEST.

THERE IS SOMETHING OF *POETIC JUSTICE* IN THIS, I THINK.

"JUSTICE"? *BAH!* THE VERY WORD *SICKENS* ME!

HOLD IT RIGHT *THERE*, LADY. ZAHL AND MADAM ROUGE MAY BE GONE, BUT *YOU* CREEPS ARE JUST AS BAD AS *THEY* ARE.

OUR FIGHT AIN'T *OVER* YET.

CLIFF... DON'T *DO* ANYTHING!

I--I MADE A *DEAL* WITH THEM TO HELP SAVE THE TITANS.

THIS TIME, AT LEAST, THEY'RE *FREE* TO GO.

FREE, HUH?

LOGAN, YOU HAVE SERVED THE BROTHERHOOD *WELL.* WE SHALL LONG *REMEMBER* ROUGE AND ZAHL'S DEATH.

SO GLORIOUS... *SO GLORIOUS.*

YOU ACTUALLY *BELIEVE* KILLING ACCOMPLISHES SOMETHING POSITIVE.

WE KNOW THERE'S *NOTHING* POSITIVE ABOUT MURDER... IT'S NOT ONLY WRONG...IT'S *SAD!* AWFULLY, *AWFULLY* SAD.

SURE, WHY *NOT?* WHO WANTS *ANOTHER* FIGHT AFTER THIS, RIGHT?

GLORIOUS? Y'KNOW, BRAIN, I GUESS THAT'S WHAT SEPARATES THE *GOOD* GUYS FROM THE *BAD* GUYS.

25

GARFIELD HAS LEARNED *WELL*, WALLACE. BEFORE THIS HE WAS A BOY STRUGGLING WITH HIS OWN FEARS.

NOW HE IS A *MAN* COME TO GRIPS WITH HIS OWN *MORTALITY*.

HE HAS SEEN HOW WASTEFUL IT IS TO *HATE*. HOW *IMPOVERISHED* THE SOUL BECOMES WHEN *VENGEANCE* CONSUMES THE *HEART*.

OH, WE TITANS FIGHT *BATTLES*, AND I ALONG WITH YOU, BECAUSE I FEEL WE TRULY BELIEVE THAT SOMEDAY EVIL WILL BE *DESTROYED*.

I LIVE FOR *THAT DAY*, WALLACE, WHEN THE ONLY TEARS AN EMPATH SHEDS ARE THOSE *TEARS OF JOY.*

CLIFF, YOU KNOW, I USED TO FEEL SO *EMPTY*. BUT NOW--

GAR, MY GOD-- *GAR!*

HUH?

DAYTON?

I WAS SO *SCARED* FOR YOU, GAR... SO VERY SCARED. I *CARE* FOR YOU. I KNOW I HAVEN'T *TOLD* YOU THAT BEFORE, BUT I *LOVE* YOU, SON.

OH, *STEVE...* ST--

--*DAD!*

IT IS ALL *OVER*? JUST LIKE *THAT*?

YEAH. YOU WANT *EVERYTHING* TO END WITH A BANG, GOLDIE?

OVER... *NEVER* THOUGHT I'D SEE THE DAY.

I'VE BEEN LIVING WITH THIS EVER SINCE *RITA* DIED.

AND I'M *GLAD* IT'S OVER. I...NO LONGER FEEL THE *HATE*.

YOU KNOW, DAD, I ONCE THOUGHT WHEN THIS ENDED, IT WOULD END ALL MY MEMORIES OF THE DOOM PATROL.

BUT IT *DOESN'T*, YOU KNOW. I THINK *WITHOUT* THE HATE CLOUDING MY MIND --THAT THEY'RE *BRIGHTER* IN MY HEART THAN *EVER*.

26

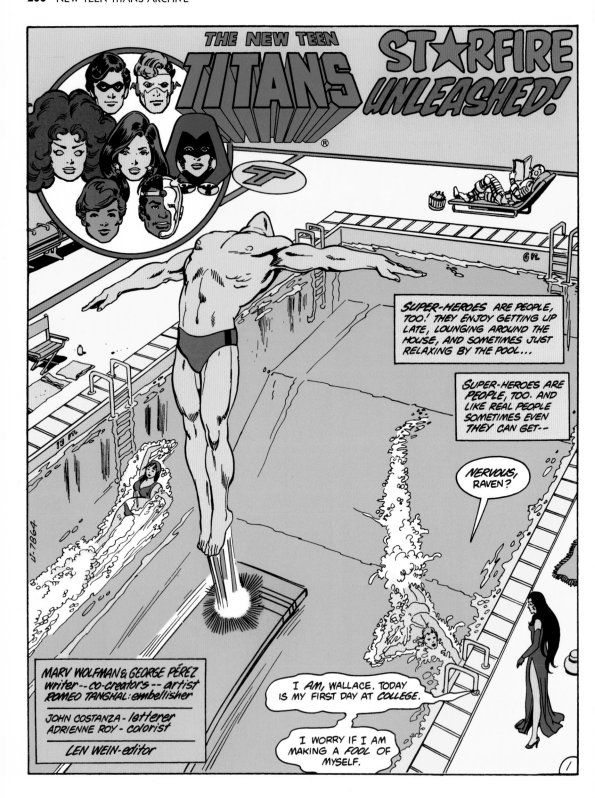

I HAVE NO REAL *KNOWLEDGE* OF YOUR WORLD. I SPENT ALL MY LIFE HIDDEN AWAY IN THE *TEMPLE AZARATH!*

DON'T SWEAT IT. EARTH IS JUST LIKE YOUR *HOME TOWN*--

--ONLY WE *SMILE* A HECKUVA LOT MORE!

♫ OH, I FLY THROUGH THE AIR WITH THE GREATEST OF EASE... ♫

...THE DARING YOUNG MAN ON THE FLYING TRAPEZE! ♫

IMPRESSED, DONNA? A *QUADRUPLE* SOMERSAULT?

EARTH TO DONNA! EARTH TO *DONNA!*

OH, DICK, DID YOU SAY SOMETHING? I WASN'T PAYING *ATTENTION.*

SO I NOTICED. IS IT *ME,* OR DO YOU HAVE *TROUBLES?*

NAH! JUST CONCERNED ABOUT *KORIAND'R,* THAT'S ALL.

HER NEW *BOYFRIEND?*

YEAH. EVER SINCE THEY MET I'VE HARDLY *SEEN* HER.

SHE'S SUCH AN *INNOCENT* IN MANY WAYS, DICK, I *WORRY* ABOUT HER.

I DON'T WANT TO SEE HER *HURT.*

"WELL I'M GLAD SHE FOUND SOMEONE. I STILL REMEMBER *OUR CONFRONTATION.*"

KORY, WE CAN'T KEEP *SEEING* EACH OTHER LIKE THIS. IT'S BAD FOR OUR *TEAMWORK.*

BUT, DICK, I THOUGHT YOU *LIKED* ME.

I *DO,* KORY... REALLY, BUT NOT THE WAY YOU *THINK.*

OH, DICK, I THOUGHT I WASN'T *ALONE* HERE ON THIS PLANET, I THOUGHT I HAD SOMEONE WHO *LOVED* ME.

I *DO*... AS A FRIEND.

THAT'S ALL, KORY-- AS A VERY GOOD *FRIEND!*

I KNEW SHE'D FIND SOMEONE *ELSE*-- JUST DIDN'T EXPECT IT WOULD BE SO *SOON.*

AND NOW THAT SHE HAS, I'M A LITTLE *JEALOUS* OF THE GUY. WHAT'S HIS *NAME*--?

FRANKLIN CRANDALL, SHORT-PANTS... AN' YOU *KNEW* IT.

MEBBE YOU LIKED GOLDIE MORE'N YOU LET ON, EH?

ACROSS THE EAST RIVER FROM TITANS' TOWER AND NORTH TO THE EAST EIGHTIES...

A SHADOW CREEPS ACROSS THE NARROW HALLWAY LEADING TO A CERTAIN PENT-HOUSE APART-MENT...

A SHADOW THAT PAUSES EVER-SO-BRIEFLY BEFORE TWO VERY FAMILIAR NAMES...

A SHADOW THAT MOVES SWIFTLY, ENTERING THE APARTMENT WITH AMAZING EASE...

WHILE BACK IN TITANS' TOWER...

YEAH, SHE MET HIM LAST MONTH, AFTER WE RETURNED FROM ZANDIA...

DONNA, DICK...RAVEN AND I HAVE TO GO.

IT'S YOUR FIRST DAY IN COLLEGE, ISN'T IT?

AND I AM LOOKING FORWARD TO IT, DONNA.

I HAVE BEEN A STRANGER HERE ALL TOO LONG.

WELL, GOOD LUCK, HOPE IT'S WHAT YOU REALLY WANT.

SEE YOU TONIGHT, OKAY? WE STILL HAVE THAT DINNER DATE, DON'T WE?

WE DO, DONNA. I WILL BE THERE.

WHEW, SHE'S GONE. Y'KNOW, SOMETIMES SHE SPOOKS ME. SHE PUTS ON THAT COLD ACT SO CONSISTENTLY, IT REALLY BOTHERS ME.

WE DO HAVE AN AMAZING GROUP, DON'T WE?

RAVEN'S SO INTRO-SPECTIVE, KORIAND'R'S SO OUTGOING...AND ME--

-- SOMETIMES I FEEL LIKE I'M THE MARY TYLER MOORE OF THE SUPER-HEROINE SET!

ANYWAY, WHAT WAS I SAYING--? OH YES, HOW KORY MET FRANKLIN...

③

"I WAS TAKING *PHOTOS* FOR CARL AT THE 'SILVER FOX ADVERTISING AGENCY'-- THEY'RE ONE OF MY FREELANCE CLIENTS..."

"KORY'S BEEN DOING SOME MODELING WORK THERE FOR ME-- SHE'S THE 'GOLDEN GIRL' FOR SERGIO DE LEVI'S JEANS."

SHE'S A *'BEAUT*, I TELL YOU. WE'RE 'A GONNA SELL A *BILLION* JEANS WITH 'A MY GOLDEN GIRL!

AN' *YOU*, LADY PICTURE-TAKER-- WHERE YOU *GET* THIS WONDERFUL IDEA--

--PUTTIN' MY GOLDEN LADY IN 'A *SPACE?* IT'S 'A *WONDERFUL!*

OH, I DON'T KNOW, MR. DE LEVI--IT JUST SEEMED *NATURAL*, I GUESS.

"WE WERE SHOOTING MOST OF THE DAY BEFORE I NOTICED HE HAD BEEN WATCHING KORY."

"WATCHING--? HECK! HIS EYES WERE BUGGING OUT LIKE *DAFFY DUCK* IN THOSE OLD CARTOONS!"

"ANYWAY, HE STOOD THERE FOR ANOTHER HOUR UNTIL I FINALLY *CALLED IT A WRAP!*"

"SERGIO TRIED TO MAKE A MOVE ON KORY. SHE BRUSHED HIM ASIDE LIKE A PRO. THE GIRL'S NOT AS NAIVE AS WE THINK."

"FRANKLIN KEPT STARING, I THINK KORY *NOTICED* HIM THEN. SHE SEEMED TO SMILE BACK..."

"AND AS CARL AND THE OTHERS PACKED UP TO LEAVE..."

THAT WAS *WONDERFUL*, KORY. WE'LL SEE YOU IN A WEEK FOR ANOTHER *SHOOT*, OKAY?

I GUESS SO, CARL. AND *THANK YOU!* THIS WAS *FUN!*

SHE THANKS *ME--?* GORGEOUS AND *HUMBLE*, TOO. WOW!

EXCUSE ME--?

"HE MOVED CLOSER TO KORY. FOR SOME REASON MY NECK HAIRS *BRISTLED.*"

④

MISS, I HAD TO TELL YOU-- YOU'RE JUST *BEAUTIFUL.*

I FEEL *SILLY,* BUT I CAME IN HERE BY *ACCIDENT.* AND WHEN I SAW YOU POSING THERE, I COULDN'T *LEAVE.*

I FEEL I HAVE TO *TALK* TO YOU, MISS--

KORY ANDERS. I THINK *YOU'RE* RATHER *HANDSOME,* TOO.

C'MON, PLEASE DON'T *EMBARRASS* ME. GOSH, PLEASE, I'D REALLY LIKE TO TAKE YOU *OUT.* COFFEE? LUNCH? DINNER? YOU *NAME* IT?

JUST PLEASE DON'T SAY *NO!*

KORY, DID YOU REMEMBER, WE HAVE A *LUNCH--*

OH, DONNA, I'D LIKE YOU TO *MEET* THIS NICE MAN-- OH, I DON'T KNOW YOUR *NAME...*

FRANKLIN CRANDALL. PLEASED TO *MEET* YOU, MISS--?

TROY! *DONNA* TROY.

DONNA, HE ASKED ME *OUT...*

KORY, YOU DON'T EVEN *KNOW* HIM.

IS THAT *IMPORTANT?* HE SEEMS LIKE SUCH A *NICE* MAN.

GEE, KORY, I DON'T *KNOW...* DONNA, EVER SINCE I *CAME* TO YOUR WORLD I'VE SPENT *ALL* MY TIME WITH YOU AND THE OTHERS...

I HAVEN'T *MET* ANYONE, AND NOW--

OH, GAWD! I'M TALKING LIKE I'M YOUR *MOTHER* AND THIS IS YOUR *FIRST* DATE...

"OF COURSE, GO OUT, HAVE FUN. JUST PLEASE, KORY-- DON'T TELL HIM WHERE YOU'RE FROM.

"SOME PEOPLE... WELL, THEY WOULDN'T UNDERSTAND."

ONLY I DON'T THINK KORIAND'R *HEARD* WHAT I WAS SAYING.

5

AND THEY'VE BEEN *SEEING* EACH OTHER EVERY DAY FOR A *MONTH* NOW.

I DON'T THINK I'VE EVER SEEN KORIAND'R SO *HAPPY.*

SO WHAT'S THE *WORRY?* EVERYTHING'S *NIFTY!*

HEY! I'M *FAMISHED,* WANNA GRAB A HAM-BURGER OR SOMETHING?

SURE. JUST LET ME STOP OFF AT MY *APARTMENT* FIRST.

YOU WANNA COME *WITH* US, VIC?

NAH! I GOT SOME *HEAVY* READIN'!

Y'KNOW, LIKE HOW TA FIX YOUR RUN-OF-THE-MILL *CYBORG BODY* WHEN IT BREAKS DOWN.

'SOKAY, PAL. SEE YOU *LATER.*

SO EVERYTHING'S *NIFTY,* IS IT, SHORT-PANTS?

NOT FOR *THIS* SECOND-RATE ERECTOR SET, IT AIN'T.

KORY'S GOT HER-SELF A NEW *GUY.* DICK 'N' LOGAN'S GOT A DOZEN GALS *EACH.*

WALLY'S GOT THE *WITCH,* AN' DONNA AN' THAT *TERRY LONG* DUDE ARE TIGHTER 'N BROOKE SHIELDS' *JEANS!*

CAN'T EVEN BRING MYSELF TA CALL *SARAH SIMMS* AN' TELL HER I'M BACK IN *TOWN...* NOT AFTER I JUST FLEW OFF WITHOUT LETTIN' HER KNOW.

A SHADOW GLIDES THROUGH THE LIVING ROOM TOWARD THE BEDROOM BEYOND.

BUT ME, I GOT *ZILCH!*

BLAST! MEBBE *VIC STONE* WAS A BIG COLLEGE HERO, BUT *CYBORG'S* NOTHIN' MORE 'N A CHROME-PLATED *CHICKEN!*

IT IS LOOKING FOR SOMETHING...

NO, NOTHING HERE.

BUT THEN...

DARK ROOM

DARK ROOM

DO NOT ENTER WHEN RED LIGHT IS ON!

...IT *KNOWS!*

6

THE RED GLOW OF DONNA TROY'S DARK-ROOM GIVES WAY TO THE GOLDEN GLOW OF A MID-AFTER-NOON SUN THAT CLEARLY EXISTS FOR ONLY THESE TWO...

I...I REALLY THINK I *CARE* FOR YOU, FRANKLIN.

I DON'T THINK I'VE EVER *FELT* THIS WAY BEFORE.

OH, COME ON, KORY, ANYONE WHO LOOKS LIKE YOU MUST HAVE A *HUNDRED* GUYS DROOLING AFTER YOU.

NO, NOT *REALLY.* WHERE I'M FROM, I DIDN'T MEET MANY MEN.

YOU'RE *SPECIAL,* KORY... *VERY* SPECIAL, I DOUBT IF THERE'S ANOTHER ON EARTH LIKE YOU.

AND MAYBE THE GUYS WHERE YOU'RE FROM ARE *BLIND*-- BUT I'M NOT. I'M NOT LETTING YOU GET *AWAY* FROM ME.

I *LOVE* YOU.

OH, FRANK, I--

X'HAL!

FRANKLIN-- *GET BACK!* THAT CAR IS *OUT* OF *CONTROL!*

SKEEEEEEEE

SKRAK...

BTRAKK!

HELP ME! *HELP ME!!* MY BRAKES WON'T HOLD!

I--I *CAN'T* STOP!

SPAM

SKREEEEEE

WHAK

OH, *LORD,* SHE'S GOING TO *CRASH!*

MAYBE *NOT,* FRANK.

7

I THINK I CAN DO THIS WITHOUT REVEALING WHO I AM.

THAT DOESN'T *MATTER* TO ME, BUT IT SEEMS SO IMPOR-TANT TO *DONNA!*

EVERYONE'S EYES RIVETED ON THE *RUNAWAY CAR,* NO ONE SEES STARFIRE UNLEASH A CRACKLING, BLAZING *STARBOLT...*

...WHOSE HEAT INSTANTLY MELTS BOTH RUBBER TIRE AND STREET TARMAC...

...FUSING BOTH TOGETHER...

...AND BRINGING THE RUNAWAY CAR TO A SLOW, STICKY HALT.

INCREDIBLE! THAT WAS FANTASTIC! DID YOU *SEE* THAT, KORY?

THAT WOMAN MUST HAVE A *GUARDIAN ANGEL!*

I GUESS SHE *DOES* AT THAT, FRANKLIN.

DOWNTOWN NEW YORK, ON THE CAMPUS OF MANHATTAN COLLEGE...

WELL, THIS IS IT, RAVEN.

I KNOW, WALLACE, AND I HAVE TO KEEP TELL-ING MYSELF THIS IS THE RIGHT THING TO *DO.*

ALL I KNOW ABOUT THE OUTSIDE WORLD IS FROM READING *BOOKS.*

BUT I MUST MINGLE WITH *REAL PEOPLE,* MUSTN'T I?

JUST EASE UP, KID, AND YOU'LL BE *FINE.*

SEE YOU AFTER CLASS. I'LL BE HERE *WAITING!*

SHE'S GOING, AND SHE DOESN'T REALIZE HOW ALL THIS CUTS ME UP.

BEING WITH HER, *LOVING* HER, AND KNOWING SHE WON'T COMMIT HERSELF TO ME UNTIL SHE UNDERSTANDS HERSELF.

WHY DOES IT HURT *LOSING* SOMEONE YOU NEVER REALLY EVER *HAD* IN THE FIRST PLACE?

8

AND NOW, LET US RETURN TO THAT EAST EIGHTIES PENTHOUSE, WHERE...

WHAT IN--? I-- I DON'T *BELIEVE* IT!

MY OWN APARTMENT GETS RIPPED OFF-- *MY OWN APARTMENT!*

I WANNA *SCREAM!*

THE LOCK WAS JIMMIED--NOT AT ALL A *PRO-FESSIONAL* JOB.

I THINK I HAVE SOMETHING THAT CAN *HELP* US.

OH? A RADAR DETECTOR FOR *BAD GUYS?*

WHAT HAPPENS WHILE I'M OUT THERE, SWEATING, STOPPING CRIME ALL OVER NEW YORK?

NOPE! DUSTING POWDER FOR *FINGERPRINTS.* MAYBE I WAS NEVER A *BOY SCOUT,* BUT NEVER LET IT BE SAID THAT I'M NOT ALWAYS *PREPARED!*

AN HOUR PASSES, AND AFTER A COMPLETE SEARCH OF THE PREMISES...

OKAY, THIS TAKES THE CAKE-- ONLY THING *STOLEN* IS ONE OF MY PHOTO SESSION *CONTACT SHEETS.*

WHO IN THEIR RIGHT MIND WOULD--

WE'LL FIND OUT AFTER THE POLICE COMPUTER RUNS A CHECK ON THESE *PRINTS* I LIFTED. C'MON, LET'S *HURRY!*

WITH LUCK WE'LL HAVE OUR WOULD-BE THIEF *NAILED* WITHIN THE HOUR.

I DON'T WANT TODAY TO *END,* FRANKLIN, IT'S BEEN *HEAVEN!*

I DON'T WANT *ANY* DAYS TO END, KORY, EVERY TIME I LEAVE YOU I GO *CRAZY...*

I'M JEALOUS THAT YOU'LL FIND SOMEONE *ELSE.*

FURIOUS AT SPENDING MY TIME ALONE!

KORY, CAN WE GO UP TO *YOUR* PLACE? I WANT TO *ASK* YOU SOMETHING...

OF COURSE... OF COURSE! ⑨

AND... DONNA?

STRANGE, SHE'S NOT *HERE* AND SHE SAID SHE *WOULD* BE.

AND THAT *MESS* ALL AROUND.

I'D BETTER *CHECK.*

TERRY? TERRY *LONG?* THIS IS, UHH... KORY ANDERS. IS *DONNA* THERE?

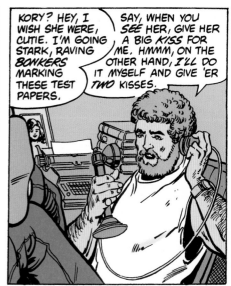

KORY? HEY, I WISH SHE WERE, CUTIE. I'M GOING STARK, RAVING *BONKERS* MARKING THESE TEST PAPERS.

SAY, WHEN YOU *SEE* HER, GIVE HER A BIG *KISS* FOR ME. HMMM, ON THE OTHER HAND, *I'LL* DO IT MYSELF AND GIVE 'ER *TWO* KISSES.

NOT THERE. HMMM. ODD, SHE'S ALWAYS SO WORRIED ABOUT *ME*...LEAVES A *NOTE* WHENEVER SHE GOES OUT. SHE TELLS ME *EVERYTHING.*

DO YOU *RECIPROCATE?* DOES SHE KNOW YOU'RE *STARFIRE?*

HUNH? YOU *KNOW?*

OHH, DONNA WILL BE *FURIOUS* WITH ME. HOW DID YOU *FIND OUT?* DID I MAKE A *MISTAKE?*

OH, I'VE KNOWN FOR *DAYS,* HONEY... YOU KNOW I FIRST CHALKED UP YOUR *COMPLEXION* TO BEING A MEDITERRANEAN *TAN*--

--BUT THEN THE OTHER DAY WHEN YOU WERE LEANING OVER--I SAW YOUR *EYES.*

BUT YOU DIDN'T *SAY* ANYTHING?

I FIGURED YOU DIDN'T *WANT* ME TO KNOW SO I DIDN'T *LET ON.* BUT I HAVE TO *NOW*...BECAUSE OF WHAT I WANT TO *ASK* YOU...

YOU MEAN YOU *STILL* LIKE ME EVEN KNOWING WHO I *AM?*

LIKE YOU? KORY ANDERS-- I *LOVE YOU!*

MANHATTAN COLLEGE...

MISS RAVEN-- UHH, IS THAT YOUR FIRST OR *LAST* NAME?

MY *ONLY* NAME, PROFESSOR HOLLIS.

YOU ARRIVED A BIT *LATE*. WE HAD BEEN DISCUSSING WHY YOU STUDENTS ENROLLED IN 'COMPARATIVE ANCIENT PHI- LOSOPHIES.'

WOULD YOU CARE TO ENLIGHTEN US AS TO YOUR *REASONS*?

PROFESSOR, FROM THE MOMENT WE ARE *BORN* WE ARE INUN- DATED WITH *PROPAGANDA.*

MUCH OF IT *BENEFICIAL,* SUCH AS 'DO UNTO OTHERS'... GENERAL RULES TO LIVE BY.

WE LEARN COMMUNICA- TION THROUGH MUTUAL *ACCEPTANCE* OF THESE RULES. WE BUILD SOCIE- TIES *BASED* ON THIS MUTUAL ACCEP- TANCE.

BUT *SOME* OF THOSE ANCIENT PHILOSOPHIES -- THEIR PROP- AGANDA HAS NOT ALWAYS BEEN FOR THE COMMON *GOOD.*

MANY PHI- LOSOPHIES PREACHED *INTOLERANCE.* SOME JUSTIFY WANTON *VIOLENCE* --

-- OTHERS COMPAS- SIONLESS *PACIFISM* SUCH AS THE CULT OF AZAR.

BUT THESE EXTREMIST CULTS, THESE PHILOSOPHIES, ALL EXIST TO *DESTROY* A COMMON BOND OF GROWTH BY *LIMITING* PER- SONAL FREEDOM AND PRODUCTIVE GOALS THAT--

OHH. I PRATTLE ON. I AM *SORRY.*

I HADN'T MEANT TO *EMBARRASS* MYSELF WITH... NO, I *STILL* TALK TOO MUCH. I--

I AM SO SORRY... SO *SORRY*...

MISS RAVEN, SOMETHING TELLS ME THIS YEAR'S CLASS IS GOING TO BE ANYTHING BUT *ORDINARY.*

SIGHHH...

WOW! YOU WERE *INCREDIBLE!* YOU MENTIONED *AZAR* -- I THOUGHT NO ONE KNEW ABOUT THEM EXCEPT *ME.* I STUDED THEIR WAYS... EVEN PRACTICED --

EXCUSE ME. THE PROFESSOR HAS ASKED FOR YOUR *ATTENTION.*

OH.

11

AN HOUR PASSES BEFORE WE RETURN TO DONNA TROY'S PENTHOUSE...

DO YOU REALLY HAVE TO GO. NOW, FRANKLIN?

PLEASE SAY YOU CAN STAY.

I WANT TO, HONEY. BUT I CAN'T. I'LL SEE YOU TONIGHT, THOUGH.

I CAN'T WAIT TO TELL THE OTHERS.

NO, PLEASE DON'T. NOT UNTIL I CAN BE WITH YOU.

I WANT TO SEE THEIR EXPRESSIONS.

OKAY. I PROMISE. BUT HURRY BACK.

GOSH.

DONNA, I NO LONGER ENVY YOU.

I'M IN LOVE!

LOVE!!

AND SUDDENLY, ANY PROBLEMS THAT MIGHT HAVE BEEN ARE GONE...

12

...BUT HARDLY FORGOTTEN...

FRANKLIN CRANDALL SAUNTERS AWAY FROM A SMALL, PRIVATE PARKING SPACE IN GREENWICH, CONNECTICUT...

HE WHISTLES MERRILY, PLEASED AT THE DAY GONE BY...

CRANDALL, YOU WERE GONE *LONGER* THAN YOU WERE SUPPOSED TO.

WHAT DO *YOU* CARE? STARFIRE'S *IN LOVE* WITH ME. ISN'T THAT WHAT *THE H.I.V.E.* WANTED?

THAT IS WHY *I* HAVE PAID YOU, CRANDALL.

HAVE YOU THE *INFORMATION* I WANT?

COME ON. I JUST TOLD HER I KNEW WHO SHE WAS. IT'LL TAKE *TIME* BEFORE I CAN ASK HER *THOSE* KINDS OF QUESTIONS.

I DO NOT *HAVE* THAT SORT OF *TIME*, CRANDALL.

I WAS BROUGHT INTO *THE H.I.V.E.* TO REPLACE THE MEMBER KILLED BY *THE TERMINATOR.**

*NTT #10. --LEN.

I WISH TO *DEMONSTRATE* TO THE OTHERS THAT THEY HAVE MADE A *WISE* DECISION.

LOOK, I REALLY DON'T LIKE *DOING* THIS TO KORY.

SHE'S A *GOOD KID* AND I FEEL LIKE *FILTH*, PLAYING HER THIS WAY.

YOU *ARE* FILTH, CRANDALL. YOU'VE MADE *HUNDREDS* OF WOMEN FALL IN LOVE WITH YOU-- ONLY TO TURN AGAINST THEM WITH *BLACK-MAIL.*

HEY, THOSE WERE ALL *RICH* BROADS CHEATING ON THEIR HUSBANDS.

KORY'S *DIFFERENT.* SHE'S INCREDIBLY SWEET, AND I ACTUALLY *LIKE* HER.

WHAT IF I PAY YOU BACK EVERYTHING YOU GAVE ME... CALL THIS *OFF--*

SWAK

NO! YOU WILL NOT BACK AWAY AND MAKE ME LOOK LIKE A *FOOL.*

YOU WILL DO WHAT I *WANT*, OR I SWEAR THIS STARFIRE WILL BE THE *LAST* FEMALE YOU EVER LOVE.

DO YOU *UNDERSTAND* ME, CRANDALL?

AFRAID FOR THE FIRST TIME IN HIS LIFE, FRANKLIN CRANDALL NODS.

13

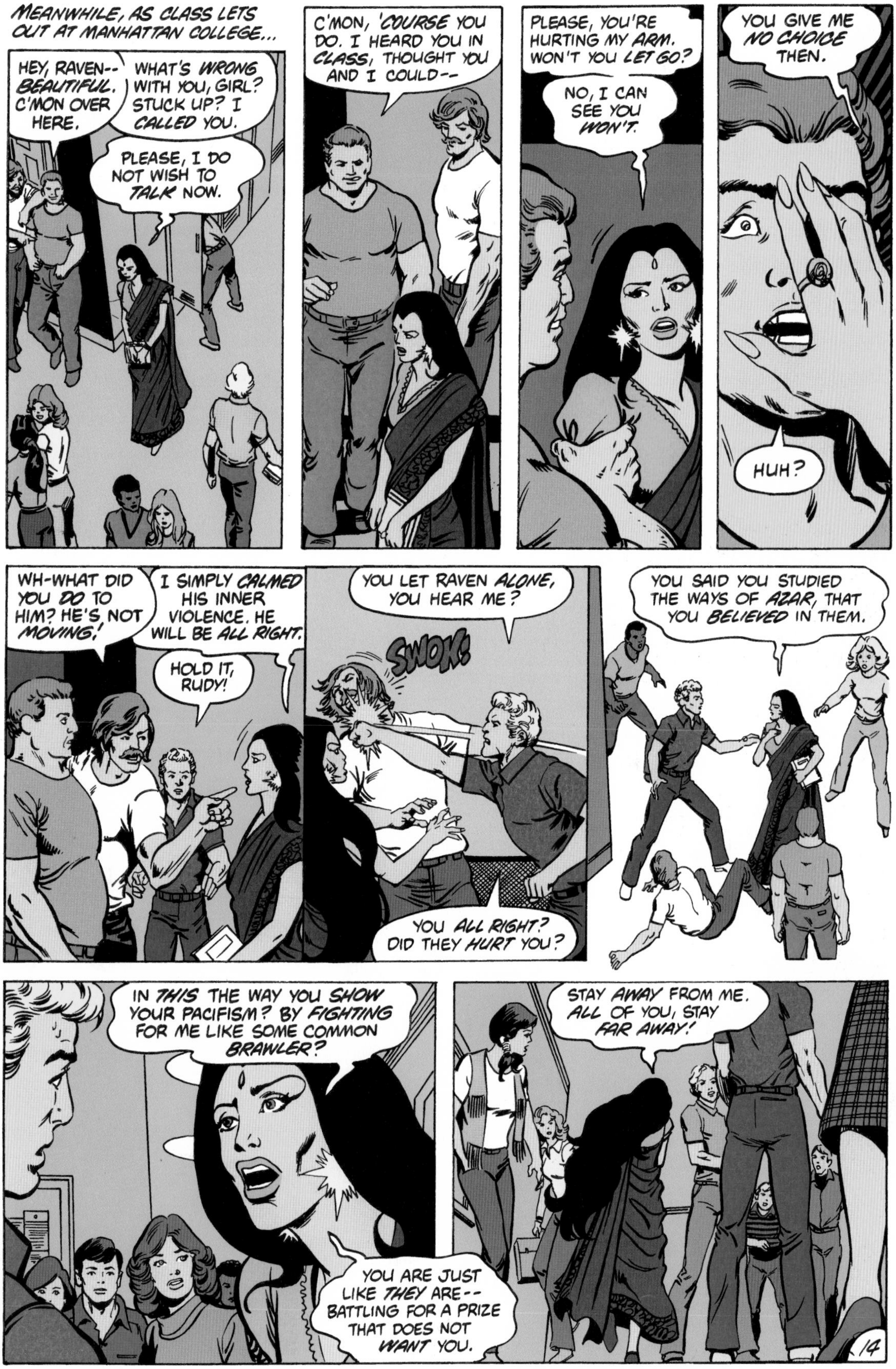
MEANWHILE, AS CLASS LETS OUT AT MANHATTAN COLLEGE...
HEY, RAVEN-- BEAUTIFUL. C'MON OVER HERE.
WHAT'S WRONG WITH YOU, GIRL? STUCK UP? I CALLED YOU.
PLEASE, I DO NOT WISH TO TALK NOW.
C'MON, 'COURSE YOU DO. I HEARD YOU IN CLASS, THOUGHT YOU AND I COULD--
PLEASE, YOU'RE HURTING MY ARM. WON'T YOU LET GO?
NO, I CAN SEE YOU WON'T.
YOU GIVE ME NO CHOICE THEN.
HUH?
WH-WHAT DID YOU DO TO HIM? HE'S NOT MOVING!
I SIMPLY CALMED HIS INNER VIOLENCE. HE WILL BE ALL RIGHT.
HOLD IT, RUDY!
YOU LET RAVEN ALONE, YOU HEAR ME?
SWOK!
YOU ALL RIGHT? DID THEY HURT YOU?
YOU SAID YOU STUDIED THE WAYS OF AZAR, THAT YOU BELIEVED IN THEM.
IN THIS THE WAY YOU SHOW YOUR PACIFISM? BY FIGHTING FOR ME LIKE SOME COMMON BRAWLER?
YOU ARE JUST LIKE THEY ARE-- BATTLING FOR A PRIZE THAT DOES NOT WANT YOU.
STAY AWAY FROM ME. ALL OF YOU, STAY FAR AWAY!
14

TITANS' TOWER...

THANK HEAVEN FOR THE *COMPUTER.* I'VE FIT ALL THE *PIECES* TOGETHER.

I *KNOW* WHO RIFLED THROUGH YOUR *APARTMENT,* DONNA.

PERSONALLY, BAT-BOY, I THINK IT WAS *LOGAN*-- SEARCHIN' FER SOME CHEESECAKE PICS OF *STARFIRE!*

VICTOR, BE *SERIOUS.* WHO *WAS* IT, DICK?

FIRST, LET'S GO OVER WHAT WE KNOW: THE ONLY THING STOLEN WAS CONTACT PROOFS ON *ANGELA DOVE,* A MODEL.

WE WENT TO ANGELA'S PLACE, AND SHE WAS *GONE.*

THERE WERE SIGNS OF A BREAK-IN AND A STRUGGLE. SHE WAS PROBABLY *TAKEN.*

NOW, ACCORDING TO THESE PICTURES, ANGELA WAS THE GIRLFRIEND OF ONE *JASON SILVER,* A SMALL-TIME NUMBERS RUNNER IN HARLEM.

SILVER WORKED FOR-- AND IS TESTIFYING NEXT WEEK IN COURT *AGAINST*-- MOB BOSS *BIG PHIL CERULLO.*

NOW SILVER'S *ALSO* DISAPPEARED. MY BET IS CERULLO TRIED TO *GET* TO SILVER THROUGH ANGELA--

--AND HE GOT ANGELA'S ADDRESS THROUGH *YOU,* KNOWING SHE WAS *MODELLING* FOR--

GUYS, GUYS, I'M SO GLAD YOU'RE ALL *HERE!*

I FEEL SO *GOOD,* AND I HAVE A *SURPRISE.*

LOGAN'S BACK FROM HIS *VACATION* WITH DAYTON AN' STEELE AN' HE'S GONNA *RUIN OUR DAY.* RIGHT?

OH, NO... A *REAL* SURPRISE, VICTOR, BUT I CAN'T *TELL* YOU YET. YOU'LL FIND OUT WHEN I TAKE YOU TO FRANKLIN'S APARTMENT TONIGHT.

DONNA, HE'S THE MOST UNDERSTANDING, *GLORIOUS* GUY IN THE WORLD. I MEAN, HE FOUND OUT WHO I AM AND HE *STILL* LOVES ME.

OBOY! KORY, YOU AND I HAD BETTER *TALK.*

OH, FRANKLIN, I'M GLAD I *CAUGHT* YOU. WHEN CAN WE COME *OVER?*

HOW'S *EIGHT O'CLOCK* SOUND, HONEY?

FINE, JUST FINE. I *LOVE* YOU.

I LOVE YOU, *TOO,* KORY.

I LOVE YOU, TOO.

IT'S STILL *EARLY--* PLENTY OF TIME TO FIND YOUR *MODEL FRIEND,* DONNA.

IF I'M *RIGHT,* SHE SHOULD BE IN CERULLO'S HARLEM *DROP PLACE...* AN ADDRESS THE COMPUTER HAD ON *FILE,* FORTUNATELY.

NO, GIRL, YOU JUST TAKE IT *EASY,* EH? WE'RE NOT GONNA *HURT* YA NONE.

SURE WOULDN'T WANNA SCAR UP THOSE BEAUTIFUL *FEATURES* ANY...

...'CAUSE I GOT *PLANS* FER YA, YER GONNA MAKE ME A *BUNDLE--*

--YER GONNA BE ONE FINE PONY IN MY *STABLE...*

...PROVIDIN' YER BIG-MOUTH BOYFRIEND, SILVER, *COOPERATES* WITH ME WHEN TALKIN' TA THE *FEDS.*

YOU UNNERSTAND WHERE I'M *COMIN'* FROM, DON'T YA, BABE?

ANGELA DOVE, ORIGINALLY *LUWANDA BROWN,* NODS. SHE WILL AGREE WITH *ANYTHING* NOW... JUST SO LONG AS SHE ISN'T *HURT...*

(17)

A PROBLEM THAT WON'T BE MUCH OF A PROBLEM IN LESS THAN FIVE SECONDS...

PARTY'S *OVER*, CREEPS!

AND THE NEXT TIME YOU SADISTS GET THE DESIRE TO *TORTURE* HELPLESS GIRLS--

-- REMEMBER NOT *ALL* OF US ARE HELPLESS!

SWAK

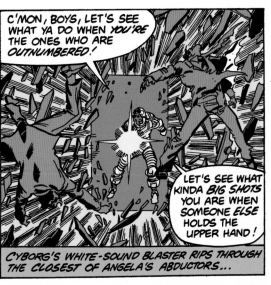

C'MON, BOYS, LET'S SEE WHAT YA DO WHEN *YOU'RE* THE ONES WHO ARE *OUTNUMBERED!*

LET'S SEE WHAT KINDA *BIG SHOTS* YOU ARE WHEN SOMEONE *ELSE* HOLDS THE UPPER HAND!

CYBORG'S WHITE-SOUND BLASTER RIPS THROUGH THE CLOSEST OF ANGELA'S ABDUCTORS...

...WHILE ROBIN, THE ACROBATIC TEEN WONDER, EASILY MOPS UP THE REST...

WE USUALLY FIND OURSELVES FIGHTING *COSTUMED* CREEPS--

-- JERKS OUT TO CONQUER THE *WORLD* AND SUCH...

...BUT Y'KNOW SOMETHING, STOPPING SLUGS LIKE YOU IS MUCH MORE SATISFYING!

BECAUSE WHAT *YOU* PUNKS DO MAKES ME PERSONALLY VERY *MAD!*

NOT A BAD *SPEECH*, KID. MEBBE I'LL HAVE IT CARVED ON YOUR GRAVESTONE!

HUH?

ANGELA--?

18

YA MADE CREAM CHEESE OF MY *MOB*, BUT NOW YER JUST GONNA SPIN AROUND AN' LEAVE...

WHAT'S *MORE*, YA AIN'T GONNA SAY A *WORD* 'BOUT THIS, RIGHT?

'CAUSE IF YA *DO*... WELL, MISS DOVE HERE'S GONNA MAKE HER *LAST FLIGHT*, IF YA UNNERSTAN' WHERE I'M COMIN' FROM.

NO WE *DON'T*, KILLER!

ARRGH!

SKREEEE

OH, NO...

STARFIRE, DID YOU--?

YOU *SKRAG* 'IM, GOLDIE?

KILL HIM? OH, NO. I WANTED TO, BUT YOU KEEP TELLING ME TO *CONTROL* MY STARBOLTS.

I JUST *STUNNED* HIM.

HE *HURT* ME. H-HE WAS GOING TO *KILL* ME.

YOU'LL BE *ALL RIGHT* NOW. JUST TAKE IT *EASY.*

HOW *IS* HE?

BREATHING, BUT JUST *BARELY.* STARFIRE, YOU USED TOO MUCH *POWER.*

WELL, HE CERTAINLY *DESERVED* IT, WONDER GIRL. HE WASN'T EXACTLY A *GOOD* MAN.

OBOY, WE REALLY HAVE TO *TALK* ABOUT HOW YOU USE YOUR POWERS... AND TALK *SOON.*

19

MEANWHILE... I'M CALLING OFF OUR DEAL.

AND YOU CAME HERE TO KILL ME?

I DID. BUT I'VE NEVER KILLED BEFORE...

...AND I'M NOT STARTING NOW. SO HERE-- TAKE MY GUN--

--IT DOESN'T HAVE ANY BULLETS IN IT ANYHOW.

I'M SEEING THE TITANS TONIGHT AND I'M TELLING THEM EVERYTHING.

YOU WOULDN'T DARE, CRANDALL. YOU KNOW WHAT THE H.I.V.E. DOES TO TRAITORS.

I'M NO FOOL. I CHECKED AROUND.

YOU'RE WORKING ALONE ON THIS TO SCORE BROWNIE POINTS WITH THE OTHERS.

THEY PROBABLY DON'T EVEN KNOW YOU'RE DOING THIS.

I... JUST HOPE KORY CAN FORGIVE ME. I REALLY DO LIKE HER.

SO, GOODBYE, MISTER-- AND GOOD RIDDANCE.

HEY, STOW IT, WILL YOU?

INDEED, MR. CRANDALL...

GOODBYE...

...AND GOOD RIDDANCE!

BAM!

20

I CAN'T *WAIT.* YOU'RE ALL GOING TO BE SO *SURPRISED.*

THAT DIDN'T TAKE *LONG.* WE'LL GET TO YOUR FRIEND'S PLACE *EARLY.*

WILL WE, *KORIAND'R?* I CERTAINLY *HOPE* SO.

BUT THEN, WHY AM I *WORRYING* SO MUCH?

THIS IS IT... HE'S WAITING *INSIDE.*

FRANK? FRANK--

OH, X'HAL! X'HAL!

FRANKLIN!

Y-YOU'RE *BLEEDING!* YOU'VE BEEN *HURT!* WHAT HAPPENED, FRANKLIN? WHO *DID* THIS TO YOU?

TELL ME WHO *DID* THIS?

K-KORY... *H.I.V.E.* ... WANTED... YOU... 276 ARCHER-- TWO... TWO BLOCKS...

¡*COUGH*¡ WANTED YOU...WAN-- OH, KORY--

I-I... LOVE... YOU...

OH, X'HAL-- D-DON'T TALK, FRANKLIN. DON'T *TALK.* WE'LL GET *HELP.*

DICK! DONNA! YOU'VE GOT TO *HELP* HIM.

I...LOVE... YOU...

AND I LOVE *YOU,* FRANKLIN... BUT PLEASE... PLEASE DON'T *TALK.*

YOU'LL BE *ALL RIGHT.* YOU WILL BE, I *KNOW* YOU WILL.

21

DICK, HE'S *OKAY*, ISN'T HE? HE'LL BE *ALL RIGHT--*?

YOU CAN *HELP* HIM, CAN'T YOU?

HE WON'T *DIE*, HE WON'T. I *KNOW* HE WON'T.

I'LL CALL *GREENWICH HOSPITAL*, TELL THEM WE'RE BRINGING HIM *IN.*

WONDER GIRL... DON'T *BOTHER--*

--IT'S TOO LATE.

NO! YOU'RE *WRONG.* CHECK HIM AGAIN AND YOU'LL SEE YOU MADE A DREAD- FUL *MISTAKE.*

HE'LL PULL *THROUGH*. I *KNOW* HE WILL.

KORY, HE'S *GONE*, THERE'S NO *CHANGING* THAT.

BUT YOU, I'M *WORRIED* ABOUT YOU. PLEASE, LISTEN--

NO!

I'VE *HAD IT* WITH LISTENING TO YOU, DICK!

SWAK!

ALWAYS TELLING ME WHAT TO *DO*... TELLING ME TO HOLD IN MY *POWER!*

WHERE DID IT *GET* ME, DICK?

THAT FILTHY *KILLER*--THE ONE WHO KILLED FRANKLIN--

--HE'LL SEE HOW *TERRIBLE* MY POWER IS, DICK. HE'LL SEE.

HE'S A DEAD MAN!

WE GOTTA *STOP* HER! SHE'LL *KILL* HIM!

NO, VICTOR, YOU TAKE *CARE* OF *DICK*.

I'M AFRAID THIS IS SOMETHING I'D BEST DO *MYSELF*.

SHE IS AN ANGRY, FIERY COMET BLAZING THROUGH THE CONNECTICUT SKIES...

22

NEVER HAS SHE FELT THIS WAY BEFORE; NOT WHEN RUTHLESSLY KIDNAPPED AS A FRIGHTENED TWELVE-YEAR-OLD...

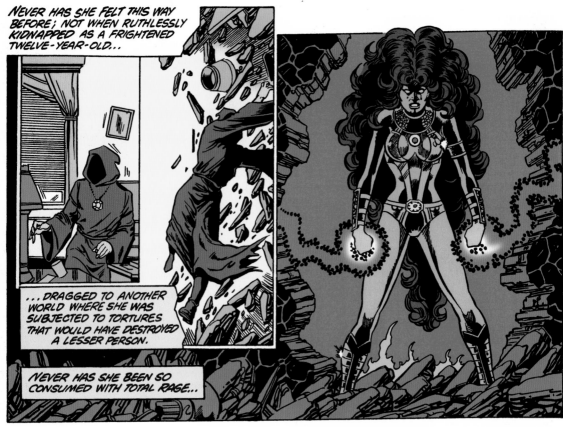

...DRAGGED TO ANOTHER WORLD WHERE SHE WAS SUBJECTED TO TORTURES THAT WOULD HAVE DESTROYED A LESSER PERSON.

NEVER HAS SHE BEEN SO CONSUMED WITH TOTAL RAGE...

NEVER HAS ONLY ONE DESIRE BURNED SO BRIGHTLY IN HER FURIOUS HEART:

PRINCESS KORIAND'R OF TAMARAN WANTS ONLY TO KILL!

STOP IT, GIRL. THAT WAS BUSINESS, THAT'S ALL.

I WANTED TO SHOW THE OTHERS THEY HAD CHOSEN WELL IN ME--

--THERE WAS NOTHING PERSONAL--

LORD!

SKREEEEEEE

SHE'LL KILL ME, UNLESS--

SPAKK!

SHE STARES AT HER FALLEN FOE AND THERE IS NO PITY IN HER COLD HEART.

ALL SHE SEES IS THE MURDERER OF THE MAN SHE HAD LOVED.

ALL SHE SEES IS A MAN WHO IS GOING TO DIE! 23

SHE STEPS CLOSER...

THERE IS NO JOY IN HER WIDE OPEN EYES.

NO JOY, ONLY CASCADING TEARS OF SORROW.

STARFIRE-- STOP! DON'T DO IT!

X'HAL!

WHAT ARE YOU *DOING?* DO YOU KNOW WHAT THIS MADMAN *DID?*

I *DO.* AND I STILL CAN'T LET YOU *KILL* HIM!

YOU CAN'T *STOP ME!*

KRAK!

HE'S *MINE!* HE'S GOING TO *DIE!*

THEN YOU'LL HAVE TO KILL *ME* FIRST.

WE HAVE *LAWS* HERE, STARFIRE. IF YOU *STAY* ON THIS PLANET YOU'LL HAVE TO *OBEY* THEM.

BECAUSE IF YOU *DON'T,* NO MATTER HOW MUCH WE *LOVE* YOU AS A *FRIEND*--

--WE'LL BE FORCED TO *HUNT YOU DOWN.* WHAT IS IT GOING TO *BE?*

24

"IT'S NOT FAIR!"

"IT'S NOT AT ALL FAIR!"

"BUT IT HAD TO *BE* THIS WAY."

"I'M *SORRY.* I REALLY *AM!*"

"NO MATTER HOW THINGS ARE DONE ON *YOUR* WORLD, IT HAD TO BE *THIS* WAY!"

"EH? THE *H.I.V.E.* KILLER--HE'S *GONE!*"

"HE GOT AWAY WHILE STARFIRE AND I WERE *ARGUING.*"

"BUT I'LL *FIND* HIM FOR YOU, KORY... I SWEAR I'LL *FIND* HIM."

"AND HE'LL *PAY...* BUT ACCORDING TO *OUR* LAWS..."

"THE WAY THINGS *HAVE* TO BE..."

"...WHETHER WE *LIKE* IT OR *NOT.*"

NIGHT...

SO DARK AND CHILLING...

NOT AT ALL A NIGHT FOR COMFORTING A SUNDERED HEART... 25

...OR A GUILTY SOUL.

NUMBER SEVEN, YOU *DISOBEYED* THE RULES OF *THE H.I.V.E.*

BEHIND OUR BACKS, YOU WORKED AS AN *INDIVIDUAL!*

TO ACHIEVE OUR GOALS *THE H.I.V.E.* ALWAYS WORKS AS *ONE.* NO ONE MEMBER *DOMINATES* THE OTHERS. NO ONE EVER WORKS *ALONE.*

BUT I DID IT TO *PROVE* MYSELF TO YOU.

AND IT *WORKED.* I GOT INFORMATION ABOUT THE *TITANS...*

THEN YOU WILL *TAKE* THAT INFORMATION TO YOUR *GRAVE.*

YOU STAND NOW BEFORE US FOR *JUDGMENT.*

AND OUR *JUDGMENT* IS--

IT IS A LONG, BLOODCURDLING SCREAM THAT ALL-TOO-SLOWLY DIES UPON THE COLD NIGHT WINDS...

MORNING FINALLY COMES...

THEY FOUND HIS *BODY,* DICK. SIX *BULLETS*-- ALL IN THE HEART.

HE *PAID...* AND IT WASN'T *KORY* WHO MADE HIM PAY. SHE DIDN'T *KILL* HIM-- EVEN THOUGH, IN HER *HEART,* THAT'S ALL SHE *WANTED.*

I THINK SHE'S *GROWN* SOMEWHAT, DICK.

DO YOU THINK SHE KNOWS THE *TRUTH* ABOUT FRANKLIN?

NO. I THINK SHE THINKS HE WAS JUST CAUGHT BETWEEN HER AND *THE H.I.V.E.* SHE THINKS HE WAS AN INNOCENT *PAWN...*

AND, AS FAR AS *I'M* CONCERNED, SHE DOESN'T *EVER* HAVE TO KNOW ANY *DIFFERENTLY!*

HE DIED *LOVING* HER, AND AS KORY HERSELF SAID-- ISN'T THAT ALL THAT'S *IMPORTANT?*

DAILY N GANGLA SLAYIN

DR. WILLIS DARROW SH TO DEATH FORMER CRIMINAL SCIENTIST FOUND SLAIN

26

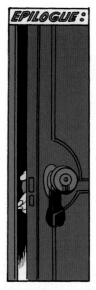

EPILOGUE:

A FULL MOON HANGS OVER THE DOMINICAN REPUBLIC THIS HOT HUMID NIGHT.

A FULL MOON: SOME SAY IT IS A HARBINGER OF MADNESS.

THANK NEPTUNE! MY INFORMATION WAS *CORRECT!*

TONIGHT WILL GIVE THAT THEORY CREDENCE.

MAN, AM I GLAD I GOT HERE *IN* TIME--

--OTHERWISE POOR *SPEEDY* WOULD BE VISITING *DAVY JONES'S LOCKER* --THE *HARD* WAY!

AQUALAD TAKES LONG, POWERFUL STROKES, PROPEL-LING HIS WELL-MUSCLED BODY THROUGH THE WARM CARIBBEAN WATERS AT AN UNBELIEVABLE SPEED.

MARV WOLFMAN *writer*
CARMINE INFANTINO *penciller*
ROMEO TANGHAL *embellisher*
ADRIENNE ROY *colorist*
BEN ODA *letterer*
LEN WEIN *editor*

REUNION!

ONE HOUR LATER: *TITANS TOWER* STANDS TALL AND PROUD ON THIS SMALL ISLAND IN *MANHATTAN'S* EAST RIVER...

RAVEN SAID SHE'D BE HERE *LATER*... I THINK SHE'S BUSY ENROLLING IN *MANHATTAN UNIVERSITY.*

IT'S GOOD FOR HER TO GET OUT, WALLY -- SHE'S ALWAYS BEEN SO *WITHDRAWN*... ALMOST *SHY* ABOUT--

GLANG! GLANG!

IT'S THE *ALARM!* WE'RE BEING *ATTACKED!*

STARFIRE -- *STOP!*

DON'T TELL ME THE *FEARSOME FIVE* IS BACK!

SHE'S NOT *LISTENING,* WONDER GIRL -- SHE'S *CHARGING* AHEAD WITHOUT *THINKING!*

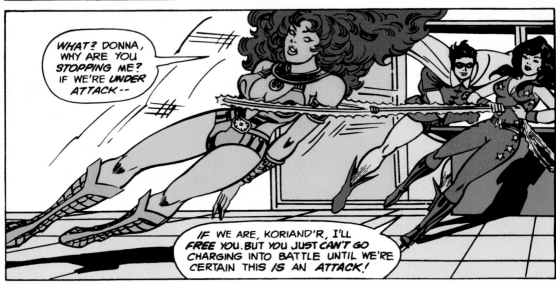

WHAT? DONNA, WHY ARE YOU *STOPPING* ME? IF WE'RE *UNDER ATTACK*--

IF WE ARE, KORIAND'R, I'LL *FREE YOU.* BUT YOU JUST *CAN'T* GO CHARGING INTO BATTLE UNTIL WE'RE CERTAIN THIS *IS* AN *ATTACK!*

BUT, A MOMENT LATER, AS THE TITANS' OUTER DOOR SLIDES OPEN...

AQUALAD?!?

SO, *THAT'S* HIM... I'VE HEARD YOU SPEAK HIS *NAME,* BUT-- WHO IS HE *CARRYING?*

IT'S *SPEEDY!* WHAT HAPPENED TO HIM?

IS HE *ALIVE?*

2

YEAH, BUT JUST *BARELY.* MAN, MY BODY ACHES IN PLACES I DIDN'T EVEN KNOW I *HAD.*

WALLY, DICK... DONNA... IT'S REALLY GOOD TO *SEE* YOU AGAIN.

I HAD HEARD *RUMORS* THAT THE TITANS HAD RE-FORMED.

ROY, WHAT *HAPPENED?* I'M SURE YOU TWO DIDN'T DROP IN JUST FOR A *SOCIAL CALL.*

YEAH, SOMETHING'S *WRONG,* DICK... *REAL* WRONG, AND I NEED YOUR HELP.

YOU'VE *GOT* IT, ROY-- YOU *KNOW* THAT.

THANKS, REALLY. YOU KNOW, EVER SINCE MY *PROBLEM* A FEW YEARS BACK, I'VE BEEN WORKING ALONGSIDE THE *NARCOTICS BUREAU...*

...TO STOP THE MILLIONS OF DOLLARS' WORTH OF *ILLEGAL DRUGS* THAT ENTER OUR COUNTRY EACH YEAR.

"I FELT IT WAS MY DUTY TO TRY TO HELP *OTHERS* BEFORE DRUGS CAN ABUSE *THEM* THE WAY THEY DID ME.

"WELL, I TRACED ONE NARCOTICS GANG TO THE DOMINICAN REPUBLIC--THEY PROCESSED DRUGS SMUGGLED OUT OF TURKEY.

"AND THEY WERE GETTING READY FOR A BIG SHIPMENT *STATESIDE.* AS I WATCHED THEM, I GREW ANGRY...

③

"...AND, UNFORTUNATELY, CARE-LESS AS WELL. I WAS SPOTTED.

"OF COURSE, BEING TUTORED BY GREEN ARROW DIDN'T HURT ME.

"I MANAGED TO STOP ABOUT HALF THEIR GANG USING MY BOXING GLOVE ARROWS.

"BUT HALF A GANG ISN'T EVERYONE. YOU SEE, THEY HAD THIS MACHETE EXPERT.

"SOMEHOW HE GOT BEHIND ME, AND WHILE I WAS MOPPING UP THE JUNGLE WITH HIS PARTNERS--

"--HE TOOK ME OUT WITH ONE QUICK THROW!

"MY WHOLE BODY'S STILL SMARTING OVER THAT.

ANYWAY, I WAS UNCONSCIOUS, AND THEY DUMPED ME IN THE OCEAN... FIGURED I'D DROWN.

ONLY ONE OF MY FISH SAW SPEEDY ...TELEPATHICALLY ALERTED ME...

...AND I SWAM THERE ...JUST ABOUT IN TIME, TOO.

THESE DRUGS YOU ARE TALKING ABOUT... WHAT ARE THEY?

THEY'RE A SUBSTANCE THAT TAKES OVER YOUR MIND... ALTERS YOUR PERCEPTIONS...

THEY'RE BAD, BUT PEOPLE USE THEM ALL THE TIME.

THAT DOES NOT MAKE *SENSE*... IF THEY ARE BAD, WHY *USE* THEM?

OH, THERE ARE *REASONS* --AND *EXCUSES* -- BUT IN THE LONG RUN, MOST OF THE EXCUSES ARE *LIES*.

TROUBLE IS, BY THE TIME THEY START DAMAGING YOUR BODY, YOU'RE *HOOKED* ON THEM. IT'S ALMOST *TOO LATE* TO STOP.

BECAUSE, WHEN YOU *TRY* TO STOP, YOU GO THROUGH A TERRIBLE *WITHDRAWAL PAIN* ... AND THAT PAIN DRIVES YOU RIGHT BACK TO THE *DRUGS*.

IT'S A *CATCH-22* ... BUT THE GAME YOU'RE PLAYING CAN *KILL* YOU.

I DON'T KNOW ABOUT THE *OTHERS*, BOWMAN, BUT COUNT *ME* IN.

BACK IN COLLEGE I SAW TOO MANY OF MY FRIENDS *FRY THEIR BRAINS* ON THAT GARBAGE.

WE'RE *ALL* IN ON THIS, CYBORG. OKAY, SPEEDY-- YOU KNOW WHAT'S COMING DOWN.

SO WHAT'S OUR NEXT *MOVE*?

5

SHORTLY, ALONG A DESOLATE STRETCH OF BEACH IN THE DOMINICAN REPUBLIC...

JUST REMEMBER, FLY *LOW*... UNDER THE COAST GUARD *RADAR*. WE DON'T WANT THIS SHIPMENT *PICKED UP*.

ONCE THIS JUNK IS CUT AND CLEANED IN OUR MIAMI WAREHOUSE, WE'LL CLEAR *TWENTY MILLION*--IN *CASH!*

ROBIN, WE COULD TAKE THEM *NOW*.

WE *COULD*, KORY, BUT I WANT THEIR *MIAMI* CONNECTION AS WELL.

STARFIRE, YOU AND WONDER GIRL FOLLOW THE *CHOPPER*. WHEN THEIR GANG IS TOGETHER, DO WHAT YOU MUST TO *STOP* THEM.

CHANGELING, CYBORG -- THE REST OF YOU... FOLLOW *ME!*

WE'RE *WITH* YA, SHORT-PANTS!

THIS ONE I'M *LOOKIN'* FORWARD TO!

6

Speedy is grim as he leads the others toward the main processing plant. He knows full well that the evil represented here is as great a threat to mankind as any super-villain or alien invasion. For this is an evil that insinuates itself into the body... and into the helpless mind...

MOVE IT! WE AIN'T GOT ALL NIGHT!

I WANT THIS STUFF *BAGGED* FOR ANOTHER SHIPMENT *TOMORROW.*

WE GOT MORE'N TWENTY DISTRIBUTORS *BEGGIN'* TO PAY US BIG BUCKS--!

SO LET'S GET THIS JOB *DONE* WITH--AN' GET IT OUTTA HERE--*FAST!*

FORGET IT, SLOBBO-- THE ONLY THING LEAVING HERE IS *YOU*--

--AND THE ONLY PLACE *YOU'RE* GOING IS *BEHIND BARS!*

FWIPPP!

WHAT--? *YOU*--? BUT IT *CAN'T* BE!

YOU THOUGHT I WAS *DEAD*, DIDN'T YOU?

WELL, PAL--I'M STILL *TICKING.* I'M STILL *MAD AS HELL!*

AND THIS BATTLING BOWMAN IS GONNA *DO* SOMETHING ABOUT IT!

7

THESE ARE THE TITANS, AND AS ONE THEY MOVE INTO ACTION.

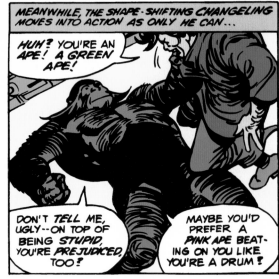

KID FLASH'S SUPER-SPEED ROUNDS UP THE GUARDS IN LESS THAN THREE SECONDS.

NEXT TIME, HE REMINDS HIMSELF --HE MUSTN'T MOVE SO SLOW.

AS FOR ROBIN, THE TEEN WONDER...

FIGHTING THESE CREEPS ISN'T THE SAME AS TAKING ON BADDIES LIKE TRIGON OR THE TERMINATOR--

--BUT PUTTING THEM OUT OF ACTION IS JUST AS SATISFYING!

MEANWHILE, THE SHAPE-SHIFTING CHANGELING MOVES INTO ACTION AS ONLY HE CAN...

HUH? YOU'RE AN APE! A GREEN APE!

DON'T TELL ME, UGLY--ON TOP OF BEING STUPID, YOU'RE PREJUDICED, TOO?

MAYBE YOU'D PREFER A PINK APE BEATING ON YOU LIKE YOU'RE A DRUM!

AQUALAD:

YOU DON'T MIND HURTING OTHERS, DO YOU? SO LET'S SEE HOW YOU LIKE BEING HURT INSTEAD!

AND, AS FOR SPEEDY...

STUPID IDIOT. HE THINKS HE'S GETTING AWAY. BUT THERE'S NO WAY HE'S ESCAPING FROM ME.

I OWE IT TO TOO MANY PEOPLE TO MAKE SURE HIS KIND NEVER GETS AWAY AGAIN!

MEANWHILE, IN MIAMI...

AS THE HELICOPTER LANDS UNDER A CLOAK OF DARKNESS, PILOT HENRY WELLE GRINS. HE WILL MAKE THOUSANDS FOR TONIGHT'S RUN--

--MORE MONEY THAN HE COULD EVER HAVE MADE FLYING TOURISTS FROM CARIBBEAN ISLAND TO ISLAND.

MONEY IS ALL THAT MOTIVATES WELLE...

...NOT THAT HE'LL HAVE ANY PLACE TO SPEND IT IN PRISON.

THEY ARE UNLOADING THE CRATES, DONNA ...

GIVE THEM A MINUTE MORE, KORY--THEN YOU TAKE CARE OF THE CHOPPER...

I DON'T WANT THEM GETTING AWAY.

STARFIRE WAITS FOR WONDER GIRL'S SIGNAL. THEN, SUDDENLY, SHE SPEEDS INTO ACTION...

...HER ALIEN BODY FAIRLY SEEMS TO GLOW WITH THE AWESOME SOLAR POWER IT CONTAINS.

SKREEEE!

ENERGY THAT IS SUDDENLY UNLEASHED IN A SINGLE DEADLY STARBOLT.

WELLE AND THE OTHERS TURN IN FEAR. THEY TRY TO FLEE, BUT WONDER GIRL, TRAINED BY THE AMAZONS ON PARADISE ISLAND, IS WAITING...

...AND READY!

THIS ONE WAS INSIDE, WONDER GIRL...

...PLANNING TO ESCAPE.

HE FAILED!

9

IT IS MORNING WHEN WE RETURN TO TITANS' TOWER, AND THIS MORNING HERALDS A SLIGHTLY BRIGHTER DAY TO COME...

WE GOT 'EM *ALL,* GUYS... RIGHT DOWN TO THEIR SLIMY INNER-CITY *DISTRIBUTORS.*

TROUBLE IS, THIS WAS JUST *ONE* OUTFIT... THERE ARE *DOZENS* MORE JUST *LIKE* 'EM.

SO, I GUESS THIS IS MY ROUNDABOUT WAY OF SAYING "THANKS BUT *NO THANKS"* FOR THE OFFER TO *REJOIN* THE TITANS.

MAYBE I'LL SHOW UP NOW AND THEN, BUT I HAVE A WHOLE LOT OF *WORK* AHEAD OF ME THAT I JUST CAN'T PUT ASIDE!

SAME WITH *ME,* GUYS... MY DUTIES IN ATLANTIS KEEP ME BUSY, AND AS MUCH AS I *ENJOYED* THIS REUNION AND MEETING THE NEW TITANS--

--I CAN'T BECOME A FULL-TIME *REGULAR!*

I AM VERY SORRY TO *HEAR* THAT, AQUALAD. I HAD HEARD *SO MUCH* ABOUT YOU AND SPEEDY...

AND YOU ARE AS GOOD AND VALIANT AS I HAD BEEN *TOLD.*

WORKING *ALONGSIDE* YOU MAKES ME EVEN *PROUDER* THAN BEFORE TO CALL MYSELF A *TITAN!*

THESE ARE THE NEW TEEN TITANS...

...AND THEY ARE THE *BEST* THERE IS!

MARV WOLFMAN

One of the most prolific and influential writers in modern comics, Marv Wolfman began his career as an artist. Realizing that his talents lay more in writing the stories than in drawing them, Wolfman soon became known for his carefully crafted, character-driven tales.

In a career that spans nearly 30 years, Wolfman has helped shape the heroic careers of DC Comics' Green Lantern, Blackhawk and the original Teen Titans, as well as Marvel Comics' *Fantastic Four*, *Spider-Man*, *Nova* and *Tomb of Dracula*. In addition to co-creating THE NEW TEEN TITANS and the universe-shattering CRISIS ON INFINITE EARTHS with George Pérez, Wolfman was instrumental in the revamp of Superman after CRISIS, the development of THE NEW TEEN TITANS spinoff series VIGILANTE, DEATHSTROKE THE TERMINATOR and TEAM TITANS, and created such characters as *Blade* for Marvel, along with NIGHT FORCE and the retooled DIAL "H" FOR HERO for DC.

In addition to his numerous comic-book credits, Wolfman has also written several novels and worked in series television and animation, including the *Superman* cartoon of the late 1980s and currently the hit *Teen Titans* show on Cartoon Network.

GEORGE PÉREZ

George Pérez started drawing at the age of five and hasn't stopped since. Born on June 9, 1954, Pérez started his professional comics career as an assistant to Rich Buckler in 1973. After establishing himself as a penciller on Marvel Comics' *Man-Wolf* and *Sons of the Tiger*, he moved on to such Marvel titles as *The Inhumans*, *Fantastic Four*, *Marvel Two-in-One* and *The Avengers*. Pérez first came to DC in 1980, where his highly detailed art style was seen in such titles as JUSTICE LEAGUE OF AMERICA and FIRESTORM THE NUCLEAR MAN.

After co-creating NEW TEEN TITANS with Marv Wolfman in 1980, Pérez and Wolfman collaborated again on the landmark miniseries CRISIS ON INFINITE EARTHS.

In the midst of the revamps of BATMAN and SUPERMAN that came in the wake of CRISIS, Pérez took on the difficult task of revitalizing WONDER WOMAN. As the series' writer and artist, he not only reestablished Wonder Woman as one of DC's preeminent characters, but also brought in some of the best sales the title has ever experienced.

Pérez returned to Marvel for a celebrated three-year run on *The Avengers*, paired with writer Kurt Busiek. He later joined forces with CrossGen Comics, pencilling a number of stories for *CrossGen Chronicles* while launching the series *Solus*. He recently completed work on the long-awaited JLA/AVENGERS crossover miniseries.

DICK GIORDANO

Dick Giordano's formative professional years were forged at Charlton Comics, where he freelanced as an artist beginning in 1952. In 1965, Giordano was made editor-in-chief of the Charlton line and introduced a tremendous amount of new talent into the comics field, working with Jim Aparo, Steve Skeates, Denny O'Neil, and many others, all of whom came with him when he moved to DC Comics in 1967. From 1983 to 1993, Giordano served as DC's Vice President-Executive Editor and was instrumental in shaping the current DC Universe. Upon retiring from his executive role, Giordano returned to his first love, art. He now pencils and inks for a variety of publishers.

CARMINE INFANTINO

Carmine Infantino began working in comics in the mid-1940s as the artist on such features as Green Lantern, Black Canary, Ghost Patrol...and the original Golden Age Flash. Infantino lent his unique style to a variety of super-hero, supernatural, and Western features throughout the 1950s until he was tapped to pencil the 1956 revival of the Flash. While continuing to pencil the FLASH series, he also provided the art for other strips, including Batman, Elongated Man, and Adam Strange. Infantino became DC's editorial director in 1967 and, later, publisher before returning to freelancing in 1976 since which time he has pencilled and inked numerous features, including the Batman newspaper strip, GREEN LANTERN CORPS, and DANGER TRAIL.

BEN ODA

Ben was one of the most prolific letterers in the world of comic books and comic strips. His work has graced literally thousands of pages for every major and minor publisher, dating back to comics' Golden Age. Ben died in 1984.

ADRIENNE ROY

Adrienne began work in DC's famed bullpen before graduating to freelance colorist. She enjoyed long runs on numerous titles including BATMAN, DETECTIVE COMICS, and, of course, THE NEW TEEN TITANS.

ROMEO TANGHAL

A veteran comic-book inker, Romeo's work has been seen in such books as JUSTICE LEAGUE OF AMERICA, WONDER WOMAN, GREEN LANTERN and, of course, NEW TEEN TITANS.

LEN WEIN

A mainstay of the comics field, Len Wein has created dozens of characters and held numerous editorial positions at both DC and Marvel Comics. Perhaps best known as the co-creator of DC's SWAMP THING (with artist Bernie Wrightson), Wein was the editorial guiding light for the early years of THE NEW TEEN TITANS. He was also instrumental in the genesis of CRISIS ON INFINITE EARTHS (working again with Wolfman and Pérez) and the original edition of WHO'S WHO.